Oconaluftee

Contents

Illustrations

FIGURES

MAP

Acknowledgments

A PROJECT ABOUT a community illuminates the need for neighbors and friends. During the years that I have researched and written the chapters of this book, I have benefitted from countless instances of professional helpfulness and personal generosity. The best stories of Oconaluftee Valley residents highlight similar experiences. "Friendship found," the benediction of Smokemont Baptist Church meetings, joined hearts and minds long ago. The phrase rings true today. This lesson emerges again and again from the history I have discovered, patched together, and, finally, recognized to be in plain view everywhere. My understanding of human interconnection as key to rich and stable lives, as well as good scholarship, did not arise solely from the books, records, and lore of the valley. It became embodied in others: friends, family members, colleagues, professional associates, and contacts who assisted, advised, encouraged, and put up with me. Along with my imaginings of those who once lived in a mountain township, while I worked on this book, I have resided within a parallel, present-day community, discontinuous, scattered, sometimes far-flung and virtual, sometimes nearby. Kind, wise, knowledgeable, and charitable people sustained me.

I am thankful for those who permitted me to meet with them, attend their events, and use their collections, libraries, and archives. History cannot be traced without these repositories. First and foremost, Michael Aday, archivist of Great Smoky Mountains National Park, and Annette Hartigan, park librarian, were essential to this project. In addition, I was advised by Kent Cave, Smokies expert extraordinaire and longtime ranger, Lynda C. Doucette, Oconaluftee supervisory park ranger, and Terry Maddox, retired director of the Great Smoky Mountains Association.

Moreover, many professionals provided suggestions and access to materials, including Mikey Littlejohn, Evan Mathis, Dakota Brown, Lucia French, and Robin Swayney of the Museum of the Cherokee Indian; George Frizzell and Jason Brady, special collections librarians at Hunter Library, Western North Carolina University; Kelly Kerney of the Valentine Museum, Richmond, Virginia; Anne Bridges, humanities reference librarian at the University of Tennessee, Knoxville; Vann Evans of the State Archives of North

Carolina; Arlene Royer of the National Archives in McDonough, Georgia; Daisy Njoku of the Anthropology Archives of the Smithsonian Institution; and Rori Brewer, Amy Thompson, Ashley Hoffman, and other interlibrary loan staff members of Sturgis Library, Kennesaw State University. Park archaeologist Erik S. Kreusch, Michael G. Angst, senior archaeologist, UTK Archaeological Research Laboratory, and Melissa Crisp, Parks as Classroom project coordinator in Gatlinburg graciously hosted me at the archaeological dig described in chapter 1. Raymond Matthews, pastor of Tow String Baptist Church; the late Dan Lambert, pastor of Wrights Creek Baptist Church; Leslie Gass; and other descendants kindly shared family stories and answered questions about Tow String, Smokemont, and Ravensford, especially during the Smokemont Reunion of 2014.

A number of individuals replied enthusiastically to requests via social media posts, phone calls, emails, and letters, including Swain County historian Don Casada; railroad expert Ron Sullivan; Cherokee scholar and emeritus professor of history Dr. John Finger, University of Tennessee, Knoxville; Kevin Watson, publisher and editor in chief, Press 53 and *Prime Number Magazine*; Neil Olson of Massie & McQuilkin; Jeff Delfield of Bryson City, North Carolina; and Ann Miller Woodford, artist and author of Andrews, North Carolina. Sincere thanks to Jennifer Ehle and Rosemary Harris for permission to use a quotation from John Ehle's *The Land Breakers* as my epigraph. Tom Robbins, legendary retired Oconaluftee ranger, provided encouragement and vital comments on early drafts of the book, as did Steve Kemp, as interpretive products and services director of the Great Smoky Mountains Association. I have been so fortunate to have the benefit of sharp-eyed and insightful anonymous peer reviewers of the University of North Carolina Press. These scholars pushed me to expand and improve the original manuscript and to make it as inclusive, appealing, and accurate as possible. I have enjoyed the luxury of having one's work examined carefully.

This work was supported by the Norman J. Radow College of Humanities and Social Sciences of Kennesaw State University, particularly via my English Department chairs John Havard and Bill Rice and the invaluable Department of English program coordinator Rhonda Nemeth, and the cheerful and ever-helpful office manager Rose-Marie Trujillo, who both know how to manage and win with bureaucratic paperwork.

The University of North Carolina Press staff has guided my project to publication with talent, care, and warmth. Lucas Church has patiently shepherded me and the manuscript; his professionalism is supreme. I also thank Thomas Bedenbaugh, Elizabeth Orange, Joanna Ruth Marsland, Laura Jones

Dooley, and Valerie Burton for their many efforts to make the book shine and reach readers. Margaretta Yarborough and Fred Kameny are due recognition for their sharp eyes and good humor during the proofing and indexing phase. Thanks are also due to Mapping Specialists for creating the map of the valley for me.

To those who listened to my doubts and nudged me to continue my work, you were my mainstay. If not for you, Sandra Ballard and Toney Frazier, Sally and Pat Govan, Laura Davis and Lynn Boettler, Vickie and Steve Reddick, Bonnie Winsbro, Pat Parr, Amy Leventhal and David Thompson, and Sue and Nate Marini, I would have given up long before anything respectable existed. Thank you for the long conversations, the favors large and small, the many good points, and, especially, your wisdom. Finally, my sweet and loving family has kept me on the trail of this long journey for over a decade. My family first taught me the meaning of community; it is fitting to find it as the message of this book.

Oconaluftee

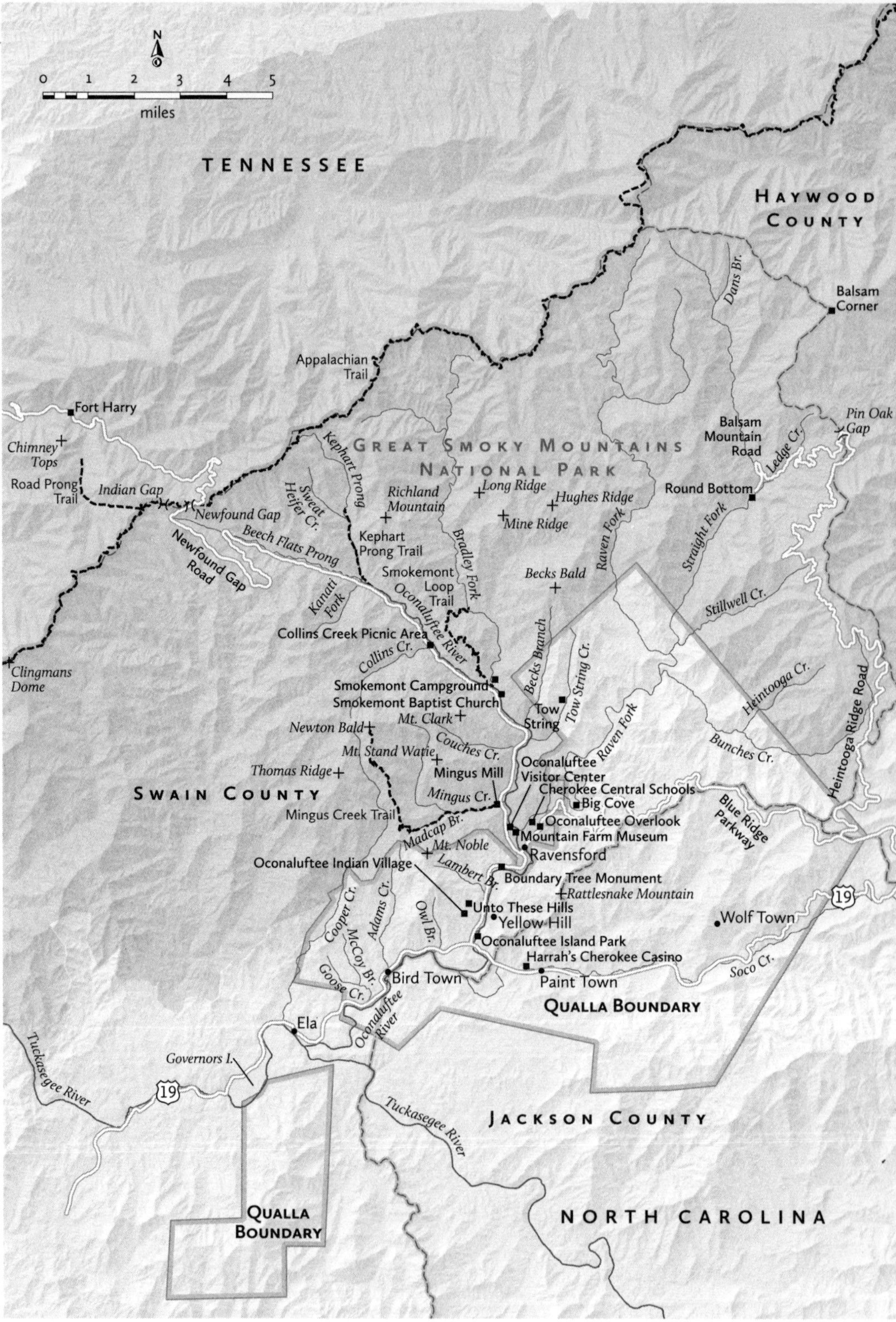

Oconaluftee Valley.

INTRODUCTION

AN INVITING SPOT

OCONALUFTEE VALLEY has simple, direct appeal: it is a beautiful, wide V-shaped valley formed by a river of the same name flowing down the North Carolina side of the main ridge of the Great Smoky Mountains National Park. The river, the largest on the North Carolina side of the park, gathers from streams coming off Richland Mountain and Thomas Ridge and broadens and deepens as it follows a southern course through the park and then through Cherokee, North Carolina. Its largest tributaries, memorializing the mountain family history of the valley, are Bradley Fork and Raven Fork, but plenty of other creeks flow into the Oconaluftee, such as Upper Grassy and Lower Grassy Branches, Sweat Heifer Creek, Coon Branch, Kephart Prong, Beech Flats Prong, Smith Branch, Kanati Fork, Cliff Branch, Jim Mac Branch, Shell Bark Branch, Will Branch, and Collins Creek—all coming off Richland Mountain. Outside of Cherokee, the Oconaluftee turns west until its confluence with the Tuckasegee River at Ela, North Carolina, which flows into and through Bryson City, emptying, eventually, into the Little Tennessee. Formed by the river's erosion, Oconaluftee Valley opens gracefully via curves to east and west. Today, park visitors trace these curves as they descend along Highway 441 from Newfound Gap to the base of the mountains. Each curve yields a terrace along the spine of the highway, often a shelf cleared at some point for a camp or home. As one descends, the clearings enlarge into broad floodplains, and these are the locations of prehistoric villages, mountain family farms, and twentieth-century towns.

Cherokee legend tells us that, as the earth was forming, a buzzard created the mountains and valleys. Sent by all the other animals to look for dry, habitable land, the buzzard had to fly for a long time, and, becoming tired, it gradually drifted lower and lower over the wet clay of the world. Its wings touched the earth, shaping the valleys on the downstroke and the mountains on the upstroke. Oconaluftee looks like a place made by the flight of a large, weary raptor, so the tale accurately captures the mood of the landscape. According to another cosmography, geologists explain that a fault (eponymously titled the Oconaluftee Fault) lying along the floor of the valley is primarily responsible for the area's topography. As the valley broadens along this fault, the two dominant rock formations of the Smokies are exposed: Thunderhead Sandstone and the highly acidic Anakeesta Formation. Both metamorphosed formations are late Precambrian, that is, more than 570 million years old. Even older rock appears south of the Smokemont Campground where the oldest rock of the park, the Precambrian basement complex, begins to become visible in roadcuts. This rock, also metamorphic, is more than 1 billion years old and composed largely of granite gneiss, formed over eons by heat and pressure on granite. As geologist Henry Moore explains, the basement complex comprises "the ancient crystalline foundation on which all the other strata of the area have been deposited."[1] In other words, it is the rock bottom of the park and of the valley. Of course, much of it is covered by stream sediment and forests, allowing for the arable fields of Mississippian cultures, Cherokees, and, later, mountain families of European descent.

The buzzard- or fault-formed slopes lining the valley sides welcome human habitation in their gentle S-curve outlines. The river offers the necessities of life: freshwater, good soil for crops, forest for game hunting and timber for manufacture, and comforting views of surrounding, protective mountains to the east. Rattlesnake Mountain dominates the vista east from the park's visitor center in Oconaluftee. Anyone looking for a place to live would recognize the valley as a premier choice. Many people from prehistory until the establishment of the park in 1934 did just that. They came here to live and farm and have families, so the valley that today looks open and uncluttered by the trappings of human life is very different than it was for centuries, when human occupation teemed in dozens of camps, villages, and towns.

Which brings us to the name: Oconaluftee. Could its euphony be more inviting or entrancing? One must slow down to say the name, forming five long vowels in turn, easing the pace of thought and then the pulse. In Cherokee, the word means “by the river.” *Egwâni* is Cherokee for river, and *nu’lti* or *nulti* means “near” or “beside.” That word, *Egwânul’ti*, first referred to a Cherokee village outside the park area that had a sizable mound and was located by the river as it turns west in Nick Bottom, close to present-day Bird Town in the Eastern Band’s Qualla Boundary.[2] As the years passed, colonial landowners and mountain families mistakenly applied the name of the village, which was destroyed during a Revolutionary War raid, to the river. So, odd as it is for a river to be the “by the river river,” that’s literally what one says when one says “Oconaluftee River.” But to the ears of English speakers, the name’s sonority suggests the river’s character: a sparkling, wide, often friendly stream for fishing, swimming, and wading. Fittingly, people have always wanted to live in the valley’s fertile bottomlands.

For these reasons, the valley has been an important location to the Eastern Band for centuries. In addition, everything that happened in the park’s history happened here, one way or another. That is, all the periods of the region’s history have a chapter or two set in Oconaluftee: prehistoric civilizations, traditional Cherokee culture, fur traders and trading posts, colonial conflict and settlement, Trail of Tears–era drama, mountain farming communities, Civil War soldiers and raids, logging camps, New Deal Civilian Conservation Corps camps, World War II–era conscientious objectors, tourists, and descendants of a distinctive triracial community, some remaining in the parts of the valley that were not absorbed into the park and others returning to annual church revivals to remember a lifestyle that has been curtailed. The park portion of the valley has been unsung, but it offers legends and historical accounts of watershed events and influential individuals. It is the famous place you drive through without knowing its distinction, perhaps because it is a gateway to the high peaks, but perhaps also because the tale is so long and old that much of it no longer comes to mind. The Cherokee portion, of course, has been much celebrated, though the association between the two dominant ethnic groups has been somewhat neglected. The simple appeal of the valley lulls us into vague reminiscences and nostalgia. Brought to light, one finds much to take in about personal and community resilience in the face of international, national, and regional external forces and trends.

Horace Kephart, the influential park proponent and journalist, called the high peaks of the Smokies “an Eden still unpeopled and unspoiled.” He referred to his camp on Hazel Creek as the “Back of Beyond” (capitalized as a proper noun), a title that has become an alluring phrase to characterize the whole park area before commercial logging arrived in the last decades of the nineteenth century.[3] This term suggests isolation and autonomy, but neither was absolute, particularly for a watershed such as the Oconaluftee Valley. Perhaps valley residents felt distant from village, county, and city doings as they tended their farms and sat on their front porches spinning fiber into thread, churning butter, playing music, and attending to all the essential chores of keeping a home repaired and a family fed. But they were not beyond the reach of outside political, administrative, economic, and social forces. At turns, they faced challenges, gained support from government agents, and were swept into systems, conflicts, and initiatives that they did not seek and did not have a part in creating. Though remote, the valley's location and resources situated its residents within transformational events, sometimes centrally, rather than exempting them from involvement and participation. Further, the vision of the valley as an isolated place inhabited by self-sufficient yeoman farmers was never true because its denizens willingly engaged in far-reaching trade networks throughout decades, even centuries.

When I began this project, I was advised to focus on the part of the valley that became parkland, which meant a story of white families who bought land from the federal or state government and settled in the valley. For a brief time, I thought this approach was possible. But as I began to recognize the significant, numerous, and consequential interconnections between them and the Cherokee community, this approach became untenable. There is simply no way to separate the two ethnic groups and chronicle the valley's history; further, attempting such an effort would only diminish its value and meaning for readers today. Similarly, understating the presence and impact of slavery in the valley (and region, for that matter) would be misleading, inaccurate, and insulting. Though the white mountain families and the Cherokees may not always have preferred their propinquity to another ethnic group, and though their different status meant that they faced different challenges and options in response to crises, they were and behaved as neighbors. The groups were not fully integrated into all aspects of one another's lives, but ongoing connections with few hostilities among residents marked life in the valley. The records about the two groups are largely separate, yet I suspect that there was far more personal contact and everyday community between the Cherokee and white families than I have discovered. Most of the individuals included in this history were not public figures and would not have anticipated the appearance of their names in a book decades after their deaths. They lived private lives.

This book offers an account of the lives of all the people of the valley that can be constructed from published and archival sources. It traces events that illustrate how people were confronted with situations that they could only partly define but that tested individual and social morality, ethics, and justice. In quests for security, people exercised their power—physical, material, economic, and political—so that their dreams could take shape and their families, communities, and cultures could survive. Although open questions abound, what can be learned is entertaining and informative, especially in regard to how people survive and thrive when overtaken by external forces.

Chapter 1

BELOW THE PLOW ZONE

THE VALLEY'S HUMAN PREHISTORY

"I DON'T KNOW what this is, but . . . ," says a black-haired, dark-eyed high school student holding a handful of dime-size, dirt-covered objects. The hand reaches toward Melissa Crisp, a Parks as Classrooms project coordinator in Gatlinburg, Tennessee, who has also taught students in the field for several summers now. She is voluble, full of energy and information. The student looks hopeful.

"That's beautiful!" Crisp picks up a small whitish-gray flake from his palm and holds it up. Looking again to his palm, she picks through the rest of the items. "That's a rock. That looks like pottery. That's a rock. But that," she says, going back to the first, small flake, "is a beautiful piece of chert. That's what that is. See, that's lighter, but it's that Knox chert." Chert was used for projectile points like arrowheads and Knox chert, not locally available, was traded by prehistoric residents with others in Tennessee. So the small chert flake is the remnant of someone's effort to make an arrowhead many years ago. The young man, palm empty now, tosses the rocks but keeps the mysterious bits and puts them in a labeled paper lunch bag. As part of a Parks as Classrooms summer program, this intern and others like him methodically dig below the plow zone, the dark layer of soil that had been disturbed by farming, to find artifacts from Native American groups who lived or camped in this spot hundreds and thousands of years ago.

By 10:00 A.M. on a humid July morning, a cluster of high school and college interns have dug a half dozen square meters of dirt on one of the valley's terraces. Shaped like a crescent, the level land is about the length of two football fields alongside Newfound Gap Road, the main road of the park. The field's vegetation was cut short last week in anticipation of the workshop, but it still harbors poison ivy, so those digging wear gloves and watch where they put their hands. They are also on the lookout for curious mice that might have hidden under a tarp overnight and, as a consequence, for mice-hungry snakes. Both have made cameo appearances over the course of the week. Yesterday, a mouse ran up someone's pant leg. It's a funny story now but caused some excitement then. A couple of folks are rather leery of touching or even standing near a tarp. A constant roar and swoosh of road noise provides a soundtrack. Nearby, a camping canopy serves as an office; under its small square of shade lie clipboards for data collection details, artifact bags kept in large plastic bins, rain jackets, a cooler of water, snacks.

The interns are creating an expanding checkerboard of one-meter squares on the north end of the field. Some look about six inches deep and others about twelve; a couple of promising squares are marked off with string and nails to maintain a boundary line and to facilitate mapping later. They are being dug deeper and more carefully, with trowels instead of shovels. Whatever the tool, students scrape the dirt from a single "unit" at a time and place it in plastic buckets for screening.

A second young man, sunburned and sandy-haired, shows Crisp more objects, simultaneously implying a question: "This is charcoal and it stayed in the sifter so that's why I kept it." Crisp looks and replies, "Actually, it's not charcoal; see the sand and the grit in it? That's just sort of a sandstone." But she sees another piece: "That's really good! That's chert!" The chert piece, like all the finds, goes into a bag marked with unit number, site, and date.

Another student, an African American college student, approaches. "My rock senses are tingling. Is it fire-cracked rock?" Crisp picks the egg-sized rock out of her hand. "No. Look for reddish rock and a sharp break. You're right; it's just a rock." The student returns to her team of three interns who are laughing as they screen their dirt through a hip-high, wood-frame sieve. The sieve stands on two legs and is held parallel to the ground by one intern. One young woman pours dirt into the top of the sieve, and another, who is holding the frame, shakes the dirt through. When only clumps remain, all three use their hands to pick out objects that might be artifacts. Below the sieve, a pile of light-brown, flour-like dirt grows.

"Oh, those are good pieces of chert! I tell ya, Deronya's got the touch. This unit has just been gold!" Digging is "almost like a puzzle in reverse," Crisp explains.

This dig is the result of an ongoing partnership between archaeologists at the University of Tennessee, Knoxville, the Eastern Band of the Cherokee Nation, and the Great Smoky Mountains National Park. Its purposes include expanding the knowledge about archaeology of the park area; exposing local students, and especially Cherokee youth, to archaeological practices and career possibilities; and providing college-age interns with training. The program, with support from the university, the park, and the nonprofit Friends of the Great Smoky Mountains, has been in place for several years, and has enabled research providing new insights into the heavy use of Oconaluftee Valley by people from the Archaic, Woodland, and Mississippian periods of prehistoric archaeology as well as by the Cherokees, who have continuously inhabited the area for more than a thousand years.

Mike Angst, one of the directors of this weeklong workshop and a senior archaeologist at the University of Tennessee, explains that "archaeologists are historical trash collectors" who remove the topsoil of a site and look for "features," which can be any kind of evidence of previous use or inhabitance of a place, such as the discolored soil that shows the location of postholes that once held timber that supported a home, the cracked rock and charcoal remains of an earth oven, pottery shards, spear points and arrowheads, and even pollen and plant remains suggesting prehistoric diets. On occasion, evidence of burial sites is found, but these features are left undisturbed. Guidelines established by the landmark Native American Graves Protection and Repatriation Act of 1990 require that federally recognized Native American groups be consulted on archaeological digs. The Eastern Band and Great Smoky Mountains National Park consult regularly on park archaeology and have agreed not to excavate gravesites out of respect for Native American cultures and peoples.

"If you find a good place to live, it's going to continue to be a good place to live for years to come," Angst tells a half dozen interns at the beginning of the day, orienting them to the current dig and explaining why artifacts from multiple historic periods turn up at single dig sites. Though lab work will later confirm the dating that he and park archaeologist Erik Kreusch estimate in passing, in this field alone the students find remains suggesting several homesites. A Cherokee summer home from the 1700s emerges on the north end. In addition, the dig this year includes completing the processing of a home structure from the 1300s that was partially excavated two years before. It lies at the south end of the same field where the crowd of interns is just breaking the surface, about thirty yards away.

With roughly 500 archaeological sites in the park, archaeologists have found evidence of Native Americans' presence during every era, from Paleo, Archaic, Woodland, and Mississippian to Cherokee. In the Paleo period (ca. 10,000 BCE–8,000 BCE), nomadic peoples migrated east from the Great Plains following megafauna like mastodon, woolly mammoth, horses, and camels that they hunted for subsistence. Though no Paleo sites have been discovered in the park, Paleo-era spear points have been found. Archaeologists speculate that Paleo peoples did not live in the Oconaluftee Valley but traveled up it to mountaintop hunting areas. Other experts believe that villages or camps along the valley, if they did exist, would have been "destroyed or deeply buried" by the increase in rain and snow at the end of the Pleistocene.[1]

By the Archaic period (8000 BCE–1000 BCE), the temperatures would have warmed considerably, leading to the extinction of megafauna but also to more tolerable mountain living conditions.[2] Consequently, Archaic peoples established camps both in the upland areas and valleys and coves of the Smokies. Though they continued to gather seasonal nuts and berries, by the end of the Archaic period they began developing agricultural practices. They cultivated squashes and gourds and domesticated sunflowers and plants such as maygrass, whose seeds could be ground for flour, and goosefoot, also called lambsquarters, which is related to quinoa and produces a pseudocereal.[3] Archaic residents of the Oconaluftee Valley still hunted, of course, but focused on smaller game such as deer, elk, buffalo, bear, raccoon, opossum, squirrel, and turkey. Artifacts of stone sinkers for nets suggest that fishing was a source of food and that mussels were consumed, which can be inferred from shell middens, or trash piles. A much larger variety of artifacts establishes the Archaic presence in the park, with more diverse and skilled projectile points found with both lanceolate shapes and notched forms. Also, the atlatl, which is a stick that was used to guide the throwing of a spear, appears during this period.[4] This tool works like a cradle for the back end of a spear; it steadies the spear as the hunter pulls back his arm; when the spear is thrown, the atlatl provides increased leverage and thrust. Consequently, the tool allowed for more accurate and powerful throws. Stone weights were lashed to the atlatl as well, and these steadied the stick and made for even longer throws. In addition, grooved axes, grinding slabs, cruciform drills, and fire-cracked rocks from pit cooking are common in Archaic sites.[5]

Under a green canopy used to provide shade, a smaller group of three, or sometimes four, interns, led by Kreusch, digs deeper and deeper on a few previously unexcavated features at the 1350 house site, the one at the south end of the field. This date places the house in the Mississippian era, and a circular pattern of postholes reveals that it was a structure more or less resembling a Cherokee winter residence, which would have been a small but well-insulated home with a vestibule entrance.[6] The diggers follow the clues of dark patches in the orange-brown dirt. Some of these patches turn out to be mole holes, but others are revealed to be additional postholes.

Digging continues. Every so often park visitors stop their cars along the roadside and walk over to see what's happening under the canopy and out in the sun. The visitors, archaeologists, interns, and volunteers chat about arrowheads and other finds as the digging continues. A consensus emerges that digging in the dirt is just about the best way to spend time. Lunchtime comes with a break. An afternoon shower arrives, and everyone huddles under the canopy. Midafternoon, Kreusch focuses on a feature that merits his professional and exclusive attention. Actually, its presence was noted a couple of years ago when the site was first identified, but limited time did not permit this feature's excavation. At day's end, a tarp is thrown over the entire house site. From the road twenty yards away, the site is unremarkable. No cause for passing cars to stop.

The next morning, the digging continues. Same canopy and tools. Same mouse in the folds of the tarp. Kreusch is back at the big, ever deeper, and more intriguing feature. Crisp joins in to dig what turns out to be a mole hole. Her son Jordan becomes Kreusch's assistant. Angst and several other University of Tennessee and park archaeologists direct the work at the north-end site. But under the south-end canopy, the trio settles into their tasks as they joke and complain about their feet falling asleep and their hands cramping. The main feature's dirt is quite black. Kreusch scrapes and digs with a trowel or, sometimes, a big cooking spoon, the kind you would use to stir a gallon-size soup pot. The hole becomes deep and difficult to reach into. Kreusch puts the dirt he excavates into buckets. Jordan sifts the soil for artifacts, and then he bags all the dirt in plastic five-gallon trash bags so that it can be taken to the university lab for analysis.

At last, something interesting happens. One after another, Kreusch pulls out fist-size fire-cracked rocks until a pile exists. They suggest the remains of an earthen oven, rather like a pit barbecue. The oven cavity, about two feet in diameter, yields, at the bottom, roughly three feet below the surface of the field, the find of the season: five large shards of pottery. Kreusch pulls them out of the pit in the space of twenty minutes. They are all alike in design, composition, and color, which is a dark, grayish black. They are a bit damp. After few moments spent arranging the pieces on a clipboard, Kreusch shows how they fit together into a partial cooking vessel. Maybe about 30 percent of the whole vessel is found. The rest does not appear, even after more digging. The vessel has been paddle stamped, giving it a cross-hatched external texture as a design as well as tempering for improved firing success and shortened cooking times.

"Woodland," Kreusch says. "This is from the year zero." The pot shards probably come from the middle Woodland period, or the Pigeon Phase, because its maker used crushed quartz as a tempering agent in the clay. Though the vessel shards do not include the base, this kind of jar might have had four feet to support it in the oven, a design and functional feature that was very common.[7] By the late Woodland period, the quartz was replaced by sand. Ceramics mark the beginning of the Woodland period, and growing sophistication in their composition and design are hallmarks of the increasing technical skill of its potters. Residents of this era constructed villages in the large floodplains of the valley.[8]

Woodland culture, spanning between 1000 BCE and AD 1000, was based in part on cultivating corn as well as crops of squash, beans, and pumpkins, so the necessity of tending the fields meant that people were less nomadic and stayed in established villages for years at a time.[9] In turn, more leisure time led to decoration and ornamentation, so Woodland peoples carved combs and jewelry like pendants from antlers and seashells.[10] Ceremonial burials in earthen mounds also began during this time in the Appalachian Summit, although the practice had begun earlier elsewhere. Trade between residents of the Appalachian Summit area and others in Tennessee and the Ohio River Valley was well established. The mountain communities traded quartz for "copper, prismatic blades of chert and chalcedony, beads, pins, and clay figurines," among other items such as ceramics.[11]

Even though Woodland culture was based on farming, hunting still provided a significant part of these peoples' diet. Woodland-era hunting camps were located on ridges and upland valleys.[12] Spear hunting with the help of the atlatl continued, but the bow and arrow became a major Woodland-era innovation for bringing down deer, elk, buffalo, and bear.[13]

Of course, artifacts from the Woodland era make up just a fraction of prehistoric objects found in the Oconaluftee Valley. Far more remains exist from Mississippian culture, which spanned the years 1000–1540. In fact, the structure above the Woodland earthen oven is a prime example of what recent archaeological work has, so to speak, turned up. Though some work had been done in the valley in the early days of the park and in the 1970s, more recent archaeology digs began in 2007 when old water and sewer lines for the Smokemont Campground were replaced. At that time, four separate sites along the Newfound Gap Road and in the valley were excavated, and the most promising of those with the most intact deposits was found to be this site that the team has returned to for a number of years. Four structures were found on this one site: two from the Qualla phase (1450–1838) and two others from the earlier Pisgah phase (1000–1450). The structure "above" the Woodland oven was one of the Pisgah structures and has been determined to be a house.[14]

This house, known formally as Structure 2, could be identified by the remains of the wooden posts, called postmolds, that would have supported its walls and roof. Two parallel trenches marked an arched, vestibule-like entryway. So the house itself was about a sixteen-foot-square building with an entrance on the northeast corner.[15] It had four large supports inside the exterior walls to support a roof of thatched cane or bark, and the walls may have been composed of sunbaked clay; that is, "lathed with cane and plastered with clay before being thatched with grass."[16] Inside, the house had a raised clay hearth in the center of the structure with a hole in the peaked roof for smoke to escape.[17] Sleeping areas made of cane benches may have been stationed around the walls with partitions between them; household items would have been stored around the sides as well. These details are all typical of this era's domestic structures. And although this home seems quite small, it is important to recall that Mississippians mostly lived outdoors except during bad weather, so they did not spend much time inside such dwellings.[18] The artifacts from the home include "four triangular projectile points" and some suggestive floral remains, including corn, tobacco, and the quinoa-like chenopodium. These crops may have been cultivated in the surrounding field.[19]

Importantly, archaeologists speak of their jobs as destructive in nature. Unlike the preserved Italian town of Pompeii, which was buried beneath the lava and ash from Mount Vesuvius's eruption in the year 79 and then excavated and preserved as ruins, for the most part excavation means destruction. Angst explains to the interns, "You can only dig a feature once. It's very important that we record everything we do. Plan view, test view, photographs—kind of tedious paperwork, but essential." After the event of the dig ends, that site is gone, so all archaeologists can do is to create as accurate a record of it as possible.

After decades of work throughout the region, southeastern archaeologists have learned that life became more varied and complex in the Mississippian era. Agriculture based on corn, beans, and squash was the dominant means of subsistence, though hunting continued.[20] There was more: more leisure than the Woodland peoples had, more trade, more ceremonies, and more elaborate social structures and social classes. Ceramics and jewelry became more elaborate. The Mississippians are known for their platform mounds and a class of chiefs and elites whose homes were located on top of mounds along with a temple and altar.[21] These were the central features of large villages that were ringed for protection by palisades, or post walls finished with clay.[22] Though no mounds currently exist in the park, it is possible that a mound, now long plowed down, was once near the Mountain Farm Museum, adjacent to the Oconaluftee Visitor Center. Evidence of archaeological features and artifacts suggests that a number of Mississippian homes were located there.[23] An even more likely candidate for a mound is Ravensford, an area defined by the Raven Fork tributary of the Oconaluftee River that once fell inside the park. After a land swap in 2003, the area now belongs to the Eastern Band and serves as the site of a K-12 school complex.[24] Before the construction of the schools, the Cherokees excavated the area. The valley has other mound sites as well. Mounds certainly existed at Kituwah, Nununyi, and Bird Town. Kituwah was the location of an early Cherokee town, and stories establish that before the Cherokees moved into the region, other peoples were settled there in an established town. Nununyi, or Potato Town, also boasts a mound. It was an eighteenth-century Cherokee settlement.[25] And, of course, a mound existed at Bird Town, the site that was once called Egwânul'ti, the Cherokee village for which the valley and river are named.

The Mississippian presence in the valley is eloquently described in Angst's conclusion to a 2012 report he wrote for the park: "One could easily imagine a series of contemporaneous household clusters along the lower reaches of Raven Fork, at its mouth in the broad alluvial valley, downstream at least as far as Nununyi and then up to the Oconaluftee River to [the excavated site] and beyond. Furthermore, many non-contemporaneous sites undoubtedly occur here that span the entire duration of the archeological Qualla phase."[26]

One wonders, then, not where prehistoric peoples lived in the valley, but where they didn't live. Twenty-first-century visitors to the park should imagine the valley as a place of continuous and significant habitation from the close of the Ice Age until the park's establishment. The findings from archaeology help park officials understand how best to manage the park going forward. Kreusch explains, "What is the current park supposed to look like? [From archaeology] we can learn what the forest used to look like and know more about the exotics that have appeared. We can learn what we can do and what we are managing the park to be and become. How does the past environment relate to what we see today? With climate change, we can see what is changing, compared to the past." These are the thoughts that surface with each season of research in the bottomlands of the Oconaluftee Valley.

Chapter 2

THE PRINCIPAL PEOPLE

TRADITIONS OF HARMONY AND SHARING

▲▲▲

On a chilly morning in April, along with two dear friends and a small group of other "pilgrims" from the park's annual wildflower pilgrimage, I find myself on a section of the Appalachian Trail headed toward the rock outcrop called Charlies Bunion. Minutes before, we left Newfound Gap, a mountain pass where the crest of the Smokies is transected by the central overmountain road of the park. Our mission is birdwatching, but it's breezy, foggy, misty, and quite cool, probably in the fifties, though the temps feel freezing. Not the best conditions to see birds, certainly not the migrating warblers we hope for. Some crows showed up in the parking lot. (No raven; sigh.) We've got on layers topped by rain jackets—hoods up—and gloves. Binoculars in hand, we're ready to see something, ever hopeful. We listen and hear a black-capped chickadee's song: fee-beeyee. A junco darts by. But, honestly, there's not much bird action because no insects are out and about. It's too early and too raw.

Sun rays reach through banks of fog now and again, lighting the mist itself and showing shiny wet rosebay rhododendrons on the downhill side of the trail. The trail here is about four feet wide, punctuated by cross logs to slow erosion and create very long steps. It is sunken below the ridge of the mountain from decades of foot traffic, so there's some protection from wind despite an altitude over 5,000 feet. That's North Carolina over my right shoulder, but the vista is obscured by the foggy mist (or misty fog). Below, entirely out of sight, are the multiple headwaters of the Oconaluftee River. I don't hear any water, just the shuffle of feet and the murmur of voices. I imagine what the headwaters might look like: seeps emerging demurely from rocks framed by club moss and wood sorrel, rivulets off inaccessibly steep slopes eventually joining into tiny streams. If I were a bird, any bird, could I see them, or are they shielded by rhododendron thicket or tightly packed yellow birch and ash trunks? Are they obscured by the pervading dampness of the mist, the rocks, the soil—the all of it? Origins can be secret, like where life begins.

In this enchanted moment, the rich relationship between place and people asserts itself from the fog, the mystery. If I'm going to think about Oconaluftee Valley, I need to acknowledge the cultural legacy of the Cherokee people. I need to understand how their beliefs and values shaped their community and influenced their subsequent responses to European colonization, the choices they made in times of crisis, and the actions they took to keep their families together.

As for the birding stop that day, we soon moved on to lower, sunnier, and warmer slopes. But even in the clouds of the crest, we were happy to be there and happy to be together as old friends visiting a familiar but ineffable place.

▲ ▲ ▲

"THIS IS WHAT the old men told me when I was a boy."[1] These words announce the telling of a Cherokee myth to a listener. Because an elder usually tells a story to a younger person, the sentence emphasizes the connections between generations. The teller shares stories and knowledge that he or she was told by elders years before. The listener is young, as the teller once was, and now needs to learn. Through understatement, the teller indicates the inherited role of each subsequent Cherokee generation to learn about Cherokee culture and pass it on, in turn, to Cherokee children for their personal development and for the practical use and benefit of the people.

Early on, Cherokee children learn that they are Ani-Yunwiya, the principal people of the earth. Other peoples exist, including not only whites but, previously, members of nearby ethnic groups such as the Creek and Shawano. Other kinds of people have existed; for example, the Cherokees traditionally believe in little people and immortal ones who share the mountains with them but are rarely seen. These peoples have their homes and town council houses below mountains though they may, on occasion, help a lost Cherokee find the way home. All these people should be respected. Nonetheless, the Cherokees call themselves the principal or real people, and for centuries the Cherokees were the dominant ethnic group of a vast part of southeastern North America, occupying western North and South Carolina, eastern and middle Tennessee, and northern Georgia and Alabama. Though they occupied only a portion of this land, Cherokee hunting grounds extended to 40,000 square miles.[2] So the proud title is based in fact.

Several theories have attempted to explain the origins of the Cherokee people. European colonists and nineteenth-century U.S. citizens believed that all Native Americans, including the Cherokees, descended from one of the lost tribes of Israel, the tribe of Shem, one of Noah's sons.[3] In particular, a prominent nineteenth-century missionary to the Cherokees, Daniel S. Butrick, stated that he had found evidence of this heritage.[4] This claim of ancestry was an attempt to counter the growing racism of white (Christian) colonists against the Cherokees and give them a status equal to Europeans. It was the explanation Cherokee sympathizers used to rationalize why Native Americans should not be enslaved as were Africans. However, because anti-Semitism was not uncommon among white colonists, the theory was of limited value over time and did not greatly lessen white hostility toward the Cherokees.[5]

Late nineteenth-century anthropologists recognized the linguistic similarity of the Cherokee language with that of the Iroquois of New England and Canada and theorized that the Cherokees broke away from the Iroquois and moved south to establish their own territory. Twentieth-century archaeologists speculated that since artifacts and dwellings did not show a dramatic change from the Mississippian to the Qualla (or Cherokee) phase, the historic Cherokees may have descended from the Mississippians in the region rather than migrating from the north.[6] Contemporary scholars think that the scenario may have played out a bit differently. Using multiple research methods such as linguistic analysis, archaeology, and DNA mapping, scholars now think that the Iroquois and Cherokees were once one people who occupied present-day Virginia.[7] At some point, probably late in the Archaic period, and for reasons that are unknown, the Iroquois and Cherokees split and moved apart, with the Iroquois going north and the Cherokees south. The Cherokees first established themselves in the Carolinas.[8] The ancient settlement of Kituwah, located on the Tuckasegee River and just downstream of the Oconaluftee Valley, is considered one of the seven mother towns of the Cherokees.[9] Once settled in the southern Appalachians, the Cherokee people developed a distinctive language, mythology, and lifeways, and, once established, they spread throughout more and more of the Southeast.

TOWNHOUSE COMMUNITIES

The Cherokees adopted several settlement patterns, but all were based on town life.[10] The largest towns were organized around preexisting Mississippian ceremonial mounds; Kituwah may have been one of these. These towns were no longer palisaded like Mississippian towns, but they were arranged around a large rectangular earthen mound on which a town council house stood. Townhouses were similar in construction to winter Mississippian and Cherokee homes—square-shaped, with thatched walls and roofs and a central clay hearth. But they were much larger than homes to accommodate the gathering of the town's people inside.[11] By the mid-eighteenth century, townhouse architecture consisted of eight-sided buildings that could accommodate large numbers of people and seat them according to their clans along seven of the sides, reserving the last side for entrance.[12] Outside, in front of the mound was spread a large, flat field for ball playing and for dances and ceremonies. Homes surrounded the mound and field. In addition, a summer townhouse, rather like an outdoor covered pavilion, and summer structures attached to each home would have been present in each community.[13] Smaller communities did not have mounds, so they were organized around townhouses (or council houses), and "very small communities of hamlets and farmsteads . . . may have looked to a distant community center based on kinship or clan ties."[14] Beyond these small communities were the "fields, [fishing] weirs, trails, orchards, meadows, and woods" that the Cherokees used for hunting, fishing, and agriculture.[15] The relative sizes and prosperity of the towns, hamlets, and farmsteads fluctuated according to soil fertility, the abundance of game, the political dominance of the Cherokees among the other Native peoples, periodic population loss from smallpox epidemics, and the threat of attack from other Native groups or, increasingly in the eighteenth century, from colonial settlers.

Cherokee lifeways and culture flourished before European traders arrived. Between 1450 and 1700 the Cherokees practiced a diverse subsistence living that provided them with food, shelter, and clothing but also structured their society by gender, clan, and kinship. The primary value of Cherokee life was harmony achieved by "a balance of opposite forces, such as war and peace, men and women, and plants and animals."[16] Importantly, harmony was more prized than material wealth; the land and its bounty were made available to humans to use as they needed but not to gather in excess. In this society that practiced communal labor and redistribution of goods to all to meet subsistence needs, individual wealth was not a goal and did not command community esteem or political power.[17] Instead, individuals' contributions to community life and their ability to lead in peace or times of war for the restoration of harmony were most highly esteemed, as exemplified by the high regard of brave warriors, expert hunters, and wise healers.[18] Historian William McLoughlin explains how the ethic of harmony provided a comprehensive outlook for Cherokees: "There was no secular area of life free from spiritual meaning; sports, war, hunting, agriculture, family, town, and tribal affairs were all woven together into a unified pattern of religious rules and connections involving harmony with the world above, the world below, and the world around them."[19]

This social structure resonates in the Cherokee mythology and illuminates values and beliefs that have always sustained the spirit of the Cherokee people. Though many sources of the Cherokee mythology are available today, James Mooney was the first anthropologist who devoted years to collecting and documenting Cherokee history, myths, and lifeways. In the late nineteenth century, he lived in Cherokee, North Carolina, for several summers while working for the U.S. Bureau of Ethnology collecting myths, stories, and sacred formulas from individuals who experienced firsthand what life was like in the Oconaluftee Valley before the Cherokee Removal of 1838. His versions of Cherokee stories remain a good starting point for understanding Cherokee culture.

A BASIC BUT SUFFICIENT LIVING

One of the foundational myths of the Cherokees, the story of Kanati and Selu, describes the social system and division of labor in the pre-European subsistence economy. Kanati (the Lucky Hunter), was a master hunter; Selu (Corn), his wife, was responsible for growing and harvesting corn, beans, and squash and preparing food.[20] Each played a vital role in feeding their two children, both boys. One of these boys was their biological child, but the other was an incarnation of the blood from a deer Kanati had slain that Selu dripped into the river when she cleaned the meat. He was a wild boy, full of curiosity and mischief, who suggested devious schemes to his brother. The boys observed that Kanati always returned to their home with meat; finding game was never difficult for him. So one day the boys followed their father up the mountain and watched as he rolled a stone away from a cave entrance. A buck ran out. Kanati shot him with an arrow and then replaced the stone. After Kanati had left, the boys moved the stone away to open the cave, inadvertently freeing all the animals trapped inside. After that moment, humans had to roam the mountains to find their game.

Another day, the boys noticed that Selu was always able to prepare them a dinner of corn, beans, and meat after a short trip to the storehouse. Thinking that she was a witch, they peered between the logs of the storehouse when she went inside. There Selu rubbed her belly and sides, and corn and beans fell into a basket on the floor. She returned to the home to prepare dinner, but when she saw the boys, she could tell that they had watched her. She also knew that they would kill her, so she told them what to do with her body after she was dead. They were instructed first to clear a field and then to drag her body around the perimeter of the circle seven times. Next they should drag her body seven times inside the circle. If they stayed up all night to watch over the circle, in the morning they would have plenty of corn. But the boys, perhaps because of their youth, failed to follow Selu's directions completely. They cleared only seven little spots instead of a large area. Rather than drag her body around the circle seven times, they did it only twice. These are the reasons why corn does not grow everywhere and why Cherokees work their crops twice each season. Even so (and most happily), the boys succeeded in watching over the corn all night, so in the morning it was ripe and ready to eat. Consequently, the Cherokees will always have corn to eat. By the way, other repercussions of the boys' violence toward their mother came about once Kanati discovered what they had done.

This story establishes the basic subsistence pattern of the Cherokees and their gendered spheres of influence: men were hunters, and women were farmers and were in charge of the home. Both men and women fished and gathered nuts and berries, but on the whole women dominated community life and men were the major actors outside the community in hunting and in matters of war.[21] Because women dominated the domestic scene, the clans that determined a person's identity were matrilineal, always following the mother's line. Family homes belonged to the wife of a marriage, and all children belonged to the mother's clan, with her brothers having the primary masculine child-rearing role for sons rather than the father. Marriages were only allowed outside of clan ties, and if a marriage ended, the woman kept the home and the children. This sharing of key responsibilities and division of labor meant that women held equal status to men in the community. They were not dependent on their husbands for their identities or their personal well-being. Even though men were more often decision makers in matters of going to war, women were respected elders with important voices in key decisions. For example, an elder woman of a town, a "beloved woman," would decide what to do with prisoners of war, whether they would become slaves, be tortured or killed, be accepted into a clan, or, worst of all, be forced to live without an identity outside of clan society.[22] Notably, both women and men could become conjurers and healers and could hold positions of great authority and respect in a town.

A MORAL NATURAL ECONOMY

The concepts of balance and mutual respect also emerge from Cherokee myths about animals and plants. The Cherokees believe that human beings are not essentially superior to either plants or animals and must respect the lives of both. Hunters may kill animals for food, but they must say thanks for their game. The character of Little Deer makes this point clearly. Little Deer is a small, invisible deer that watches over all deer.[23] When a hunter kills a deer, he must say thanks for it immediately because Little Deer appears to observe every kill scene. If the hunter neglects to give thanks, then Little Deer will follow the hunter home by the drops of blood on the trail and give him rheumatism. It's simple to infer the outcome of disrespect: future hunting will be more difficult and less successful for a hunter disabled by rheumatism. Similarly, someone collecting herbs, particularly ginseng, must first pass by three plants and take only the fourth in the same area.[24] It is not appropriate to take too many.

Perhaps the most direct connection between animals and humans emerges from the traditional story of the origin of bears.[25] Bears, myth tells Cherokees, once were a community of humans. But they decided that they wanted to live in the mountains, so they left their town and townhouse to become a bear clan. As they walked to the mountains they grew claws and tails, turning into physical bears. Even so, the bears maintained some of their human practices such as occasionally walking on two legs and maintaining townhouses for community events. Four bear townhouses are said to be located within different high peaks of the Smokies. At these places the bears hold a dance before disbanding to hibernate during the winter. One of the townhouses is Kuwahi, or Mulberry Place, now known as Clingmans Dome, the highest peak in the Smokies.[26] The grand White Bear, the chief of the bears, lives below Mulberry Place. This townhouse is near the Enchanted Lake at the headwaters of the Oconaluftee River.[27] Although the lake is invisible to humans, it is a medicine lake for all animals and birds. If an injured animal swims across the lake, it will be healed of any wounds from arrows or from sickness. The lake preserves the balance between animals and humans. Bears, recalling their past lives as humans and retaining some sympathy for them, have also helped lost hunters from time to time, even allowing them to den with a bear over the winter. Finally, when humans kill a bear, if they cover the blood remaining from a kill with leaves, as they leave the site and look back, they will see that the killed bear will rise up, ghostlike, and return to the woods. In such an instance the bear helps humans by offering them meat but not its life.[28]

In general, because of humans' numbers and pride, their relationships with animals are more adversarial than their relationships with plants. Plants serve as friends to humans, providing remedies for the wounds and diseases that animals (especially insects) cause. Ginseng is a primary example of a plant that helps humans. Mooney calls it "a sentient being," and J. T. Garrett, a Cherokee healer, explains that it helps to build immunity and is good for many purposes, including "headaches, nervous conditions, [and] vertigo," as well as for stopping bleeding.[29]

CLEAR-CUT JUSTICE

Another key component of traditional Cherokee life was a law of vengeance for aggression to fellow clan members and swift retaliation for aggression against the community from those who were not Cherokee. Cherokees believed that "crying blood is quenched with equal blood."[30] In situations where an aggression occurred between two Cherokees, the clan of the victim would seek vengeance from the clan of the aggressor in precise proportion to the original offense. This vengeance, however, would not spark a cycle of subsequent revenge. In cases of aggression between ethnic groups or nations, retaliation was not limited to a single act of proportional vengeance. In such international conflicts, Cherokee law permitted warriors to take as many lives as possible, and of course, subsequent cycles of retaliation often occurred. Clan vengeance and community liability were duties, not choices.[31] They constituted the only legal protections Cherokees had against aggression. In their view, if they did not retaliate, then they essentially accepted the status of game that could be killed at will by anyone. According to Mooney, when the bears stopped avenging the deaths they suffered from hunters, they became game rather than humans, and of course, this situation was unacceptable for the Cherokee people.[32] Consequently, the Cherokees valued skill in physical competition and warfare. This skill was developed in *anetso*, the Cherokee ball game, a game like lacrosse with important community ritual meaning because it tested the bravery and physical ability of men who would need to serve as warriors. The ball game has always been a key part of Cherokee culture, involving the whole community as spectators and in celebratory events before and after matches. It survives today as one of the important features of Cherokee life.

The ball game's cultural significance can be seen in its role in the story of Kanati and Selu after the corn goddess's murder.[33] When Kanati returns home and finds that his sons have murdered his wife and placed her head on the roof, he becomes angry and abandons the boys, going to live with the Wolf people. Once he reaches their town, Kanati enters the townhouse where a council is in session and sits in silence until the chief asks why he is present. Kanati requests that the Wolf people go to the boys in a week's time and "play ball" with them, meaning that he wants the Wolf people to kill the boys. The boys have secret knowledge of their coming battle and prepare for it; in the end, they prevail over the warriors, killing almost all of them. In the meantime, Kanati leaves the Wolf people and continues traveling west. The boys go to find Kanati, who is surprised to see them. He then tests them with two other mortal ordeals, and through cleverness, perseverance, and skill they survive. After each test they seek out Kanati. After the final ordeal, they find him at the end of the world, in the east where the sun rises, sitting with Selu. The couple welcomes the boys and visits with them for a week but will not let them stay for long. Instead, the boys must go to the Darkening Land, where the sun goes down (the west), to live. There, they are called The Little Men. When they talk, people hear low thunder, so they are also called the Thunder Boys.

This story of the Thunder Boys' survival directly associates the ball game with war and vengeance. It also shows how the boys win challenges through their ability to compete in physical tests as well as through strategy and preparation.[34] Finally, it suggests that balance between the impulses toward war (or vengeance) and peace (or the hunting and agriculture needed for subsistence) is essential to maintaining harmony on Earth. This is the reason why the boys cannot live with their parents at the end. Similarly, the Cherokees designated separated leaders and even separate towns for purposes of war and peace. Some towns were peace towns, or towns of refuge, and criminals could seek protection from their victims' kinsmen there; also, towns often had two leaders, one a peace chief, who led treaty negotiations, and the other a war chief, who led braves into battle.

Because it is a sport that requires collaboration among team members, the ball game also illustrates the harmony ethic of the Cherokees.[35] The story of the Ball Game of the Birds and Animals tells how two small individuals, the bat and the flying squirrel—"two little things hardly larger than field mice"—help the birds win over the animals, a team with powerful players like the bear, tough ones like the terrapin, and fast ones like the deer.[36] Though the bat and flying squirrel should belong on the side of the animals, they are rejected because of their small size. The birds accept them and help them find ways to fly. When the game begins, these unexpected heroes control the ball and score, winning the game for the birds. The story further suggests that the ball game functioned as a substitute for war, bringing members of one village together in a contest against another in a ritualized fashion.[37] Because a lost game was likely to lead to a rematch, this cycle of continued encounters follows the pattern of ongoing vengeance seeking—but at a far less consequential level since casualties were rare.

INDIGENOUS SUSTAINABILITY MEETS CAPITALISM

All together, these elements of traditional Cherokee culture, in place before European contact, point to some of the reasons that colonists and Cherokees had difficulty understanding each other. In the subsistence Cherokee economy, individuals were not motivated to seek personal wealth, or even surplus, as capitalist Europeans generally were. The Cherokee economy depended on a gendered division of labor but recognized the contributions of both sexes as equal and essential to survival and happiness. This view gave women status equal to but distinct from that of men. Both women and men held positions of respect and responsibility within communities and also had authority in "state" matters such as peace negotiations. The clan and kinship systems gave individuals their identities, provided for the raising of children, and governed social life as well as most legal issues. Because Cherokees did not own land individually but used it as they needed in the cultivation of corn, beans, and other staples, or through the use of collectively held tribal hunting grounds, private property, and particularly the ownership of land, was not relevant to them. Finally, Cherokee vengeance and retaliation were regarded as clan or community duties, and they were practiced outside what Europeans understood as individual liability for aggression, since a clansman of an aggressor could be made to answer for a relative's crime and since wars against one non-Cherokee community could be provoked by the actions of another one of the same group, or even by a single individual. When disputes about white families settling in hunting grounds arose and when they led to bloodshed, acts of vengeance and retaliation were often understood differently by the Cherokees and Europeans. It is important to note that the Cherokees had contact with other societies before Europeans arrived in their villages. After contact, the Cherokees continued their existing traditions, including the ways they regarded those who were not Cherokee, responded to trade opportunities, and reacted to violence and aggression. They were not an isolated people without strategies to cope with competing peoples. Further, whether they were in fact "the principal people" would be fully tested as their identity and status shifted in the eighteenth and nineteenth centuries.

Though much has changed for the Cherokees since the seventeenth century, the core values, stories, and rituals remain to unite them. In the late 1990s, Lynne Harlan, cultural director for the Eastern Band of the Cherokee, illuminated the traditional Cherokee outlook and its persistence to the present: "There's a continuum of culture that makes us one, that makes us a family. We have always been in this place together. This is where the Creator put us. The fundamental thing that makes us Indian is that spirit of community that keeps us together."[38]

Chapter 3

LIFE IN THE OUT TOWNS

CRISES OF THE COLONIAL ERA

▲ ▲ ▲

Oconaluftee Island Park offers a reprieve, right in the middle of the Cherokee tourist district, just across the river via several pedestrian bridges. The island, a small sandbar in the river, is ideal to wander, picnic, fish. Usually, mallards are on scene. There's not much wild about it, but okay, we're in a city. The trail around the island leads into a stand of bamboo, which arches grandly overhead, creating shaded corridors and a room. Yes, bamboo is nonnative and invasive, but it does provide a pleasant outdoor enclosure. Think of a place to meet a friend for a chat.

But bamboo? Why, oh why, is an invasive species right here in the middle of a world-renowned refuge for native plants and animals? The answer is, simply, European settlers and their livestock. Once, river cane, *Arundinaria gigantea*, might have thrived here. Alas, cattle happily eat native river cane; their hooves trample its rhizomes and roots. Over time, it dies and new plants take root. Invasive and exotic plants displace native flora.

River cane is more than a feature of the landscape, though it is that, too. Canebrakes prevent erosion and offer streamside habitat for birds and other critters. The stand of exotic bamboo is testimony to ecological, cultural, and economic losses the Cherokees endured in the eighteenth century. River cane is the essential material for many traditional items: blowguns, fishing rods, mats, and, most important, baskets, the kind known as double-walled and dyed with bloodroot and black walnut. These provided home furnishings and subsistence tools before the time of European traders and settlers. Next they became part of the trade business itself, especially toward the end of the nineteenth century and the beginning of the twentieth as the craft and tourist trades developed. Unfortunately, as native canebrakes disappeared, the abundant supply of free craft material shrank and became rare, particularly as demand for them increased as the Cherokee craft business grew.

River cane is making a comeback in the twenty-first century. Cherokee, state, and academic groups are all working to establish new stands nearby. So although losses from European settlement and the capitalist capture of Native culture have been transformational for the Cherokees, key remnants of the culture have persisted and, over time, are reemerging.

▲ ▲ ▲

CONTACT BETWEEN the Cherokees and Europeans grew in North America during the seventeenth century, mostly in the form of trade. The English and French traded with Native American peoples for deer and other animal skins, providing firearms, ammunition, and goods in return. By 1700, the deerskin trade was well established throughout the Cherokee territories because of the high quality of Cherokee skins.[1] Charleston exported more than 50,000 skins each year to England.[2] This activity led to a shift in Cherokee society from a sustainable, subsistence economy to a market economy.[3] British traders lived and traveled among the Cherokees, exchanging rifles and other manufactured goods for skins. The British traders were somewhat supervised and regulated by the royal governor of South Carolina, who set size standards for skins and their trade value in goods. As the British trade increased and outcompeted the French, the British mapped the Cherokee Nation as extending to "five geographically distinct areas that each contained ten to twelve independent towns."[4] These five areas comprised the Lower Towns in South Carolina; the Middle Towns on the upper Little Tennessee River; the Valley Towns around the upper Hiawassee, Valley, and Cheoah Rivers; the Overhill Towns in Tennessee; and, finally, the Out Towns along the Tuckasegee and Oconaluftee Rivers.[5] Though the Out Towns were near key places such as Kituwah, and though they were important culturally because of the centrality of the mountains in Cherokee legend, they were literally outposts. Not well known to colonists before or after the Revolutionary War, the Out Towns were at a remove because of the ruggedness of the surrounding mountains. In fact, in many Euro-American period sources, the Out Towns are loosely grouped with the

Middle Towns, likely because comparatively little was known about them.[6] Ultimately, by the nineteenth century, the Out Towns became a stronghold of traditional Cherokee culture, and this conservative social temperament ironically—though in a way quite logically—caused the area to become the center of the Eastern Band after the Indian Removal of 1838.

For Cherokees living in the Out Towns, trade was their first contact with Europeans. Spanish explorers of the mid-sixteenth century such as Hernando de Soto and Juan Pardo did not travel far enough into the mountains to reach the Out Towns even though they spent a good amount of time in other Cherokee territories, including some Middle and Valley Towns not very far away. In 1721, the United Society of the Propagation of the Gospel in Foreign Parts sent Francis Varnod to the Out Towns to collect census data about them, and he visited Tuckareechee, Kituwah, Stecoe, and Nununyi.[7] Varnod recorded that Stecoe (or Stecoa) was the largest town, with a population just under 300. Tuckareechee and Kituwha both had about 225 people, and Nununyi was the smallest community at the time with 160 individuals. From that time forward, the Out Towns appeared on both English and American maps, mostly to facilitate surveillance of Cherokee towns for news about the nation's shifting alliances with other European countries.[8] Additional Out Towns appear on these maps: Tuckasegee, Connawisca, Conuntory, Evanga, and Dick's Village, as well as Oconelufty with its alternative names of Bird Town, Nick Bottom, and Cunnulrasha. Of these towns, Tuckareechee, Stecoe, Nununyi, and Oconelufty lay in the Oconaluftee Valley.

THE DEERSKIN TRADE

Hunting deer was a long established practice for Cherokees. The vast majority of Cherokee territory consisted of hunting grounds rather than land used for towns or even for crops. As the deerskin trade developed, the Cherokees folded hunting for trade purposes into the men's seasonal routine: they hunted in the winter, sold skins to traders in spring, went to war with neighboring tribes in the summer, and bought ammunition from traders in the fall before the men set out for their mountain hunting camps as the weather turned cold and crop harvest ended. Women, too, were involved in the trade; they laboriously stretched and cleaned the skins.[9] Once prepared, skins were bartered on a credit system rather than sold for cash value. The traders credited hunters the guns and ammunition that they needed before the hunt; in the spring when the hunters' cache was ready, the Cherokees were compensated for the value of the skins they had minus that of the credited supplies. Hunters, then, could easily fall into debt to traders, especially during poor years or when other problems arose such as disease, continuing hostilities with neighboring groups, or encroachments by settlers into hunting grounds. Traders were also often in debt to partners who financed their business.

The immediate benefits of trade to the Cherokees were enormous: guns and ammunition for better hunting and for warfare; cloth and blankets for clothes and comfort; pots and utensils for easier cooking; and metal farming tools for easier work putting in and tending to crops. But other effects with more ambiguous outcomes were also set in motion. The deerskin trade shifted the subsistence economy to a market economy. Cherokees who once focused on fulfilling their clan and town's immediate survival needs eventually began to see the appeal of surplus goods and material wealth.[10] Over time, areas became overhunted and wildlife populations declined, affecting Cherokees' diets and hunters' ability to supply the necessary number of skins to traders. Financial debt resulted from lean hunting years. European diseases like smallpox, measles, and influenza decimated the Cherokees in the eighteenth century, and for the most part, the traditional remedies and healers were powerless against the ravages of these diseases. Deaths from these diseases often wiped out whole towns and areas. Three periods of disease occurred: a smallpox epidemic in 1738, said to cause the death of half the tribe; epidemics of smallpox, measles, and influenza between 1759 and 1760, right in the middle of the confusion of the Cherokee War; and another smallpox outbreak in the years 1780–83.[11] Such devastating population losses during times when the Cherokees needed to defend themselves from attacks by other tribes led to cultural losses: the loss of faith in traditional medicine surely challenged the Cherokees' sense of themselves and their understanding of the world.

In addition, the Cherokees became embroiled in an international power play among the English, French, and Spanish; without the material needs and the complex relationships ushered in by trade with the Europeans, Native Americans would not have become entangled in such affairs. Before the deerskin trade, ethnic groups had regularly waged war over territory, to retaliate against past injustices, or even to take prisoners, who could become slaves. But trade in hides came alongside the Europeans' struggle for continental dominance. The English held the Atlantic Coast, and the French were powerful along the Mississippi, in the Midwest, and in the Great Lakes. The Spanish dominated Florida and the West. Each European power wanted to reap maximum economic benefits for its home country and to secure and strengthen its position on the continent. In May 1751, South Carolina governor James Glen described the seriousness of these shifting relationships to New York governor George Clinton: "To one unacquainted with Indian Affairs, the Designs of the French may seem dark and doubtfull, their Projects improbable, and their Views very Distant. However, they are not less to be minded upon that Account. If British Governors are either indolent or neglectfull, it may prove very fatal to the Provinces."[12]

On top of international competition, the English colonies competed with one another for the Native American trade: South Carolina, Virginia, and Georgia worked for their own colonies' advantage and punished the Cherokees when they tried to improve prices or increase deliveries of ammunition by bargaining with trade commissions of more than one colony. The Cherokees' traditional reasons for war among ethnic groups were expanded by new pressures placed on them because of trade agreements and allegiances with Europeans. Citing terms from a treaty of 1730, the English demanded that the Cherokees aid them in their battles against the French and French-allied Indians on the Virginia frontier.[13] Altogether, the Cherokees and other nations to the north and south found themselves in the midst of ever more complex cycles of aggression, retribution, and negotiation.

RUST ON THE CHAIN OF FRIENDSHIP

Given the Out Towns' remove, one might think that they would be protected from the international intrigue and competition that resulted in the French and Indian War (1754–63). After all, their area was bordered by the Cowee Mountains to the south, the Balsam Mountains to the north, and the Great Smoky Mountains to the west.[14] But the opposite was more the case. At midcentury, the Out Towns were known for their hostility toward the English as compared with the other parts of the Cherokee Nation. Because the Out Towns were remote, they were more exposed to northern Native American groups supported by the French.[15] The encounters that Cherokees had with these French-affiliated Native peoples were, in turn, both friendly and hostile in nature. Northern Native Americans, supplied and incited by the French, attacked the Out Towns and the Overhill Towns. Further, the northern groups preached hatred of the English to the Cherokees, and sometimes these arguments made sense when the South Carolina governor was perceived as ambivalent or inadequate in his support of the Out Towns. Allegiances were continuously shifting.

An early instance of the doubts and stresses between the Out Towns and South Carolina traders and officials became known as the crisis of 1751. That spring a rumor spread that a white trader in the Out Towns was murdered and his goods were taken by people from Conuntory, Stecoe, and Kituwha. The murder, however, was a false report, though the trader, Bernard Hughes, was beaten and driven out of town and his goods were confiscated. Unfortunately, these events happened at the same time as other incidents: white intrusion into the hunting grounds, Cherokee accusations that traders used false weights and measures that exacerbated their debt, a raid by whites of a Cherokee camp along the Savannah River and the theft of 330 of their deerskins, and, finally, the murder of a white man's servant and a Chickasaw man in an Oconee River store.[16]

A letter from the Raven, a chief of the Overhill (Tennessee) towns, to Governor Glen of South Carolina supplies an account of the Out Towns' incident and shows how serious it was to the entire Cherokee Nation. In this matter the Raven quickly and obsequiously took the side of the English against other Cherokees, whom he called rogues, because he knew that all of the South Carolina trade was affected and that his towns must maintain the trade for their own protection. In part (and via a scribe), he wrote:

> And the Raven desires that those Towns who done this Mischief should have no traders amongst them, that is Kenotory, Sticoe and Kittawa, nor yet no Indian nor Half-breed should be Factor from any white Man among them, till they acknowledge their Faults, and see the want of a white Man, and that they themselves, and their Women and Children should have wary Leggs to walk to Traders in other Towns to buy what they want.
>
> The Raven sais that he and his head Men and Warriours has not forgot all the good Talks that they have heard from Time to Time, nor never shall be forgot, as long as Grass grows and Water runs, and we will hand it down to our young People comeing up, and graft it in their Hearts, as your Excellency has done in theirs, for they do not want to know any other People but the English, and they hope your Excellency will not let them suffer for those that has been the Rogues, as he and his Parts has put a stop to it all, but that you will let their Traders come up as usual, for the Good of both, for we are in great Want of Ammunition, and as we are outside Towns, the French are daily upon us, and for the Want of Ammunition, we don't know how soon we may be cutt off.[17]

Chucheechee, the Warrior of Tuckasegee, one of the Out Towns, seconded the Raven's concern about a trade embargo, writing to Governor Glen, whom he called "father," on May 6, 1751: "The Warriour says he expects his father will send his Children Goods for they mourn for Goods, and hopes he will not stop Goods from them. . . . He hopes his Father will not stop the Traders from comeing with Amunition sonn for they are very much in Debt to the white People, and Enemies very many upon them from the Southward and Northward when they go off."[18] Just as these chiefs feared, on learning of these events, Governor Glen placed an embargo on all trade with all the Cherokee towns, not just the Out Towns or other hot spots. Glen also wrote to the chiefs of the Out Towns, stated that rust had appeared on their chain of friendship, and demanded that they turn over two men from each town, those most responsible for the attack:

> Head Men and Warriours of Ketowah, As the Chain of Friendship which has so long subsisted between the English and your beloved Men, has of late contracted Rust among you in your town of Ketowaw, and as you have forgot of late the many good Talks that have passed between us, and your beloved Men, and as in your Town in a daring and insolent Manner you have broke open the Stores of our Traders, and publickly divided and shared their Goods and Skins among you, as if they has been Spoil taken from an Enemy, and not only threatned the Lives of those white Men and forced them to fly, for the Security of their Persons, but sent out a Party of you[r] People to pursue and kill them. These Robberies and Violences we are determined not to induce, but to have the Author of them brought to condign Punishment.
>
> We therefore send you this Letter, which is to desire that you deliver up two Persons of your Town of those who broke open the Stores and divided the Goods, were met most Guilty and active against the English, and we do hereby declare that if they are not delivered up to us within two Months from the Date hereof, we will come up to your Town and take them by Force.[19]

The posturing on both sides of this correspondence, particularly the language of the Cherokee's dependence and the governor's patriarchal status, suggests that the two cultures were testing strategies to manage each other, all the while recognizing that a transition of power had already taken place.

The Cherokees responded by saying that no further negotiations would occur until trade was restored.[20] In addition, the Overhill (Tennessee) Towns began discussions with Virginia traders to defy the embargo. Forced into action by this maneuver, Glen led the South Carolina trade council in drafting reformed trade regulations. These were presented to the Cherokees in November 1751, and the treaty was accepted. It required that the Out Towns pay for the goods stolen from Hughes and that the other simultaneous wrongs be resolved. The reforms consisted of thirty-nine points that attempted to clarify regulations and prevent future injustices of trade between traders and villages. These included standard prices and measurements throughout the Cherokee Nation, the establishment of districts consisting of several towns each, with assigned traders for each, prohibition of any rum trading, prohibition of taking slaves into Cherokee territory, prohibition of using an Indian as a trader or factor, and requirements on traders to keep records, report problems, and trade fairly or risk losing their licenses.[21] The treaty resolved the crisis but did little to improve the ongoing disputes between traders and Cherokees because, after a time, accusations about high prices, inaccurate measurements, trade monopolies, and shortages of much-needed goods resurfaced. By the mid-1750s the international tensions with the French had escalated.

THE CHEROKEE WAR

In 1754, Chucheechee, the Warrior of Tuckasegee, asked that the governor build a fort in the Out Towns to supply security against attacks, as had already been promised to the Lower Towns. Knowing that the chances that this request would succeed were small, Chucheechee said he would settle for more ammunition: "If your Excellency does not think proper to settle a Fort at our Town as we have land very hilly, I beg your Excellency would assist us with Ammunition to enable us to defend ourselves against the Enemies that come to molest us."[22] But neither seems to have happened, and attention shifted from the Out Towns, primarily to the Overhill Towns but also to the nation as a whole. South Carolina became concerned that the Cherokees were developing allegiances and agreements with the French or the Virginians. They ignored the Out Towns because their location was less strategic than the Overhill Towns' in providing a buffer zone between areas of English and French influence.[23] Consequently, the Out Town Cherokees were shortchanged by the English in South Carolina and became desperate for ammunition. Their anxiety comes through clearly in a letter from the Tuckesaws (Tosate of Tuckasage and Tosate of Slocke) to Governor Glen in October 1754:

> With submission to our Brother the Governour and the Beloved Men of Carolina, we return you Thanks for the Powder and Bulletts you sent

> us to defend ourselves against our Enemies. We received but two Bags of Powder and four of Bulletts which is but a small Quantity for seven Towns, we having the Enemy as bad against us as the People over the Hills, and the Chief of the Ammunition that was sent up was carried over the Hills, and we beg that the Governor and the beloved Men will be so good as to send us up seven Bags of Powder and fourteen Bags of Bullets, that is one Bag of Powder and two of Bulletts for each Town to defend ourselves and the White People that live amongst us for the Enemy is so hot upon us that we can hardly go from Town to Town. And if you please and think proper to send us Pistols, Cutlashes, and small Hatchets, Flints to defend ourselves we shall be very glad for we have News of a great many Enemies comeing upon us, and we beg that this Letter may not be forgot as our last was as we have sent our Token as you told us to send it when we were in Want and we desire an Answer to our Letter as we remain in brotherly Freindship.[24]

Governor Glen responded by promising three bags of powder and six bags of bullets while simultaneously noting his surprise that more was needed and while proposing a meeting of Out Town and Overhill chiefs with him in Charleston for discussions about "some Things relating to the Wellfare of the Cherroekee Nation which I have much at Heart."[25] That meeting in early 1755 led to South Carolina's promise that it would build a fort near the Overhill Towns so that the Cherokee frontier would have English protection and so that the Cherokees would agree to join the English in fighting the French and their allied Native Americans in Virginia. The plans for the fort, which became Fort Loudoun in Tennessee, took years to be realized because of disputes between Virginia and South Carolina about its financing, delays in the expedition to site and construct the fort, and disagreements and rivalries between the two officers in charge of the project. Fort Loudoun was finally completed on July 30, 1757.[26] Though the Out Towns were not primarily involved in the events of the next several years owing to their location and comparatively small numbers of warriors, they suffered horrible consequences from the acts of the more powerful and political Lower, Middle, and Overhill Towns.

By this point, the Cherokees had wavered in their promise to fight for the English, but they eventually agreed when they were offered a bounty for the scalps of Frenchmen and French-allied Native Americans and after they were promised new guns and ammunition for the battle. But instead of going to war in Virginia, the Cherokees went to the Ohio River Valley. Disputes arose about the bounty paid on scalps, the insufficiency of traders and trade goods coming to the towns, and the Cherokees' debt to traders. In addition, small-scale disruptions emerged among the Cherokees in the Lower Towns and settlers in western South Carolina; these included raids, thefts of cattle and horses, and, in late 1757, the murder of four Cherokees and the theft of their skins by settlers. These events began the breakdown of trust that caused the Cherokee War of 1758–61.[27] Hostilities continued to mount, but eventually the Cherokees assembled a large force to fight for Virginia in the campaign against the French Fort Duquesne, located in what is now Pittsburgh, Pennsylvania. Once the Cherokee warriors arrived in Virginia (en route to Fort Duquesne), however, the English were slow to begin their campaign and some of the Cherokees decided to return home. They plundered as they traveled through southwest Virginia. When they refused to return stolen horses and property, the settlers attacked and killed a number of warriors. Once the Cherokees reached home, they demanded revenge and threatened attacks against the closest English settlements—those in South Carolina. In response, the South Carolina governor embargoed trade, again. Next, the Cherokees attacked settlers in the Carolina backcountry and renewed trade negotiations with the French.[28]

In an ill-fated effort to resolve these disputes, a large delegation of Cherokee chiefs traveled to Charleston to meet with the governor. After an agreement similar to the previous one was reached, however, Glen held the delegation against its will and moved them to Fort Prince George, in South Carolina, as hostages. After a few days, all but twenty-four of the Cherokees were released. The remaining hostages included Cherokee head men as well as representatives of most Cherokee towns. Although the Cherokees understood and practiced the taking of captives after war, often to supplement their own populations after losses in battle, they did not understand why the British had held their leaders as hostages; they were insulted and felt that the governor acted in bad faith. Consequently, the incident caused the Cherokees, led by Ogan'sto', also known as Oconostota, to come to Fort Prince George and lure the commander, Lt. Richard Coytmore, out of the fort for negotiations. When the British officer was ambushed (and mortally wounded) along with two others, the soldiers inside the fort shot and killed the hostages. Retaliation came as Cherokee warriors attacked backcountry white settlements and cut off supply lines to Fort Loudoun. In the spring, the Cherokees began a siege on Fort Loudoun that continued through the summer of 1760. In August, the officers of Fort Loudoun surrendered and left their ammunition in the fort. They walked out and toward Fort Prince George, seeking refuge. The morning after their departure, the Cherokees attacked them at their campsite in a meadow. Their commander was captured and tortured to death; several others died during the attack, and a few were lost in the fray. Most survivors were taken to the Overhill Towns as captives; a very few escaped and were led to safety by Cherokee friends and protectors.[29]

In response to the fall of Fort Loudoun and the attack on its soldiers, in May 1761, the English sent Lt. Col. James Grant through the Middle and Out Towns in a campaign of complete destruction. Grant set out from Fort Prince George with about 2,500 men. He razed fifteen towns, destroying all crops, an estimated 1,500 acres. This offensive reached the Out Towns on June 25 with an Indian corps and 1,500 regular troops. Over four days Grant and his men destroyed the crops and burned the houses of Stecoe, Conuntory, Kituwah, Tuckareechee, and Tessante.[30] An account in the September 19, 1761, issue of the *South Carolina Gazette* reported that the Cherokee men fled to the Overhill Towns while the women and children went to the mountains.[31] Seven Cherokees were captured and one was murdered by Mohawks serving in Grant's company. On July 9, Grant and his soldiers returned to Fort Prince George. The English and Cherokees reached a peace agreement with the same terms that had been offered before Grant's campaign, so the campaign accomplished little in the effort to resolve the ongoing disputes and misunderstandings.[32] The terms reopened trade to the Lower Towns; demanded the return of prisoners, stolen goods, and livestock; and prohibited the French from building forts in the Cherokee Nation.

The effect of Grant's campaign on the Out Towns was ruinous. It ended not only their trade with the English but, more critically, their occupation of a number of towns. After 1761, all the Out Towns but Stecoe and Tuckasegee were likely abandoned. From this date on, the English grouped the Out Towns with the Middle Towns on maps.[33] Though many Out Town residents probably relocated to other town areas, most likely the Overhill Towns, small groups stayed in Oconaluftee Valley and moved up into the mountains, where they lived in homesteads and hamlets rather than organized towns with council houses.[34] Perhaps because the Cherokee War showed many white soldiers the high-quality farmland of the area, land encroachments continued into Cherokee hunting grounds despite joint efforts by the English and Cherokees to establish boundaries.[35]

The Out Towns' defeat in the Cherokee War terminated their documentary history during the last forty years of the eighteenth century. No traders lived or traveled through them. When naturalist William Bartram traveled in the Cherokee Nation during the spring and early summer of 1776, he reached the former Valley Towns to the south near the Valley and Nantahala Rivers of North Carolina, but he did not venture north toward Oconaluftee.[36] The Out Towns seem to have been forgotten until the last of the Americans' raids on the Cherokee Nation in the late summer and fall of 1776 during the Revolutionary War.

REVOLUTIONARY WAR RAIDS

Quite reasonably, the Cherokees sided with the English in the American Revolutionary War. Cherokees valued the deerskin trade, and they appreciated the boundaries that the English had established and tried to honor between settlers and Cherokee hunting grounds. The Cherokees also believed that the Americans would quickly be defeated. Unfortunately, their choice of ally was mistaken for long-term stability; it only further endangered them. The Americans moved against the Cherokee Nation early in the Revolutionary War to suppress Cherokee attacks on illegally located white settlements. In early August 1776, Col. Andrew Williamson of South Carolina destroyed the Lower Towns, and in late August, Gen. Griffith Rutherford of North Carolina conducted raids against the Middle and Valley Towns. Rutherford reached the Tuckasegee River but did not follow it north. He sent Col. William Moore to complete the campaign in late October 1776, probably with orders to destroy Stecoe and other villages on the Tuckasegee and Oconaluftee Rivers.[37]

Moore had a small force of ninety-seven men, and over the course of twenty days they marched to Stecoe, plundered and burned it, as well as three other camps. After Stecoe, Moore and his men turned north and followed a smoke sign toward an unknown camp. They came upon the Oconaluftee River and found a deserted camp, probably Bird Town, and then traversed a mountain into a cove and found the confluence of Soco Creek and the Oconaluftee River.[38] There they apprehended prisoners, "two squaws and a lad," and followed them up Soco Creek to another quickly abandoned but well-stocked camp.[39] They plundered and then probably burned the camp. Going north, by way of Richland Creek Mountain, Moore's men found a road, which they followed back to South Carolina. In his report to Rutherford, Moore says that, against his preferences and arguments to the contrary, his soldiers insisted on selling the prisoners into slavery and the plunder for cash, for a total booty of $1,100.[40] Though the Out Towns suffered few casualties from Moore's campaign, it once again decimated Cherokee occupation of them. Just a few mountain villages and farmsteads remained. Intriguingly, a careful reading of Moore's report suggests that Nununyi, the town that once existed in the middle of today's downtown Cherokee, North Carolina, was not discovered at all during the raid because Moore and his men did not follow the Oconaluftee far enough north to reach it.[41] Sadly, it is not known whether the town even existed at the time because it does not appear on revolutionary-era or later maps. This question illustrates just how deep the mystery remains about Cherokee occupation of Oconaluftee Valley after 1761 and until the early nineteenth century.

In late 1780 and early 1781, Col. John Sevier of Tennessee made the final assault on the region. He led a small force of about 150 men over the ridge of the Great Smoky Mountains and attacked and then burned the town of Tuckasegee on the river. Before returning to Tennessee via an overmountain route, he also burned two other towns and several villages, but he likely did not reach Cherokees living along Oconaluftee River.[42]

Hostilities with militias continued until the Treaty of Paris in 1783, which ended the Revolutionary War. After that, white settlers persisted in their skirmishes over land until 1794, by which time much of the remaining Cherokee Nation, despite land cessions made in treaties, was occupied by white settlers, and the Cherokee population was greatly reduced and dispersed. Though communities continued to exist in the Out Towns, their populations were very small, sometimes just a family or two.[43]

The upheavals of the eighteenth century affected every aspect of traditional Cherokee life. With the decline and eventual loss of the hunting grounds, men were encouraged and eventually forced by the dominant market economy to abandon their roles as hunters and warriors. They had to become farmers; their families depended much more than before on agricultural production for subsistence and on surplus for participation in a growing market economy. Women lost status as they were placed within the home, a smaller and more domestic sphere of influence than they had previously held. The communal mode of town life and its traditions were disrupted, and families became more isolated on their farms, separated from extended family members within and outside of their clans. Over time, as private ownership of property replaced communal land holdings, inheritance practices shifted from matrilineal to patrilineal, a shift that further disempowered women. And psychologically, the Cherokees could no longer live in the moment as part of a nation and community; to a much greater extent than ever before, they had to accept individual responsibility for their existence and to worry about their individual prospects and futures.[44] Similarly, the settlement patterns of the Cherokees changed from "very compact, homogenous entities with social and political life revolving around the townhouses" to a town model that was "a sprawling community of farmsteads extending for as much as two miles along the bottomlands."[45] In addition, the Cherokees shifted from building houses and townhouses with a wattle and daub technique to building log cabin homes and wood shingle roofs, adopting building styles of the American settlers.[46] In the mountains, perhaps some trade goods such as plows and metal tools would have remained after the English and American raids of the second half of the eighteenth century; these would have been preserved over years of use.[47]

The last decade of the eighteenth century forced the Cherokee Nation to make additional land cessions, including the area that now comprises the Great Smoky Mountains National Park. In the Treaty of Holston of 1791, a quarter of the park area was ceded to Americans, and another section to the south was ceded in 1798. Then in February 1819 one quarter of the entire Cherokee Nation was ceded in a treaty made in Washington. These cessions included the remainder of the land in the Smokies as well as all of the area of the former Out Towns and Middle Towns.[48]

Although the towns vanished, the changing Cherokee occupation of the mountains in the late eighteenth century led to an "ecological revolution" whose vestiges are apparent even today.[49] Large cooperative Cherokee towns and communal agriculture were replaced by single family farms whose traces on the landscape persist in the settlement patterns they created between "fields, homes, and roads" and the landscape features of "mountains, forests, streams, and river."[50] In other words, the places that humans established toward the end of the eighteenth century became the basis for the roads, farms, stores, and towns that developed in the next century. These were oriented, to one degree or another, toward larger population centers, not away from them. Valley residents may have prized their peace and quiet in the mountains, but they were also engaged in agriculture, craft production, and the harvesting of forest products that linked them irrevocably to the larger world. The chain of connection that they held may not always have been one of friendship, as once existed (at least in name) between the South Carolina governor and Cherokee village head men, but it was a chain nonetheless.

Chapter 4

TWO PEOPLES SHARE A HOME

THE EARLY NINETEENTH CENTURY IN THE VALLEY

▲▲▲

The Boundary Tree Monument is a rather forlorn place this windy November afternoon. No one else stops at the pull-off. In fact, it's easy to miss the monument entirely, on a quiet stretch of Tsali Boulevard in Cherokee, North Carolina, just across from the Cherokee language immersion school, the New Kituwah Academy. Overwhelmed by a picnic pavilion, the stone monument can be mistaken for something functional because it is downstream of the Cherokee water intake facility. But steps from the road, the marker stands about six feet high. It doesn't offer much excitement. I guess that's right, but once this was a place that made a difference to many.

I read the weathered but warm-toned brown brass plaque. In formal phrases, it announces that this is the spot where a large poplar, likely a tulip tree, stood for hundreds of years and marked the division between white and Cherokee land. The divide remained under various authorities, including Great Britain, North Carolina, and the National Park Service.

Of course, the tree is long gone. An article by John Parris of the *Asheville Citizen-Times* states that the tree was cut down in 1959 because it was a hazard.[1] I imagine it as a towering 300-year-old tulip tree, one that could be readily noticed, one that a traveler marked in approach and crossing. Now, even the boundary has moved. In the 1940s, the Eastern Band purchased the 884-acre Boundary Tree tract, which included this area, from the federal government, and used the land to develop a successful Cherokee-owned hotel and diner. The school replaced these in 2009. I like to think some serendipity comes into play with this turn of events. As a result of the sale, the park boundary moved north some, which is indeed marked with a sign that folks regularly use for a photo op. In the 1970s a man living in Macon County claimed to have a coffee table top made from a horizontal slice of the actual tree. But it later burned in a house fire. Look for a photo in *Foxfire 4*.[2] The table, about a yard in diameter, sure looks small to me to have come from an age-old tree. Who can say? Everything changes. I enjoy this quiet place even if its purpose and most of its glory has passed. Here was the line.

▲ ▲ ▲

AFTER THE TREATY OF HOLSTON was signed in 1791, an era of boundary-line expeditions in Tennessee, North Carolina, and South Carolina began, effectively taking former Cherokee hunting grounds and opening them to white settlement. Federal and state agents and Cherokee chiefs worked to survey ceded land and draw clear boundaries between state land and the remnants of the Cherokee Nation. In the years between 1791 and 1802, four boundary lines were drawn that affected the residents in western North Carolina; each of these was disputed and each displaced both white mountain families and Cherokees, infuriating both groups. Also at this time, land in the Oconaluftee Valley began to be granted to homesteaders and land speculators. A process for granting land in North Carolina had existed since colonial days. Eligible citizens or Revolutionary War veterans could go to a county's land office and register an entry for vacant land. Next, the court would order the land to be surveyed via a land warrant. Once the survey was completed and the surveyor's plat of the land was approved, a patent was issued by the state, which granted the individual or family the land. As you can imagine, the process could take years, and mistakes could and did occur.[3]

Even before boundary issues were resolved, in 1796, large tracts along the Oconaluftee and Tuckasegee Rivers were granted to William Cathcart, a prominent North Carolinian. But his title to this land was subsequently disallowed in the outcome of a lawsuit, although he did successfully speculate in land elsewhere in North Carolina.[4] Another grant of this period survived similar disputes over boundaries and titles; it was to Felix Walker, a Revolutionary War veteran, North Carolina state politician, and later U.S.

Boundary Tree and monument (*in foreground on right*) marking line between Cherokee, N.C., and Great Smoky Mountains National Park, 1935.

GREAT SMOKY MOUNTAINS NATIONAL PARK ARCHIVES, TOWNSEND, TENN.

congressman. On February 2, 1798, Walker obtained grant #501, an area of 2,560 acres, from North Carolina. This tract began at the Boundary Tree and included the fertile bottomlands of the Oconaluftee up to Smokemont as well as up Raven Fork to the foot of Stoney Mountain. The Boundary Tree was a tree used as a boundary by the British earl of Granville as early as 1743 and again as the dividing line between Burke and Rutherford Counties in 1792. After 1840, the tree marked the line between white mountain families and the Cherokees. This location is now about a mile outside the national park in Cherokee, North Carolina. Walker had no intention of homesteading in the region himself; he was interested in selling the land at a profit to others. Very soon families of German and Scots Irish heritage began buying land from Walker and moving into the area. It is important to note that the best land was affordable only to land speculators and to well-off families; most white settlers could afford only inferior land—that is, land that was not cleared, on a steep slope, rocky, or all three.[5] Other families pursued state land grants independently.

THE MEIGS-FREEMAN LINE

One of the most telling stories of the drawing of boundaries comes from a fragment of a journal by surveyor Thomas Freeman as he joined an expedition led by Col. Return Jonathan Meigs. This 1802 expedition drew a line from the crest of the Smokies through Oconaluftee Valley and beyond to the confluence of the Little River and the French Broad in South Carolina. Meigs had become the federal agent to the Cherokees the year before at age sixty-three, and he served in that position until his death in 1823. The boundary that became known as the Meigs-Freeman line was initiated to settle disputes that had arisen from previous boundaries to the north and south of the new line. The Meigs-Freeman line was drawn between earlier boundary lines, the northern Hawkins line of 1797 and the southern Butler line of 1799. The new line was intended to limit disruption of both white and Cherokee settlements, placing the Cherokee Nation to the south and west of the line and the United States to the north and east.[6] More specifically, Meigs's purpose was to ensure that the headwaters of the French Broad fell within North Carolina so that white mountain families' farms in this area were protected from future dispute.[7]

Meigs set out from his office at South West Point (Kingston, Tennessee) in July with Freeman and a company of sixty white and twenty Cherokee men to carry provisions, measuring chains, and other instruments to mark blazes along the new line and, in the case of the Cherokees, to serve as guides and interpreters.[8] All were paid for their labor; when the route became too steep for pack horses, the rate per person was set at one dollar a day.[9] The expedition began in earnest in late July when the company departed from the base of what is now known as Meigs Mountain to ascend the crest of the Smokies. They proceeded slowly, blazing trees with gashes that would remain as scars and marking the line as best as possible in the rough terrain and despite views limited by clouds, mist, and rain. The western end of the new line was placed at the top of Mount Collins and was marked by a post, called Meigs Post, which has served as a key geographical point since it was established, designating the Tennessee–North Carolina boundary as well as boundaries for many later land sales and forest plots by lumber companies. Meigs Post was a key marker when these lumber companies sold their land to Tennessee and North Carolina in the twentieth century to establish the national park.

Freeman's journal records August 17, 1802, as the day the survey party reached and marked Meigs Post:

> Thermometer 51°. Ordered the Pack horses to meet us on the line in the Indian Country by going up the waters of the French Broad. Supposed to require about eight days. A Spring at our Camp being very cold was found by the Thermometer to sink the Spirit to 48°.
>
> We marched 3 miles to a position on the G. Mountain, Erected a post of Spruce pine 15 inches in diameter, Six feet high, pointed at top, drawing a line from top to bottom to designate our course & marked on the north side U.S. 1802. R. J. Meigs AWD. T. Freeman, USA. & on the south side C.N. U. and E., Cherokee Chiefs. Erected a mound of Stones around the post of about 2 Tons of Stone, wh. with difficulty we collected having no Tools for digging. From this monument we commenced our line between the Cherokee and North Carolina and descended the mountain 45 chains and Encamped on its Side, Laurel being very thick.[10]

On the south side of the post, the initials C.N. indicate "Cherokee Nation" followed by the initials of two chiefs. Possibly these men were Unaketa or Unalouskee (Junaluska, perhaps, whose first name was Gul'kalaski) and Elijah Ryan, who was mentioned in related documents.[11]

Over the next three days, the party marked the line down through Deep Creek, over Thomas Ridge, and arrived in Oconaluftee Valley on August 20: "Sunrise Thermometer 65° Our provisions being nearly out Sent our Interpreter & two Indians to the Bears Town to purchase provisions delivering him Ten dollars & 10 cents. continued our Survey on a ridge & on Over a turn of it descending the side a steep declivity over a stream of 50 links wide ascending & descending a high mountain to a fine stream of water & encamped on the West side of it. Killing two rattle snakes on the route wh[ich] makes 5 killed since commencing the Survey."[12] The stream that measured fifty links wide (about thirty-three feet) was probably the Oconaluftee, and the "fine stream" may have been Soco Creek.[13] This day would have led the party close by the Boundary Tree.

From Soco Creek, the company proceeded to John's Town and to Bear's Town (both now near Sylva, North Carolina). The Bear of Bear's Town was Chief Big Bear, or Yona Equah.[14] Whether or not Yona Equah was related to the later Chief Yonaguska, Drowning Bear, is unclear. Yonaguska emerged to become one of the pivotal leaders of the Eastern Band of the Cherokee Nation in his efforts to preserve the homeland of the Lufty Indians (as Cherokees who resisted removal were called) by successfully resisting the inducements and coercions of the United States for Indian removal to Arkansas and Oklahoma.[15] Nonetheless, the last three surviving entries of Freeman's journal suggest that Yona Equah was himself sharply focused on maintaining Cherokee lands in North Carolina:

> 23rd Thermometer 64° Sunrise Continued the line to Johns Town where five Chiefs & a number of Indians were assembled who seem much concerned at the running of the line. Having requested the Big Bear the principal chief to go with us on the survey expressed much unwillingness to attend: but will give an answer tomorrow morning. The Indians discovered a friendly disposition bringing us provisions & fruits—more than we could take with us.
>
> 24th Thermometer sunrise 68°. Met the Bear and 4 other Chiefs to renew the conversation respecting the line wh they were apprehensive would leave their Settlements on the Carolina Side. they used every argument & [behest] for us to use our discretion; & run so as to leave them on the Cherokee side. They were told [by Meigs] that it was not in our power, and that we were ordered to run the line from one given point to another given point; on our holding to this, the Big Bear refused to attend on the running of the line as he was requested to do. We told him that/ in the/if event of their houses being left out we [would] make a representation of their situation to the Executive [the secretary of war] and did not doubt their case would be favorably attended by the Government.
>
> 25th a Council of Chiefs met in the morning & agreed to send forward two of their men Lusena as Chief—the Big Bear having gone off in disgust.[16]

The remainder of the journal was lost or damaged beyond use; the surviving fragment was salvaged from the White House fire during the War of 1812. Unfortunately, no daily account of the expedition's conclusion is available. Nonetheless, we know from Meigs's own reports to the secretary of war that his line displaced five Cherokee families but no white mountain families. Also, the reports demonstrate that he did live up to his promise to intercede for the Cherokees:

> In running the line between the two points directed in our Instructions, not a single Settlement of the White People is cut off or intersected, not

> coming nearer than one & a half miles of any of their plantations.—On the other hand there is but five Indian Families left on the Carolina side of the line.—In justice to them & on their earnest solicitation, I promised to state their circumstances to the government as those Indians behaved very well but seemed much affected at the Idea of being obliged to leave their little cabins & a few acres of cleared land—I found by inquiry that they were on the land long before the treaty of 1798.[17]

Though Meigs did right by the Cherokees in this first letter, the discussion of the same situation in a letter he sent two days later, also addressed to the secretary, suggests that the Cherokees had to relocate anyway but received additional compensation, perhaps in land: "They [the Cherokees] received an addition to their amnesty in consideration of that relinquishment—in this respect the precedent they plead does not apply—they have nothing to give—There are but five Indian families cut off by the line—I took account of their number, their Cabbins, Stock, cleared land, &c."[18] Meigs had integrity and kept his word, but he was the federal agent, and in this instance and many later ones his decisions show that even though he was sincerely sympathetic to the needs and circumstances of Cherokee families, he was always loyal to the United States and its interests. A subsequent description of the entire area by Meigs attests to his grasp of the desirability of the land to white farmers and lumbermen:

> That part of the Cherokee Country on the South Side of Tennessee River except the mountainous trail, mentioned lying below the North Carolina line which was run by Mr. Freeman in 1802 is a very desirable & valuable Country, including the Highlands on both sides of the River—The Soil and seasons seem peculiarly calculated for raising Cotton & Corn & wheat has come by well in the few Instances when it has been tried—and immense numbers of Cattle may be raised with only the expense of salt being given them—large numbers raised even without the expense of that article—Mr. [name illegible], last year had five hundred head, he told me that he gave them nothing but Fatt at proper seasons.
>
> I have omitted mentioning the kinds of Timber on the different portions of The Country On the great Iron or Smoaky mountains & in other high mountains that is, particularly on the Western & Northern sides a great deal of the Spruce pine, which gives them a cold &

> dreary appearance—On the smaller mountains & hills & on the level grounds, are all the different kinds of Oak, Hickory, Poplar, Pine, Sasafras, Dogwood & frequently all these are mixed on the same tract—and the common pine is not here, as at the Northward, an indication of poor land—On the Border of the River, there is Elm, Buckeye, Poplar, Cottontree, Persimmon & Cucumbertree, Sugar beech—.[19]

Given this description of fertile farmland and valuable forests, it is no surprise that Felix Walker's land in Oconaluftee Valley was soon sold to a number of settler families. On farms from Walker's large grant in what was then Buncombe County, the families of Jacob Mingus and Rafe Hughes first settled in the Raven Fork area, known today as Ravensford (though this name was not used until the twentieth century). Abraham Enloe also bought Walker land in Ravensford very early in the nineteenth century and established a home near the current ranger station and visitor center.[20] Other early families included those of Robert Collins, Isaac Bradley, and John C. Beck, soon to be followed by the Conners, Floyds, and Sherrills, among others.[21] The names of these families now dot the map of the park, so dominant were they in the valley's nineteenth-century history.

Though not always a dependable way of locating a family's homestead, geographical names often indicate nearby homesites. The Mingus family established its mill on Mingus Creek on the west side of Highway 441. Just across Newfound Gap Road and the river lies the bottomland where they farmed and built a home around 1810. East of this original homesite, on the east side of Raven Fork, Mingo Falls suggests the approximate location of Ephraim and Sophia Mingus's farm in Big Cove. Samuel Sherrill's family is memorialized by Sherrill Cove, also on the south side of Raven Fork, which is now close to the park boundary and to the Blue Ridge Parkway. Rafe Hughes and his family established a farm at the fork of Raven Fork and Tight Run, now along the road entering Big Cove and at the base of the long ridge that carries this family name.[22] Further upstream but below Smokemont, Becks Creek indicates where the Becks settled. Above Smokemont, Bradley Fork, a major tributary of the Oconaluftee, locates the Bradleys' farm. Moving up the valley, the mouth of Collins Creek marks the location of the Collins family home, later bought by a branch of the Conner family.

Because the white community was small, families intermarried and property shifted from one to another. For example, the Mingus farm became known in 1870s as the Floyd Place because Sarah Angeline Mingus, the daughter of Polly Enloe and Dr. John Mingus, married Rufus G. Floyd. Their son John Leonidas Floyd, a great-grandson of Jacob and Sarah Mingus on his mother's side, inherited the farm after Dr. John's death. In addition, the Enloe farm was bought by the Floyd family in the first decade of the twentieth century, after the death of Wesley Enloe, who had lived there all his life and nearly all of the nineteenth century. Many of the homesites in the park changed family ownership through marriage and inheritance of the original handful of families.

At this time, the Cherokees lived in small towns and individual homesteads south of the Meigs-Freeman line, which means that they were mostly squeezed out of the park area, as well as out of Big Cove. They occupied sites within the Oconaluftee Valley around the current cities of Cherokee and Ela, North Carolina. In 1808 Meigs commissioned a census of the North Carolina Cherokees from George Barber Davis, who reported that in comparison to the more white-assimilated Cherokees in Georgia, those in North Carolina "are at least twenty years behind the lower town Indians." This assessment meant that they were more traditional in their religious beliefs and less interested in Christianity, that fewer spoke or read English, and that their subsistence lifestyle was less influenced by metal tools and colonial production processes. Farms in North Carolina were smaller than those in Georgia, and only a tiny fraction of North Carolina Cherokees owned slaves to help with farmwork. Of the 583 Black slaves in the Cherokee Nation at this time, only 5 were in North Carolina. Despite being the home of about a third of the entire Cherokee population, with 3,648 individuals, those in North Carolina owned only forty plows out of 567, 270 spinning wheels out of 1,572, and 70 looms of a total of 429.[23] In part, the reason for these impoverished circumstances was that the North Carolina Cherokees did not benefit as much as the Georgia Cherokees from federal "aid" because they were distant from the center of the Cherokee government located in the Lower Towns and, later, at the capital city of New Echota in Georgia. This is where Meigs doled out tools and other goods as part of the United States annuity to the Cherokees for land cessions. But it is also the case that the North Carolina Cherokees were generally more resistant to the federal policy goal of civilizing the Cherokees to live and believe as whites and to eventually assimilate into white society.

At this point, the North Carolina Cherokees were finding their separate answers to the pressures of white society. According to legend, in 1811, they resisted the persuasion of Shawnee chief Tecumseh when he spoke at Soco Creek in an effort to raise a pan-Indian confederation against the United

States. Although younger men were tempted to join Tecumseh, Gul'kalaski, a chief who later distinguished himself as an ally of the United States at the Battle of Horseshoe Bend in 1814, counseled friendship with whites.[24]

"PILGRIMS OF DESTINY"

By most accounts Jacob and Sarah Mingus were the first white settlers along the Oconaluftee. They farmed much of the bottomland of Oconaluftee River and Raven Fork in the nineteenth century. They had four children and became pillars of the community. The family's prominence was marked by its support for an early church and school. Both Jacob and his second son, Jacob Jr., served in the infantry during the War of 1812, enlisting as privates. Much later, in 1879, Sarah received a land warrant for her husband's service; similarly, in 1850 Jacob Jr. received 160 acres for his.

During these early years of settlement, the families focused on building cabins for shelter and clearing land for their farms. Detailed records of these first homes do not survive, but they likely would have been relatively simple log cabins with few windows, overhanging roofs for porches, stone chimneys, and loft sleeping chambers. As the families and their fortunes grew, the homes expanded as well, with additional rooms, floors, and outbuildings. The earliest farms were situated on fertile bottomland that the Cherokees had previously cultivated, but as farmers increased their acreage devoted to crops and pastures, they would have needed to take down massive trees by axe. The stumps would have been hauled out by an ox team or burned. Trees that were too large to fell were girdled by cutting a deep ring all around the trunk, which cut off the flow of sap and nutrients to the tree and, eventually, killed it in place. Later, once the tree was dead and dry, it could more readily be split and brought down and its lumber used for myriad purposes.[25] These families had to be self-reliant and inventive to manage and do the hard labor that was required. They learned, for example, to use sleds made of sourwood tree trunks for hauling because they were easy to make and forgiving on rough mountain trails.[26] Sleds made from a fork in a tree were called "lizzards" and could be cut and rigged in a brief time. Similarly, because rope was in short supply, hickory bark peeled from trees served in its stead and could be used to lash items to sleds or for assorted other purposes such as weaving a chair seat.[27]

The paramount legend of the early years of Oconaluftee Valley belongs to the Enloe family, headed by Abraham and Sarah. In the early 1800s, the well-to-do Enloe family moved from South Carolina to a farm in Rutherford County, North Carolina, then to one along Soco Creek, and ultimately to the 250 acres in the fertile bottomlands of Oconaluftee now occupied by the national park visitor center and Mountain Farm Museum. Already prosperous, Abraham owned and traded slaves and served as justice of the peace. He was known as a successful farmer as well as a good hunter with devoted dogs. Reportedly, he owned the only wagon in the early Oconaluftee settlement.

The tale that Abraham Enloe is famous (or infamous) for claims that he was the biological father of Abraham Lincoln. The story holds that while living in Rutherford County, the Enloes took in a young woman in need of a stable home to work as a housemaid. She was Nancy Hanks. While Sarah was away visiting relatives, Abraham and Nancy conceived a child, and when Sarah discovered the pregnancy after her return, she insisted that Nancy be sent away. To keep peace in the family, Nancy was either sent to live in Kentucky with the Enloes' recently married daughter, also named Nancy, and her husband, or taken there by a man named Tom Lincoln, whom Abraham Enloe paid to take Nancy Hanks away and to marry. Nancy named her child Abraham after the Enloe patriarch. As evidence of the likely truth of the story, some proponents note the physical resemblance between the two Abrahams: their height, deep-set eyes, and gaunt cheeks, though Enloe had striking blue eyes, not at all like the deep brown ones of the president. Genealogists have attempted to trace the president's paternity back to Enloe and have published articles and books on the topic, though few scholars accept the story as possible.[28] Academic historians doubt that this Nancy Hanks was Lincoln's mother at all. Two important facts complicate the legend. First, Lincoln was born February 12, 1809, three years after Nancy's transport to Kentucky; also, Lincoln had an older sister, Sarah. Finally, Abraham Enloe's son Wesley doubted the story and could provide no evidence to confirm it.

Some scholars have suggested that the tale was spun or nurtured by Democrats or other political rivals in an effort to tarnish Lincoln's reputation both before and after he was elected president. Even so, the legend lives on, and some descendants of Oconaluftee families defend it vigorously. Whether it remains a part of the lore as a scandal or a claim of Enloe superiority and fame, this uncertain link between the remote Oconaluftee Valley and one of the most influential leaders of U.S. history matters greatly to many. If the story lives as a point of pride, then it suggests how strongly the descendants of this mountain community want to establish their merit and mark on the national stage. Stepping back from the story, even if it is not true, Abraham Enloe achieved great success in North Carolina, not least of which can be attributed to being a parent to seventeen children—nine sons and eight daughters—and managing the farm until his death in 1841. Without the Lincoln celebrity, Enloe should certainly be viewed as the patriarch of a prosperous and large mountain family.

Perhaps a story that captures the determination and bravery of the early settlers as a group is that of Ephraim and Sophia Mingus, who homesteaded in Big Cove in the spring of 1814. Ephraim was the oldest son of Jacob Mingus and about twenty years old and newly married to Sophia Ellis. Haywood County historian Alice R. Cook honored them with the moniker "pilgrims of destiny" as they set off from the Mingus farm carrying their "bare necessities in split basket and a bag on their backs."[29] After hiking eight miles up a trail alongside Raven Fork, they found a valley and made a camp. All night while they lay on the ground, they heard "the night howl of the wolves, panther screams on the ridge, and the cry of an owl." By the morning, Ephraim concluded that the place was too wild for them to stay, but Sophia saw that the land was rich with edible plants, tree nuts, fruits, wildlife, and fish, and she replied to his suggestion to retreat by saying, "We have come now. Can't we stay and try out life here? It may be that we can start to live." So the couple constructed a temporary cabin using wooden pegs, vines, and other simple methods. It had a poplar puncheon floor, which was constructed of logs halved lengthwise and set parallel with the split side up. The door was hand hewn and attached with wooden hinges and a fastener. The shakes on the roof were hand rived or split, and the chimney was built of rock using clay mortar. This precarious beginning led to success and prosperity as they ultimately acquired over 1,000 acres in the valley and raised a family of eight children.[30] Ephraim and Sophia lived all their lives together in Big Cove, and Ephraim's brother Jacob Jr. joined them, establishing his own farm nearby for two decades before moving to Missouri.[31] Jacob Jr. was a preacher at the Lufty Baptist Church.

CHEROKEE "RESERVEES"

During the first two decades of the nineteenth century, the United States continued to press the Cherokee Nation for additional land cessions. Gradually, George Washington's policy of encouraging the Indians to become "civilized" (that is, Christian, patriarchal, and capitalist owners of land as private property rather than as communal holdings) and then to assimilate into white society was replaced by the view that white society needed Indian land for its own communities, farms, and industries and that true Indians would never give up hunting and tribal warfare as occupations. Consequently, the rationale went, the eastern Indians should be removed west beyond the states' boundaries into territories of their own for resettlement where they could continue their traditional ways of life. This view was championed by Andrew Jackson, a celebrated general from the War of 1812, who became president in 1829.

The transition from one policy to the next was gradual; during the first two and a half decades of the nineteenth century, the Cherokee Nation adapted to the demands of the federal government, communicated by Meigs, the longtime federal Cherokee agent. The most prominent and wealthy Cherokee chiefs in Tennessee and Georgia became proprietors of large farms and used slave labor. A number of them were of mixed heritage, with white and Cherokee ancestry; consequently, they learned to speak and read English. During the same period, Sequoya, a Cherokee who also went by the name of George Gist, or Guess, realized that his people needed the facility of a written language like the whites'. Remarkably, he single-handedly developed the Cherokee syllabary, which came into use around 1821. It is a system in which each syllable of the language corresponds to a unique symbol, and it was easy for those who spoke Cherokee to learn quickly and to use both for reading and writing. The syllabary enabled the Cherokees to write laws and keep records, as well as to publish a newspaper in their native language, bringing literacy to the culture with uncanny speed. Literacy provided a new kind of national pride and identity as well as the means to function as a nation-state. It is hard to overstate the adaptation and innovation that the Cherokees achieved during these years. William McLoughlin, a prominent Cherokee scholar, has termed the era a "Renascence" to emphasize how fully the traditional culture adapted to its challenges with creativity and aplomb.

The elite Cherokees in and around New Echota, Georgia, thought that the best way to protect their interests was to establish a Cherokee Nation along the lines of the representative democracy of the United States, with elected leaders empowered to negotiate on a continuing basis with the federal government. Rather than needing to call ad hoc national councils where weeks of deliberation might or might not lead to a consensus, the Cherokees created a central government at New Echota following the outlines of the U.S. Constitution with a principal chief and assistant chief, a canon of laws, and a national judiciary. In short, the Cherokees transformed themselves as the United States wished, but instead of dissolving their sovereignty into that of the nation of white settlers surrounding them, the Cherokee Nation was on its way to becoming an independent state within a state, a turn that neither the surrounding states nor the federal government wanted. Georgia, Tennessee, and North Carolina wanted the Cherokees' land, and these states, assisted by the federal government, whittled away at the established boundaries of the Cherokee Nation. Most always the treaties offered the Cherokees additional annuities in goods or cash for further relinquishing traditional hunting grounds and concentrating the Cherokee people into smaller and smaller pockets of communities. Land cessions also allowed Cherokees to eliminate debt that they had accrued from the decline of the deerskin trade.[32]

The treaty of 1819 between the Cherokee Nation and the United States had significant consequences for those Cherokees living in the North Carolina mountains. First, it ceded all the land in and around the Smokies to the state. It provided for the federal government to pay displaced Cherokees for all improvements to their lands such as cabins, pastures, and cleared land and created a large area in the West for them to move to, if they preferred, rather than moving into the now smaller territory of the nation. But the treaty contained an important alternative for Cherokees who did not want to leave their farms: individual heads of families could apply for a reserve of 640 acres (one square mile) and become U.S. citizens, leaving the collective protection of the Cherokee Nation. Most Cherokees affected by the new cessions did not want to move west, so they moved into the new boundaries of the Cherokee Nation. But about fifty families in North Carolina applied for reserves and stayed put on their lands as established by the Meigs-Freeman line. Among these families were Yonaguska, Utsala (or Euchella), and others who had always lived along the Oconaluftee, Tuckasegee, and Little Tennessee Rivers. Reserve plots were located at Cowee, Kituwah, along the Cullasaja and Little Tennessee Rivers, in Franklin, along Alarka and Savannah Creeks, and at the mouth of Soco Creek as it flows into the Oconaluftee. In this fashion, these Cherokees became "owners," or "reservees," of their land, now classified as private property. According to the language of the treaty, they were citizens of the United States and, by extension, of North Carolina. But this stipulation was more in name than in practice; the reservees did not exercise voting rights and were not viewed as citizens by the whites. They lived quietly, traded cattle and sheep with the white mountain families, and sold ginseng for export, ultimately, to China for ten cents a pound at the local store owned by Felix Walker Jr., the son of the land speculator.[33] Also, though the treaty stated that they would no longer be part of the Cherokee Nation, they continued to be included in Cherokee affairs and participated in the events and discussions that preceded the nation's removal in 1838; nonetheless, as reservees, they were distinct from those living within national boundaries and were disadvantaged somewhat by their distance from New Echota. Their status was precarious, to be sure, but it provided an opportunity for a sage and determined leader to embark on a path that would keep them on their homeland.

Yonaguska, or Drowning Bear, was the most prominent chief of these Lufty Indians. According to Mooney, he was "a peace chief and counselor rather than a war leader," so he is not named in any war treaties. He was reputed to be a persuasive and powerful speaker in town council as well as strikingly handsome. Mooney states that Yonaguska was six feet, three inches tall and "strongly built, with a faint tinge of red, due to a slight strain of white blood on his father's side." In 1819 he lived on Governor's Island in the middle of the Tuckasegee River, near Ela. The federal listing of reserves states that there were sixteen members in Yonaguska's family at this time.[34] He had at least two wives, five children, and a slave, Cudjo, who was treated as a member of the family and was loyal to Yonaguska throughout his life.[35] Though far too little is known about the man, several legends of his youth and adulthood suggest his unique insight and talent for leadership. Yonaguska was born in 1759, so he would have been a toddler when James Grant razed the Out Towns and a youth during the revolutionary era. During his young adulthood, he would have experienced wave after wave of land cessions. Though he advised peace and friendship with whites, he believed in traditional Cherokee legends and ways of life and resisted every inducement to move from the homelands. Mooney explains that Yonaguska thought that "the Indians were safer from aggression among their rocks and mountains than they could ever be in a land which the white man could find profitable, and that the Cherokee could be happy only in the country where nature had planted them."[36] His brother Willnotah told a story about him as a child of twelve in which he had a frightful vision of the white man's coming to the mountains that no one believed at the time.

There is no record of the role of women among the reservee Cherokees, and that is a limitation to understanding the early decades of the nineteenth century in the valley. Scholar Wilma Dunaway has established that most Cherokee women of the day (excluding elite Cherokees in New Echota and those in interracial marriages where they had accepted a patriarchal system) continued to live in traditional ways following the practices of their matrilineal clans.[37] Since the Cherokees of western North Carolina were among the most traditional of the nation, it seems quite likely that women would have been as active in their own community as they had always been in guiding the decisions that affected their households, clans, and towns. One wonders how women were involved in the actions that are today fully attributed to Yonaguska and a white man named Will Thomas.

By late in the 1810s, of course, it was obvious that Yonaguska's early vision had been prophetic. Ironically, Yonaguska's close relationship with Will Thomas set the reservees and other North Carolina Cherokees, who had become known as the Lufty Indians, down a course by which they saved part of their homeland for themselves and established the Eastern Band. At just the right time to put this tale in motion, in 1818, at age twelve, Thomas signed a contract to serve as store clerk for three years at the Soco Creek Trading Post, established on the southern bank of the creek by Felix Walker Jr. Will was the only son of a young widow, Temperance Thomas, and he accepted this position to begin to make his way in the world. He planned to use the one-hundred-dollar payment that he would receive at the end of his term to set himself up in business.

What can be thought about the legendary meeting and subsequent friendship of these two men, the sixty-year-old chief and the teenage apprentice clerk? Imagine the scene of a backcountry trading post alongside a beautiful creek just beyond the highest peaks of the Smokies. An everyday transaction led to an acquaintanceship, then to a friendship, and finally into a complex, multifaceted and lifelong relationship. The white youth became the champion of the Lufty Cherokees. It seems to have been one of those fateful encounters that changed history. The story goes that the chief had sympathy for Will because he was an orphan with no father or brother. Also, Will, according to all sources, was bright, curious, and welcoming to the Cherokees with whom he daily traded city goods for deer and other skins and ginseng. In time, Will picked up the Cherokee language, probably largely taught to him by a Cherokee companion in the store. Once the syllabary was introduced, Thomas also learned to read Cherokee. In a twist of fate, by the time Thomas's apprenticeship to Walker ended, Walker was bankrupt and wanted for debts. He had nothing to pay Will—not even part of the promised one hundred dollars.

So Thomas returned to live with his mother at a farm she had bought on the west bank of the Oconaluftee near the mouth of Soco Creek. Knowing that her son must find a way to make a living, his mother sold some of her land and invested the proceeds into a store for Thomas to run as proprietor. This store, located on Thomas land, was named Qualla, after a Cherokee woman named Polly. It was also known as Indiantown. Eventually, Walker wrote to Thomas, apologized for cheating him, and sent him his law library as substitute compensation for the apprentice's years of labor. Given Thomas's

Col. William Holland Thomas, 1858.

COURTESY OF THE STATE ARCHIVES OF NORTH CAROLINA, RALEIGH.

intellect and drive, he set about reading the law books and considered that in time he might be able to practice law. Just about this time, in early 1821, Yonaguska persuaded the Lufty Cherokees to accept Will into the tribe as Wil-Usdi, "Little Will," with Yonaguska taking the role of maternal uncle and thus giving him an identity within the tribe. To Thomas the relationship came as a surprise, but likely it was a welcome one that bound him to the Cherokees he knew and regularly encountered in his store. Having no experience in a matrilineal clan, Thomas may have thought of Yonaguska as an adoptive father, rather than an uncle. By 1822, Thomas was set up in business for himself and operated using a generous trading policy with both whites and Cherokees. His records are full of notes of debts between individuals and receipts of goods bought on credit until harvest or some other form of exchange, such as manual labor, allowed buyers to clear their tabs.

MOUNTAIN FAMILY PROSPERITY AMID CHEROKEE ANXIETY

Unfortunately, the reserves did not end land disputes for the Cherokees. In the hurry to claim newly ceded lands, the state mistakenly sold some reserves to white families, who then occupied portions of them. In 1824 both Utsala (Euchella) and Yonaguska filed suit against whites who had deeds to their reserves. *Euchella v. Welsh* was the first case to come up in the Supreme Court of North Carolina. With Utsala represented at the federal government's expense, the court upheld his right to his reserve. Because the land had already been sold to whites, however, the state offered him new territory as compensation. Yonaguska's case was similar to Utsala's, so it was dismissed with the same ruling. In August, the state offered to buy out all of the Cherokees who owned reserves. The process took several years but was completed in 1829, when Congress provided North Carolina $20,000 to cover the land purchases. Utsala moved back into land controlled by the Cherokee Nation, but Yonaguska and many of the other reservees moved to Quallatown, creating for themselves a Cherokee community that was separate from the Cherokee Nation but one in which the residents held their land in common as a means of protection against encroachment. This new settlement at Qualla was the beginning of the Lufty Cherokees as legally distinct from the Cherokee Nation. Eventually, the group, supervised by Yonaguska, built a council house on Soco Creek as their community center.[38] The experiment of having Cherokees become private property owners was short lived, and in time it became clear that communal ownership was a far better strategy to protect their land rights and community. Because the Cherokees were unschooled in the state's legal system, individually held private property left them too vulnerable to the whites. They had been "imposed on, cheated, and defrauded by some of the people of this country," so in 1829 the Lufty Indians hired John L. Dillard as their attorney.[39] This job was handed over to Will Thomas at age twenty-six in 1831, and he remained their counselor and agent until after the Civil War.

During the same decade the Lufty Cherokees determined that another cultural practice of the whites, drinking alcohol, was not for them. The Cherokees had imbibed since the beginning of the deerskin trade, when rum became widely available. Some, including Yonaguska, became addicted. At one point the chief became severely ill and fell into a trance. Though he seemed dead except for his breathing, he was carefully attended by his family. Yonaguska at last awoke, after either twenty-four hours (according to Mooney) or two months (according to Willnotah, Yonaguska's brother). Mooney's account states that during the trance "he had been to the spirit world, where he had talked to friends who had gone before, and with God, who had sent him back with a message to the Indians, promising to call him again at a later time." The experience motivated the chief to renounce liquor for himself and discourage it among his people. Once recovered, he made a moving speech to the town council and "declared that God had permitted him to return to earth especially that he might thus warn his people and banish whiskey from among them."[40] The chief then asked Thomas, who was present in the council, to write a temperance pledge, which Yonaguska signed first, followed by the members of the council. This pledge significantly decreased the Lufty Cherokees' use of alcohol, a fact that helped make them tolerable to nearby whites. In the coming years when Thomas fought for the Lufty Cherokees' legal status, he often used their sobriety as an example of their virtue.

Meanwhile, the mountain families in the valley prospered. Their families grew and expanded their farm acreage and operations. The community as a whole undertook projects to establish infrastructure and strengthen their community bonds. One such effort was to improve an existing trail over the crest of the Smokies into a road that could accommodate travelers, wagons, and livestock drives to Tennessee. An existing ancient trail, Indian Gap Trail, crossed the crest at Indian Gap, which is about a mile west of Newfound Gap as the crow flies. This trail linked the Great Indian War Path in East Tennessee with the Rutherford War Trace in western North Carolina. It ascended the Tennessee side of the mountains along the west prong of the Little Pigeon River, passed through the gap, and descended Beech Flats Prong, which becomes the west fork of the Oconaluftee River, and followed it to Whittier, North Carolina.[41] Unlike the current Newfound Gap Road (Highway 441), this trail ran on the north side of the river, though both routes follow the river's slope downhill. As early as 1826, the Haywood County Court ordered a group of valley settlers to "view and mark out a way for a wagon road," naming Ephraim Mingus, Samuel Conner, Jonas Jenkins, Rafe Hughes, Jacob Stillwell, Abraham Enloe, Aseph Enloe, George Shuler, Nathan Hyatt, and Samuel Sherrill as partners and workers. Though it is difficult to determine with confidence, a few enslaved individuals may have contributed labor to this project. The 1830 census shows that George Shuler, John Mingus, and Abraham Enloe owned a total of five enslaved males at this time, so these men may have been tasked with some of the immense physical labor that would have been required.[42] It appears that progress was slow until 1832, when the North Carolina legislature chartered the Oconalufty Turnpike Company to build a road from the gap down to John Beck's farm just below Bradleytown, the area that became Smokemont. The named commissioners of this company—Abraham Enloe, Samuel Sherrill, John Carroll, Samuel Gibson, and John C. Beck—were empowered to raise stocks to finance the venture. Once complete and "received" by appointed Haywood County officials, the company could charge tolls for those using the new road. These tolls were set:

4-wheel carriage of pleasure	75 cents
Gig or sulky	37½ cents
6-horse wagon	75 cents
5-horse wagon	62½ cents
4-horse wagon	50 cents
3- and 2-horse wagons	37½ cents
1-horse wagon or cart	25 cents
Horse without rider	2½ cents
Head of cattle	2 cents
Hog or sheep	1 cent
Traveler on horse back	6¼ cents[43]

Also at this time, Jacob Mingus was made overseer of a road from his home to Abraham Enloe's, quite possibly a segment of the turnpike project.[44] It seems likely that the commissioners invested in the road, but Will Thomas did, too, and became an enthusiastic proponent of it. In June 1839, Thomas wrote to James S. Porter of Sevierville, Tennessee, asking him to "encourage your people to complete their part of the Smoky mountain road" and promising to work to extend the North Carolina part into South Carolina. By September he was able to write business associates that the road had been received by Haywood County as complete, that he expected to make a settlement on it with the state treasurer in Raleigh, and that Robert Collins should collect tolls and keep the road in repair.[45] A statement from his Quallatown store shows that he had invested $2,417.47 on behalf of his firm, which by then included a handful of stores and several business partners.[46] Collins managed the road and took tolls, as shown in an existing record book for the month of June (year unknown), naming the person or number of livestock heads, including hashmarks counting each animal, and listing a total fee paid to the company. Though worn and difficult to read, this "Road Book" shows that business was steady.[47]

During the 1830s, the mountain families embarked on several additional community and entrepreneurial projects that served to make life in Oconaluftee Valley more manageable than it had been when every farmer had to be entirely self-sufficient. The area became an election precinct in Haywood County in 1831.[48] In 1834, a man named Couch began operating a gunpowder mill at the confluence of Couches Creek and the river.[49] Three years later Ephraim Mingus visited Alum Cave for the first time, perhaps led there by Yonaguska, though the timing of such an event makes it doubtful. Mingus, along with Robert Collins and George W. Hayes, surveyed the area, and bought a fifty-acre tract to create the Epsom Salts Manufacturing Company to mine alum and saltpeter up to and through the Civil War. The business was successful enough to employ others, who lived in camps. Some of the laborers are likely to have been men enslaved by the businesses' owners. The company came to be jointly owned by the three Mingus brothers (Ephraim, John, and Abraham), Robert Collins, David Elder, Micajah Rogers, and Ira H. Hill.[50]

"FELLOWSHIP FOUND"

The Oconaluftee mountain families also reached critical mass by the late 1820s to establish community worship services. The Reverend Humphrey Posey and Adam Corn established the Mount Zion Church in 1829. Throughout his life, Posey was associated with Baptist efforts to bring Christianity to the Cherokees; around 1820, he created a mission school for the Cherokees at Mission Place on the Hiwassee River, seven miles above Murphy, North Carolina. When the missionary school was not in session, Posey traveled the mountains as an itinerant preacher in both white and Cherokee villages.[51] He also established white churches at Cane Creek in Buncombe County and Locust Old Fields in Haywood County.[52] The first Lufty church met near Bradleytown, close to where the Smokemont Baptist Church was later built. Longtime residents such as the Minguses, Conners, and Becks attended.[53] By 1836, church members decided that they needed to change the location of services because of difficult traveling conditions, presumably due to a lack of bridges to make access possible. The meeting minutes read:

The Church at Lufty

> Being organized for the first time at Dr. John Mingus'; June 19, 1836—resolved that we have our church meeting at Samuel Conners & Jacob Mingus'. . . . Each one in their turn. For the convenience of the aged & infirm *until we get a regular meeting house* and that we have a prayer meeting at Brother S. Conners & Brother Mingus' on each fork of sd. river Between each monthly meeting. Each one in its turn. Then appointed the fourth Sunday in each month and Sateray before for our church meeting days then organized.[54]

The alternate-site meeting arrangement was short-lived. By September 1837, the two units recombined and met in an old schoolhouse on John H. Beck's land below a bridge. At this time the name of Lufty Baptist Church was adopted, and the members convened at this location until late in the nineteenth century. Several efforts to site and build a new church were begun throughout the next several years, but none of these early efforts succeeded.[55]

There were twenty-one charter members of Lufty Baptist Church. Robert Collins and Ephraim Mingus were elected to serve as deacons, and the pastors were the Reverends Adam Corn and David Elder. Elder kept the records as "moderator" during this period, including an entry summarizing the highlights of each meeting. These highlights noted appointments to the larger Baptist association, occasions when new members were received, requests for letters of "dismission" when members moved away, baptisms, and occasionally entries about a brother who "acknowledge[d] himself guilty of intoxication and made satisfaction." One source indicates that Jacob Mingus was one of the members who made this confession and that he did so while his son served as a deacon, which may have been mildly scandalous because the by-laws prohibited "any member from making or selling spirituous liquors or from using them as beverages." Despite these occasional moments of tension, every monthly entry declares "fellowship found," a comment that emphasizes the important communal role of the church in the sparsely populated valley where church meetings brought people together only once a month.[56]

The church board functioned like a court or grievance council for small civil matters. Charges included "telling falsehoods, gossiping, stealing, playing cards, drinking, profanity, general misconduct, and causing strife in the family to more serious sins of the flesh. Some of the brethren and sisters became stricken with 'disorders of passion.'" Members could be dismissed or excluded from the church if infractions were serious or if they refused to explain the charges. If a member was "churched," he or she was removed from the church. On occasion, outside ministers came to serve as impartial judges. "Habitual offenders" could be put under "watch care" of other members.[57]

At about the same time, in 1830, a Cherokee Methodist mission was established at the foot of Hughes Ridge, which forms a divide between the Oconaluftee and Raven Fork. The preacher and teacher of this log church was William Hicks. In addition, a circuit rider preacher, David Woodring, served the valley. He was sometimes called David Ring by mountain folk.[58]

The success of the Methodist mission is impressive, given Yonaguska's suspicion of all missionaries. When a Cherokee translation of the Gospel of Matthew arrived in North Carolina, he insisted that it be read aloud to him before it could be read to his people. Mooney's account states that "after listening to one or two chapters the old chief dryly remarked: 'Well, it seems to be a good book—strange that the white people are not better, after having had it so long.'"[59] Even so, Thomas encouraged Christianity among the Cherokees, seemingly for the same reasons he encouraged temperance: to assure the whites that the Lufty Cherokees were model residents. In some ways, the total immersion baptism practices of the Baptists were familiar and appealing to the Cherokees because this ceremony resembled their own Going to Water purification practice, which was regularly observed for such purposes as celebrating seasonal renewal and as ritual cleansing before warfare or its substitute, the ball play.[60] This resemblance generally made the Baptists more appealing to the Cherokees than the Methodists, though the Methodists were especially influential in western North Carolina.

The white mountain families and Lufty Cherokees managed to live side by side in the valley with apparent neighborliness during the first decades of the nineteenth century, possibly because of the Cherokees' impulse toward harmony and nonconfrontation. Both were active in trade and in efforts to strengthen their own largely separate communities. But their lives were controlled by distinct priorities. While landowning white farmers were busily establishing themselves, producing surplus goods, and building a road to get them to market, the Cherokee experience of living within the young United States was dominated by scrambling to hang on to their land and culture despite all manner of intrusions. Clearly, individuals from the two groups did forge important bonds, best exemplified by Yonaguska and Will Thomas. It is also clear that unease and distrust were as likely to be the sentiments between the groups as tolerance and cooperation. For many of us today, this frontier era has a romantic character, full of potential and mystery. The natural beauty of the land must have been astonishing and its wildness more intense than ever since, regardless of the many decades of Cherokee residence that had already transformed the land. So much about the thoughts of the valley's people during this time can only be left to musing, musing at once irresistible and unanswerable.

Chapter 5

CIRCUMVENTING THE TRAIL OF TEARS

LUFTY CHEROKEES HOLD ON

▲▲▲

"I lift up mine eyes unto the hills from whence cometh my help" begins Psalm 121. God will bring peace to the oppressed—that's what this line promises. A two-letter change to the central prepositional phrase yields *Unto These Hills*, the title of the longstanding outdoor drama interpreting the origins of the Eastern Band of the Cherokee Indians for thousands of summertime visitors since 1950.

That is an inspired title with a brilliant edit. The edit specifies the hills as the Smokies; they now represent a homeland, a sacred birthplace of a people. So the phrase offers far more than the solace that a generic vista provides when it helps troubled humans remember the size, wonder, and beauty of the world. It offers encouragement, patience, and determination to the downtrodden. Consider the resonance of this phrase for many tourists with biblical fluency and as well for Cherokees, many of whom embraced Christianity in the eighteenth and nineteenth centuries and whose descendants are devout today. Whatever criticism Kermit Houston Hunter, the University of North Carolina graduate student who wrote the drama in 1949 as his MA thesis, may deserve for skewing the role of Tsali, a Cherokee man, in the Cherokee Removal from the western Carolina mountains and endorsing an assimilationist vision of the band's future, he deserves kudos for the title. It emphasizes place and endurance. Further, the play provides a pageant of relatable characters. Hunter found a scapegoat in Tsali; villains in Andrew Jackson, cruel soldiers, and gold-hungry settlers; traitors in elite Cherokee Elias Boudinot and John Ridge; prophets in Tecumseh and Yonaguska; a learned man in Sequoyah; allies in preachers, sympathetic whites, and Will Thomas; victims in Gul'kalaski and those forced to walk the Trail of Tears; and survivors in the Eastern Band. That's a lot to impart in an evening.

I am not sure how many times I have watched the drama, several as a kid on summer trips with my family and at least twice in more recent years. Though I see its issues, I experience the play as a pastime and a ritual. At a moment about thirty minutes in, darkness arrives and the crickets begin chirping, loudly. I wait for the crickets. It's part of the soundscape that brings history forward to the present moment for me. It reminds the me that I am nestled within the protective hills of the psalm.

▲▲▲

BY THE MID-1830S, national events once again affected the lives of everyone living in the North Carolina mountains, though the Cherokees especially endured great upheaval, hardship, and uncertainty. The infamous Treaty of New Echota was signed at the close of 1835 by a handful of Cherokee chiefs representing a minority of the people. It committed the Cherokee Nation to removal west; it was ratified by the U.S. Senate by one vote in 1836 and allowed the Cherokees two years to move to the new Cherokee territory. Even though the treaty was challenged and resisted, ultimately the Cherokee Nation faced forced emigration via the calamitous and cruel journey called the Trail of Tears.

Will Thomas launched an effort to gain the state's support for the Lufty Cherokees to remain in North Carolina. He encouraged fourteen citizens of Macon and Haywood Counties to sign a statement certifying that the Lufty Cherokees followed North Carolina laws and behaved as citizens, that they were more temperate than some whites, and that they were making progress in farming. This memorial, dated January 31, 1836, is signed by business associates of Thomas's, including Scroop Enloe; three members of the Hyatt family; George W. Hayes, who was part of the Epsom Salts Company; John Shuler; and two members of the Love family, with whom Thomas had a long friendship and multifaceted business associations. Although not all of the signers were residents of Oconaluftee Valley, valley residents were represented in the group and kin to a number of the signers, so it seems likely that the white residents were not entirely hostile to the community of Lufty Cherokees.[1]

In the fall of 1836, the Lufty Cherokees held a meeting at their council house to decide what to do in the face of forced removal. Two men were asked to stand a few feet apart to form a gate, and those who wanted to remain in North Carolina were asked to walk through this gate. All present took this action, confirming their agreement with Yonaguska, who was also on the scene, that if they moved west, the white men would soon want that land, too.[2]

Next, Thomas got the Haywood County Court to send a statement to the governor describing the Lufty Cherokees as peaceful and hardworking and affirming that they were already citizens. Ultimately, the General Assembly of North Carolina passed an act to shield the Lufty Cherokees from fraud once the removal had occurred, acknowledging their right to stay only indirectly. Because of their unique status as "citizen Indians" in North Carolina, Thomas was able to argue in Washington that the Lufty Cherokees had the right to remain on the land that he was beginning to purchase for them in Qualla and along the lower Oconaluftee Valley. In September 1837, the federal commissioners responded to a petition that the Lufty group, consisting of about 330 individuals, be allowed to remain with preliminary approval, another ambiguous acknowledgment of their unique status.[3] Consequently, the Lufty Cherokees were more apprehensive observers to removal than its victims. Nonetheless, they felt that their security was at risk and worried that their status might change unexpectedly. As always, Thomas advised a nonconfrontational approach to the whites, sobriety, Christianity, and cooperation with authorities.

THE TSALI LEGEND

Even though they were not targeted by the harsh removal process, the Lufty Cherokees were closely involved in a famous episode of the Trail of Tears, that of Tsali. The story of his family's efforts to remain in their homeland was the sole incident of open Cherokee aggression against the U.S. soldiers during removal and has become the founding myth of the Eastern Band. Though many accounts have been published with varying facts, motivations, interpretations, and consequences, contemporaneous U.S. Army correspondence and a recently discovered memorial by Tsali's wife, Nanih (or Nancy), provide a factual basis of the events that later were revised into legend.[4]

By August 1838, the U.S. Army realized that about 300 noncitizen Cherokees were resisting removal by living in the fastnesses of the North Carolina mountains. General Winfield Scott, who was in charge of the removal, ordered several detachments to begin rounding up these fugitives. In late October, Thomas and Cherokee runners, who preceded the mounted troops and attempted to persuade fugitives to surrender peacefully, were assisting three lieutenants. Their involvement was an attempt to disassociate the Lufty Cherokees from those in the nation who faced removal. On October 29, one of these lieutenants, 2nd Lt. Andrew Jackson Smith, captured fifteen Cherokees along the Tuckasegee River. When he learned that Cherokees were present farther south at the mouth of the Tuckasegee, Smith divided his company, sending the captured group ahead to Fort Cass, located along the Hiwassee River, near present-day Charleston, Tennessee, while he proceeded with three soldiers to capture twelve members of Tsali's family on October 30. Tsali, or Charley, was a Cherokee in his sixties who lived along the Nantahala River; his family included his wife, Nanih, three sons, one daughter, a son-in-law, and several grandchildren. According to a subsequent account by Nanih, Tsali had requested an exemption from removal like the Lufty group but his was not accepted. This is why his extended family had gone into hiding. Will Thomas was accompanying Smith in the roundup and was likely joined by several Lufty Cherokees as runners. The next day, as Lieutenant Smith was moving Tsali's family into custody, he learned that the previously captured group of fifteen Cherokees had escaped from his sergeant, so Smith rushed his group to rejoin the rest of his command in hopes of recapturing the escapees. Though Thomas had been with Smith and Tsali, an unexplained accident caused him and the Lufty Cherokees to stay behind on this fateful travel day.

The going was rough, and the young children of Tsali's family slowed progress. The military account states that the soldiers gave up their horses so the children and Nanih could ride them, in order to ease the way and cover more ground. As dusk arrived, Smith spied that one of Tsali's adult sons had a "dirk knife," which was quickly confiscated. Shortly after, Tsali "raised the war woop," according to Nanih, and Smith saw another son draw a small axe. Before Smith could order its seizure, the second son killed one of the soldiers by splitting his head in two. A second soldier was quickly killed by a blow to the head with the butt of an unloaded rifle, carried by one of the sons. The remaining third soldier was wounded by a tomahawk. The three Cherokee men then attempted to seize Smith, but because he was on horseback, he was able to escape along the trail. Soon Smith encountered some of his own men, but by then darkness had fallen, so they stopped their search for Tsali's family after returning to the place of the attack.

The motivations for the attack have been much debated. A late-in-life account by Wasseton, or Washington, a teenage grandson of Tsali's, asserted that the soldiers became impatient with Nanih, who was tending to the needs of a young child, and that when she was hurried with the child on horseback, she fell off the horse and her foot got caught in a stirrup, causing her to drop the child, who fell to the ground, hit a stone, and suffered a crushed skull and instant death. This grim accident angered Tsali and his sons.[5] These details explaining why Tsali's family may have been incited to rebel against the soldiers, however, are not included in the military reports and correspondence. In her account, Nanih does not state that she or a child had been harassed or abused. Instead, she explains that Tsali had become enraged by the forced removal and the loss of property and security that it entailed, and he compelled his sons to join him in an attack to gain his family's freedom or die trying. She portrays Tsali as the instigator of the attack.[6] Though it is impossible to know the actual details of these events and the motivations of the participants, it seems likely that Nanih would have recalled the death of a child, accidental or not. Perhaps Nanih's version is more accurate in this regard.

Tsali's family escaped into the mountains. Local lore tells us that they hid at a site named Tsali's Rock, a rock ledge within the park boundaries, located along the Left Fork of Deep Creek, ten miles north of Deep Creek Ranger Station. Though not a cave, the rock provided shelter underneath that was large enough for several adults. It was surrounded by thick rhododendron with a stream nearby.[7]

The morning after the attack, Smith followed his standing orders and returned to Fort Cass, abandoning his search for Tsali's family. When the news of the murders reached General Scott, he ordered detachments sent to North Carolina to find and punish the family, now considered fugitives. Col. William S. Foster was the senior officer of this mission. Seven detachments set out between November 7 and 15 to different parts of the western mountains and Foster headquartered at Joe Welch's farm on the Little Tennessee River. Will Thomas offered assistance and joined 1st Lt. C. H. Larned to search along the Oconaluftee River. General Scott described the Cherokee view of the incident in a letter to the War Department:

> Every Cherokee in this neighborhood who has heard of the recent outrage has expressed the utmost indignation and regret, and it would be very easy to obtain from the emigrants on the road any number of

> warriors to march with the troops against the outlaws. I shall, however, only accept of the services of a few runners, to bear invitations of kindness, deeming it against the honor of the United States to employ, in hostilities, one part of the tribe against another.
>
> Colonel Foster will also have the aid, as runners, guides, and interpreters, of some of Mr. Thomas's Oconeelufty Indians, as well as the personal services of Mr. Thomas himself, who takes a lively interest in the success of his expedition.[8]

Utsala (or Euchella) headed another family in the environs of Valley Town along the Little Tennessee.[9] He is the same man who had successfully sued a white settler over his 1819-era reserve. Sometime after the murders, Thomas met with Utsala and his group, who were themselves hiding in the mountains and hoping to avoid removal. In an 1844 letter to General Scott, Thomas explained that he recruited Utsala and other "outlying Indians" in the hunt for Tsali's family by promising them their freedom for the effort.[10] Soon after, on November 18, Foster received a petition from thirty-two white heads of households in the area of Joe Welch's farm (including Welch) to permit Utsala and his group to remain in North Carolina because they were "a well disposed peacible inoffensive body of people . . . and have been verry useful to us the inhabitants of this district."[11]

Then, the next day, Utsala's group and some Lufty Cherokees led by Salonita, or Flying Squirrel, captured Tsali's oldest son, Nantayalee Jake, and his son-in-law, Nantayalee George, along with Nanih, Ancil, Tsali's daughter, and a granddaughter. Additionally, the Utsala and the Lufty Cherokee Indians, along with a mounted company of soldiers, were reported to be in "close pursuit" of the remaining fugitives. Tsali's son Lowan was found in the next day or so, along with some other members of the family, including Wasseton. After Smith, Thomas, and Welch identified them as the murderers, Jake, George, and Lowan were executed by some of Utsala's group and in the presence of the army regiment. According to an account published at the time in the Hamilton, Tennessee, *Gazette*, once blindfolds were tied around the captives' eyes, three warriors aimed for the culprits' hearts and three aimed for their heads.[12] Wasseton, about age sixteen, was spared because of his youth. Colonel Foster subsequently proclaimed Utsala and his group exempt from removal because of their assistance in the search for the murderers; they were to join with the Lufty Cherokees. On November 24, Foster and his company, the Fourth Infantry, departed. From the date of Nanih's statement, July 18, 1843, which was transcribed by Will Thomas, it is apparent that she and the others of the Tsali group were ultimately permitted to stay in Qualla as well.[13] On November 25, Utsala and another Cherokee, Wachacha, captured Tsali near Yonaguska's former reserve on Governor's Island on the Tuckasegee. They executed him where he was taken captive.

It is a sad tale of desperate people in dire circumstances. Unlike the popularized version, Tsali did not nobly surrender his family and life so that other Cherokees might remain in the homeland. The Lufty Cherokees had already been spared removal, yet they knew that cooperation with whites was key to their long-term survival. Utsala and his group of about a hundred benefited because of Thomas's offer. But Tsali himself was a head of a family, like many others, who was trapped between legalities and events beyond his control. If he was part of a plot among his sons to attack Smith's company, it can be seen as his last move to resist. That the tale became the founding legend of the Eastern Band shows something about how the Lufty Cherokees, with help from Thomas, crafted their image for white sympathy. Early versions of the Tsali legend were published by Charles Lanman, a journalist who visited the Oconaluftee Valley in the 1840s and made the tale into a heroic drama, likening Tsali to Julius Caesar and Utsala to Brutus, perhaps with the encouragement of Thomas, perhaps not.[14] By the late 1880s ethnologist James Mooney wrote a version, based on an interview with Thomas, that firmly established the legend of Tsali as martyr, and this one has been promoted for decades by the Eastern Band itself in the outdoor drama *Unto These Hills*.

The most detailed account of the story, reprinting and interpreting Nanih's statement, was published in 2006 in a book chapter by William Martin Jurgelski. And a volume of the *Journal of Cherokee Studies*, published in 1979 by the Museum of the Cherokee Indian in Cherokee, North Carolina, and edited by Duane King and E. Raymond Evans, reprints military correspondence between the principal military characters Scott, Smith, and Foster and others as evidence of a less glamorous tale. An introductory essay to the *Journal*'s archival sources provides an interpretation more in keeping with the facts and more congruent with Cherokee mythology. Tsali and his sons were guilty of a brutal crime, and they endangered the community of Lufty Cherokees through their acts. King and Evans suggest that these individuals were cast more in the role of social deviants or criminals than selfless heroes. They are like Selu and Kanati's sons, who bring agriculture and hunting to the Cherokees after committing serious crimes, or like Spearfinger and Stonecoat, two other legendary villains of Cherokee mythology. After Stonecoat is captured, he is burned to death, but during his immolation he shares his wisdom about medicines with the Cherokees, helping them to thrive over the ages. In these myths, deviance and crime lead to new, heightened knowledge and civilization.[15] Certainly, the Cherokees' condemnation of odious crimes and participation in their resolution through justice and a return to peace are values that the myths share with Tsali's story.

One coincidental outcome of the incident was that it brought Israel Carver to Oconaluftee Valley. Carver was one of the soldiers who searched for Tsali and his family, so he saw the lush farmland at that time. Though it is impossible to verify, Israel likely met Andrew Jackson Bradley, who also served as a private in the North Carolina Militia rounding up Cherokees before the Trail of Tears.[16] Perhaps they formed a friendship that led to Israel's meeting Andrew's younger sister Mary along with the rest of the Bradley family. Mary and Israel Carver married in 1839. By the late 1840s they joined the Bradley family members who had moved to a farm in Oconaluftee in 1841. Israel and Mary were the parents of fifteen children, eleven of whom survived to adulthood. One child, Aden Carver, was born in 1844. Aden became the quintessential mountain man. As a child, Aden tended the cattle that pastured up in the mountains above the family farm. His great-granddaughter, Janice Carver Mooney of Canton, North Carolina, told of a day when young Aden took salt to the cattle and on his return hike heard

> a sound like a woman screaming. This was a panther, only he called it a painter. He said he walked a little faster. Then, he heard it scream again, a little closer. And he ran a little bit. Then he heard it scream again and he ran as fast as he could at a full run, and he came to a rail fence. He showed me how high it was from the ground. And he said, "I riz and jumped that fence. . . . Don't know how I got across that fence. It'd taken me an hour if I'd a climbed it."[17]

As an adult Aden became diversely skilled as a farmer, carpenter, backwoodsman, and, most notably, a millwright. He lived many years of his life in the valley.

Despite the competing Tsali legends and the conflicting details, a proclamation made by the Cherokee Tribal Council in the 1990s established November 25 as a holiday in Tsali's honor. The proclamation reads: "On November 25, 1838, Tsali was executed by Euchella and Wachacha. They used to be his neighbors. They were ordered to kill him so they could stay in North Carolina. Tsali was killed. We are still here. Tsali is a Cherokee hero."[18]

THE VALLEY AFTER REMOVAL

The two decades between removal and the beginning of the Civil War saw the development of an established community among white farmers in the park area of the Oconaluftee Valley and Raven Fork and a concentration of the Cherokee community in the eastern parts of the valley. Though the white and Cherokee communities lived largely separate lives, nonetheless, they were neighbors. They certainly interacted regularly at Thomas's store in Qualla, where a post office was established in 1839.[19] No doubt they met while driving livestock along the Oconalufty Turnpike, as well as, occasionally, in church via the visits of circuit-riding preachers and cross-community congregation members. Also, they would have come together when Cherokees or whites were hired as day laborers for one of Thomas's various enterprises or as workers on other whites' farms. Harsh winters brought on sharing. Thomas gave corn and grain to Utsala's group to help them survive the winter of 1839, and in 1842 the Lufty Cherokees sold corn to local whites after harsh rains caused crop failures.[20] Albeit generally harmonious, this close contact must have been tinged with some unease on the Cherokees' part because of the fragility of their status as North Carolinians; they were wary of doing anything to annoy the whites and cause hostility.

Soon after the upheaval of removal ended, several patriarchs passed away, issuing in a new generation of community leaders. In April 1839, Yonaguska died, shortly after selling his land on Governor's Island for $1,300 and moving to Qualla. After bidding his kinfolk farewell in the Qualla council house, the story goes that he passed on the leadership of the Lufty Cherokees to Will Thomas. However, it is important to note that Thomas was not tapped to be the chief of the Lufty Indians, an exaggeration of Thomas's role propagated later, and mistakenly, by James Mooney and Thomas's daughter Sallie Thomas Avery.[21] After Yonaguska's passing, Salonita, chief of Paint Town, became the head chief.[22] Thomas became the key liaison between the whites and Cherokees because of his entrepreneurial drive and boundless energy for civic projects, his devotion to the Cherokees, and his rare legal and strategic skills for protecting their interests. He became a longtime friend and associate of Scroop Enloe, the third son of Abraham and Sarah Enloe. In 1839, he bought the Enloes' farm at Stekoa Old Fields, the site of the Indian village that was raided during the Revolutionary War, now located in Whittier, North Carolina. Abraham, Scroop, and Wesley Enloe sold the 1,000-acre site for $3,400 to pay off their debt in Thomas's store. The farm became his personal residence where he lived with his mother and later with his wife and family.[23]

In 1841, Abraham Enloe died and the homestead in Oconaluftee was inherited by his son Wesley, who lived there—near the location of the park visitor center and Mountain Farm Museum—with his family for decades. Wesley was the twelfth child of seventeen and the seventh son of nine. By 1845, Jacob Mingus also had died; his homestead became the property of his third son, Dr. John Mingus, who also lived until late in the century. Jacob and Sarah Mingus's older sons, Jacob Jr. and Ephraim, already had farms in Big Cove by this time. By the way, both Sarah Enloe and Sarah Mingus survived their husbands by several decades, late into the nineteenth century.[24]

As more and more descendants of the first white families married and needed land for farms, they moved up the valley to settle on higher tributaries of the river, once the bottomlands became full and the terraces occupied. The number of farms, the size of the earliest farms, and the acres cultivated increased gradually over time. At the high end of farm production was Wesley Enloe. Census data show that in 1849 he farmed 200 of the 500 acres he owned, producing 25 bushels of wheat, 50 of rye, 800 of corn, and 50 of oats. He had livestock worth $934 (eight horses, twelve milk cows, twenty-four beef, two oxen, fifteen sheep, and sixty hogs). On a smaller farm higher up the valley, Samuel Beck cultivated 50 of 90 acres, yielding 14 bushels of rye, 6 of wheat, 10 of oats, 300 of corn, and 50 pounds of tobacco. He owned four horses, six cows, eighteen sheep, and twelve hogs.[25]

Self-sufficiency remained the default way of life; the farm families typically did everything for themselves: planting, harvesting, blacksmithing, carpentry, care of livestock, cooking, laundry, spinning, weaving, and sewing. Family labor was the norm. A few of the most prosperous white farms in the valley hired help and owned slaves. In 1850, Rufus G. Floyd owned four slaves, as did Samuel Sherrill. By 1860, the total number of enslaved persons on white farms in Oconalufty Township was sixteen.[26] Male slaves worked the farm, though typically female slaves did domestic work indoors.[27] As one of the most prosperous farmers and businessmen in the area, Will Thomas bought, sold, and owned slaves as well; he likely owned more than a dozen in the 1840s and had thirty-eight by the time of the 1860 census. Cudjo, Yonaguska's slave, became a trusted member of Thomas's household after the chief's death. Thomas also hired Cherokee, white, and Black people as workers on his farm, in his stores, and in support of other projects. In 1840, he paid a group of Cherokees $358.95 for road repairs.

A few tradesmen lived in the valley, including Nathaniel Blackburn, a tanner, and William Davis, a miller. Gunsmith Couch resided up along the creek that bears his name, and notably, the Cherokee Salola (Squirrel) became an accomplished blacksmith and gunsmith at this time. One of his rifles survives and is part of the collection at the Museum of the Cherokee Indian in Cherokee, North Carolina.[28]

Though a few development projects such as the Oconalufty Turnpike and Epsom Salts Manufacturing Company were operating at this time, an important one began during this era. The first mill on Mingus Creek was built as "a small whirling bucket overshot wheel gristmill" owned by the Mingus family.[29] Along with other, smaller mills scattered in the valley, it served families in the area until after the Civil War, when the first turbine mill was constructed at the same site. Also, Thomas was running five stores in western North Carolina. These had tradesmen available, including a tannery at the Qualla store. Thomas accepted barter and credit. The Cherokees often traded corn, ginseng, and other herbs for cash, coffee, sugar, and fabric.[30]

THE LUFTY CHEROKEE

After removal ended, roughly 700 Cherokees comprised the Lufty Cherokees around Qualla, including Utsala's group as well as a few others who had successfully evaded the soldiers during the fall of 1838. Though some white mountain folk remained unhappy about their presence and periodically pressed the federal government to address their status, both state and federal interest in the Lufty Cherokees fluctuated mercurially in the coming years. Additional federal and state removal attempts occurred in the early 1840s, but they were poorly financed and rather half-hearted, and the remaining full-blood Cherokees in North Carolina persistently resisted them.[31] Throughout these years, Thomas lobbied in Washington, D.C., and in the state for the Lufty Cherokees' share of the subsistence funds due from the Treaty of New Echota and for a secure status for them. By September 1839, he succeeded in gaining them an allowance from the federal government, but this small victory was undermined over the years by contentious and spotty disbursements. Payments for subsistence and removal were finally won in 1855, but were not paid at all until well after the end of the Civil War, in 1875.[32] The Cherokees' poverty is one reason Thomas bought land for them with his own money, in expectation that he would be repaid once the government claims were settled. He bought many tracts of land from the original residents of Oconaluftee Valley, particularly those who owned land along Raven Fork in

Big Cove, including, eventually, Sophia Mingus, Ephraim's widow, Abraham Mingus, and Samuel Sherrill. The Cherokees were not legally sanctioned to own property independently. To circumvent this legal conundrum, Thomas created the Cherokee Company in 1845. On paper, the company was formed to build a silk and sugar industry among the Cherokees. Mulberry saplings were imported for the silk effort, but they did not thrive in the climate. In time the company became a holding company through which the Cherokees could own land. As president of the company, Thomas could buy, sell, and pay taxes on land for them.[33]

In the lower valley, Thomas helped establish five townships to organize Cherokee civic life and provide a significant measure of self-governance, despite their nominal citizenship in Haywood or Jackson County, the latter of which was established in 1851 and in honor of President Andrew Jackson. The five Cherokee towns were Bird Town, Paint Town, Wolf Town, Yellow Hill, and Big Cove; each had a chief and tribal council that resolved disputes, loaned money, and collected taxes on the tracts of Indian land that were privately owned. Once collected, the tax funds would be passed on to Thomas, who would pay them for the band as a whole, often paying personally for the taxes on communally held property. Salonita (Flying Squirrel) became chief of Paint Town, and Utsala was chief of Wolf Town.

Some records exist from the council meetings at Wolf Town, kept by Inoli, or Black Fox, during this period. They document community activity such as church attendance, loans and schedules for repayment, and the institution of new community policy.[34] For example, in May 1859, the Wolf Town council announced new, more bureaucratic rules for marriage. A loose translation of the Cherokee records reads:

> If someone wants to get married, a paper must be obtained. The man is to come get the paper, for which he will pay $0.25, then he is to choose the one to marry them. He is to think of the preacher and also the clerk that is to marry them.
>
> This rule is for the marrying of Cherokees: if one of the couple is a Negro, they are not to be married; for it would be improper for one to have to separate them. A Negro man is not to be given a paper.
>
> When a man comes to get a paper, he must have the name of the woman. He will say that they are married. They will know that the land that they have is also to be mentioned so that both the cohabitants will know that they and their children will live upon their own property.[35]

THE WANDERING STAR'S TRAVEL NARRATIVE

One of the best sources of information about the lives of residents during the 1840s is the Whig journalist Charles Lanman, who traveled to the area in May 1848 and published an account of his travels in *Letters from the Alleghany Mountains*. In Qualla, Lanman met Thomas, who supervised his visit into the Smokies and, subsequently, with the Cherokees. Apparently, Thomas wanted to promote the newly established Epsom Salts Manufacturing Company and organized an expedition to Alum Cave in the company of a surveyor employed by Thomas. Lanman described the four-day trek to the cave. After the group had to abandon their horses at the top of the crest, his party made "a pedestrian pilgrimage of about six miles up and down, very far up and ever so far down, and over every thing in the way of rocks and ruined vegetation which Nature could possibly devise, until you come to a mountain side, which is only two miles from your starting place at the peak." Next he climbed "a precipice, in a zigzag way, which is at least 2,000 feet high, when you find yourself on a level spot of pulverized stone, with a rocky roof extending over your head a distance of fifty or sixty feet." Once Lanman reached the bluff, he was impressed by its height as well as the "alum, Epsom salts, saltpeter, magnesia, and copperas" in its walls. Similarly, he rhapsodically described the view as "one of the most remarkable and impressive scenes that I ever witnessed . . . a glorious picture." These descriptions are entertaining to park visitors familiar with Alum Cave and the trail to reach it. Perhaps more informative is the account of his lodging in homes on his way up and down the crest along the Oconaluftee.[36]

On the way up, Lanman seems to have stayed with Dr. John Mingus, given the mention of the host's abilities in medicine. Dr. John, as he was known, had received some premedical training in Hamburg, Germany, early in his life but reportedly had returned home because of his poor vision.[37] In time, he became the local physician and treated patients throughout Haywood and Macon Counties in the 1840s and 1850s. A letter from the doctor on March 20, 1845, to the itinerant Methodist preacher David Ring, who was traveling in Virginia at the time, described remedies for a malady that sounds like influenza. The remedies range from the sensible (keep the bowels open and the patient neither too hot nor too cold) to the elaborate. For example, Dr. John suggested (maintaining the details of the original letter):

> a puke of Epecacuanaha follow it up with Rubarb purge then I gave them cianna peper put in good vinegar and give a spoonful Every ten

> or 15 minits through the Day and also give sulphur in large Quantityes, and if the side panes much I Blister if the throat swells I aply musterd if the sweling still advances aply a blister to the throat, and make the following salution take sugar of lead and add salamoniac and alum Equal quantity and put it [in] water untell it is Desolved and wash the throadt and mouth you may also give sweat spirtis of Nitre & of laudanum combind a tea spoonful to an adult. Repeat Every hour tell the have taken three or four Doses and do this Every Day tell the begin to mend.[38]

These remedies must have seemed effective to patients and families for years, considering that he was always known as Dr. John. After the Civil War, however, he seems to have given up medicine. Perhaps he was compelled to do so because in an affidavit from May 29, 1868, T. H. Welch states that John Mingus had not practiced medicine for the thirteen years he had known him.[39]

Nonetheless, it seems that John Mingus was the likely multitalented host of Lanman during his visit to the Smokies:

> Our first night from home we spent in the cabin of a man who treated us with the utmost kindness, and would not receive a penny for his pains. So much for mountain hospitality. And now, to prove that our friend was an intelligent man, it may be mentioned that he is an adept in the following professions and trades, viz. those of medicine, the law, the blacksmith, the carpenter, the hunter, the shoemaker, the watchmaker, the farmer, and he also seemed to possess an inkling of some half dozen sciences. Now, I do not exactly mean to assert that the gentleman is a master practitioner in all these departments of human learning and industry; but if you were to judge of his ability by his use of technical words, you would not for a moment imagine he could have a competitor. But so it is in this wild region, one man has to perform the intellectual labor of a whole district; and, what is really a hard case, the knowledge which is thus brought to so good a market is nearly always the fruit of a chance education, and not of a systematic one.[40]

The next morning, the party picked up "a guide, who happened to be one of the proprietors of Alum Cave."[41] The guide must have been Robert Collins, whose home lay along the turnpike route and who was one of the investors in the company. Pressing ahead and approaching the cave, they met two Cherokees on a bear-hunting trip and stayed overnight with them: "We were admitted under their bark roof, and with them spent the night, sleeping upon the ground. We remained a sufficient length of time to enjoy one supper and one breakfast; the first was composed of corn bread and bear meat, and the second of trout (caught in a neighboring stream) and a corn cake fried in the fat of a bear."[42] Though Lanman visited in May, bad weather shortened the trip; hail and several inches of snow fell during their trek, so the journalist and his escort spent the return evening at Collins's home:

> We spent that night under the roof of our good friend and worthy man, the guide, and it was with difficulty that we could induce him to receive a quarter eagle for all his trouble in piloting us and treating us to his best fare. On that night we ate our supper at nine o'clock, and what rendered it somewhat peculiar was the fact that his two eldest daughters, and very pretty girls besides, waited upon us at table, holding above our heads a couple of torches made of the fat pine. That was the first time that I was ever waited upon in so regal a style, and more than once during the feast did I long to retire in a corner of the smoky and dingy cabin to take a sketch of the romantic scene.[43]

Even though Lanman commented that one could judge the wealth of a mountain farmer as inverse in proportion to the number of dogs he owned and the number of children he had, he received generous, if somewhat exotic, hospitality in his overnight accommodations.[44] The locals were also free with their time and stories. It is easy to speculate that Thomas arranged the journey as part of his tireless and multifaceted public relations campaigns aimed at cosmopolitan audiences in the state capital, in Washington, D.C., and in other large cities.

This notion may be documented even more fully in Lanman's positive portrayal of the Lufty Indians in three lengthy letters. The first described their political status, advancement toward "civilization," and a church service. The second focused on a ball game, including all its rituals and settings, and the final letter provided biographical sketches of the most notable Cherokee individuals of the time: Yonaguska, the blacksmith Squirrel, Chief Utsala, and Tsali, as well as brief mentions of the achievements of Sequoya, and the leaders of New Echota before removal, Elias Boudinot, John Ridge, and Major Ridge. In particular, Lanman's account of Tsali's escape and execution launched the refugee into the Cherokee pantheon by being the first to portray him as the martyr of the tribe whose death made possible the Lufty Indians' persistence in North Carolina. Throughout, the message was consistent: the Lufty Cherokees are "the happiest community that I have yet met with in this Southern country, and no candid man can visit them without being convinced of the wickedness and foolishness of that policy of the Government which as always acted upon the opinion that the red man could not be educated into a reasonable being."[45]

Lanman offers a "comprehensive summary" that praises the Cherokees for their high levels of literacy in their native language, their achievement in agriculture and the mechanical arts (such as making their own clothing and manufacturing farm equipment), the shift of the women's domain into the house and out of the fields, and their temperance, honesty, and morality.[46] When Lanman accompanied Thomas to church at the town council, he approved of the service:

> The first hour was devoted to instructing the children from a Cherokee Catechism, and the chiefs of the several clans were the officiating teachers. At twelve o'clock a congregation of some one hundred and fifty souls was collected, a large proportion of whom were women, who were as neatly dressed as could be desired, with tidy calico gowns, and fancy handkerchiefs tied over their heads. The deportment of all present was as circumspect and solemn as I have ever witnessed at any New England religious assembly. When a prayer was offered they all fell upon their knees, and in singing all but the concluding hymn they retained their seats. Their form of worship was according to the Methodist custom, but in their singing there was a wild and plaintive sweetness which was very impressive. The women and children as well as the men participated in this portion of the ceremony, and some of the female voices reminded me of the caroling of birds. They sung four hymns; three prayers were offered by several individuals, and two sermons or exhortations were delivered.[47]

If church marked the Indians' advancement, the ball game testified to their traditionalism. The two-day event was narrated in detail beginning with the activities of the evening beforehand: a dance and going-to-water ritual afterward. The game-day account was detailed as well with descriptions of preparing the field, starting the game, maidens giving tokens to their favorite players, the "varsity" game by the young men followed by a going-to-water ritual and awards ceremony, the boys' game as a second event, and, concluding the day, a second community dance in the "lodge" or council house. The game itself was described as like lacrosse in which players use a "spoony stick" to advance a ball to a goal but involving one-on-one wrestling as well in exercise "of a character that would kill the majority of white men." The account documented the clothes of the spectators ("holiday attire, so that feathers, shawl turbans, scarlet belts, and gaudy hunting shirts were quite abundant"), the home of a chief who provided supper (a cabin of "hewn logs" on a "farm of twenty acres on the mountainside, about one-fourth of which was in a state of cultivation, and planted with corn and potatoes. He had a tidy wife and several children, and his stock consisted of a pony, a cow, and some ten or a dozen sheep"), and the shape and size of the council house ("built of hewn logs, very large and circular, without any floor but that of solid earth," but including seats for the chiefs and a large fire in the center).[48] There is no doubt that the Cherokees were just as welcoming as the whites, but their public relations objectives seem obvious to today's reader at the letter's end:

> The dancing continued until midnight, when the presiding chief addressed the multitude on the subject of their duties as intelligent beings, and told them to return to their several homes and resume their labors in the field and in the shops. He concluded by remarking that he hoped I was pleased with what I had witnessed, and trusted that nothing had happened which would make the wise men of my country in the East think less of the poor Indian than they did at the present time: and then added that, according to an ancient custom, as I was a stranger they liked, the several chiefs had given me a name, by which I should hereafter be remembered among the Carolina Cherokees, and that name was *Ga-taw-hough No-que-sih*, or *The Wandering Star.*[49]

Will Thomas must have been present to serve as interpreter and cross-cultural liaison.

AN ERA OF CHURCH BUILDING

Beyond the special occasions orchestrated for travelers, community events involving churchgoing remained prominent parts of cultural life. During the twenty years between removal and the Civil War, church buildings were constructed by the white Baptists and Methodists in the valley, and the Cherokee Methodist Mission also acquired its first building. The first log church at Smokemont was built in 1841 by the Lufty Baptist Church. Hughes Chapel Methodist Episcopal Church was built at the foot of Hughes Ridge in 1846. Constructed on land donated by Rafe Hughes, it had a hewed log structure and large fireplace, and it served as both a place of worship and a school. The

Echota Methodist Mission, located in Soco Valley, existed as early as 1840 and added a school in 1850. Today the mission operates as the Cherokee United Methodist Church.[50]

The churches functioned as places of social contact between races. At the mission, Cherokee chiefs and converted Christians led the services, though David Woodring, or, more familiarly, Davy Ring, served as pastor. Tsali and Anitsa were church leaders. A tribute to Anitsa after his death August 1, 1874, quotes his valedictory: "I talked to sinners and I prayed for them; and now if I am not able to talk to them, if now my speaking is past, I am ready to go. All of you know how I walked here below."[51]

The records for Lufty Baptist Church show that a few Cherokees and enslaved people were received as members as early as 1840. A list of members includes the following entries:

Conot, Nelly	Cherokee, Received August 1840
Conot, Tom	Cherokee, Baptized August 1840
Jane, a Black woman belonging to Widow Floyd	Received and baptized, 1849
Geesca, Van	Cherokee, Received by baptism, July 1850
Geesca, Willa	Cherokee, Received by baptism, July 1850
Black man belonging to Wesley Enloe	Received by experience, June 1858
Black girl by name of Ardilla	Received by experience, August 1865[52]

Worship by enslaved persons was regularly compelled by white masters, so it is difficult to know if they attended because of their own desire or that of their owners.[53] Ardilla, who became a member in 1865, would have done so after emancipation. Even so, these non-white members suggest that there may have been an open spirit in the Baptist congregation.

Pastors also served both Cherokee and white churches. Richard Evans of Tennessee was elected the "co-supply" pastor of Lufty Baptist Church along with C. B. Mingus in 1852. Though the census listed his occupation as a farmer, he preached in many churches, including one in Bird Town, where he used an interpreter. This church had about a hundred members, sixty of whom Evans had converted and baptized. Ultimately, Evans moved to White Oak Flats, which became Gatlinburg, in Tennessee, and started Evans Chapel. Just before the Civil War, in 1860, William Henry Conner began preaching at Lufty Baptist Church and purchased the Collins homestead. He, too, was active among the Cherokees and organized churches at Bird Town, Soco, Big Cove, and Yellow Hill; he helped establish the Cherokee Baptist Association and taught at a Cherokee church school as well.[54] In 1851, Henry Jackson Beck was ordained as a deacon in Lufty Baptist Church and remained active for decades. At some point, he conducted a mass marriage ceremony "where 400 Cherokee couples were united in matrimony. Many of them were grandparents, having already had their family before legalizing their union for the state." Beck also served as a church clerk and moderator, as Sunday school superintendent, and as a superior court clerk.[55]

Churches were important locations for education generally, though literacy was not high. Well-to-do white heads of households could read and write, but perhaps not all members of the family were literate.[56] Some Cherokees could use the Cherokee syllabary created by Sequoyah, though very few could speak, write, or read English. Despite limited formal education in the valley, during the twenty years after removal both the whites and Cherokees developed and stabilized their communities to a considerable degree. The Cherokees obviously faced monumental challenges from the state and federal government during this period, which they were able to meet with assistance from Thomas and other white neighbors. It seems likely that despite acts of generosity and recognition, however, they would have been chagrined to live in Jackson County, a new county named after the president who led the removal program. The social achievements of this time would soon be tested during the Civil War, and the bonds formed would shape the ways the community met the moment.

Chapter 6

BEGINNING TO MAP THE SMOKIES

FAMOUS MEN AND MOUNTAIN NAMES

▲▲▲

I know it's unwise to hike alone, and I do it rarely. Don't tell my family. But from time to time I set out by myself, and I enjoy it because when I'm alone there's no reason to talk. I notice more things. I detest a crowded trail; I'm most content when a few other folks are passing me or coming from the other direction. I am aware that the park is bear country. I have a plan if I meet a bear: keep car keys, ID, and phone separate from the day pack; blow my whistle when it gets really quiet so as not to surprise the bear; if approached, toss the pack with my lunch to the bear; back away slowly. (A friend of mine once encountered a bear on Spence Field and handed over his pack containing peaches, a move that ended the meeting.)

The bigger risk is getting lost or confused. My security is placed in the detailed trail map in my day pack. I've studied it beforehand, too. On occasion, I have missed a turn; I have inadvertently taken the wrong trailhead and thought I was on a different path than I actually was. It does not take long for the beauty of the woods to become terrifying once I feel I've made a mistake. At these times, I force myself, despite my elevated pulse, to stop, take out the map, check it, retrace my steps. I check my watch for how long I have been hiking and when I passed the last junction. I ask other hikers about the trail; I don't care if they think I'm stupid or annoying. Nothing new there.

I consider maps to be the ultimate sign of human intelligence. They are similar to the wonder of a hardware store that has the precise tool, among thousands, to solve my particular problem, a tool made by people who anticipated my need. I love that. Today, maps are ubiquitous and reliable, on our phones, in our hands, ready to assist. We take them for granted until the GPS signal is lost. What must tramping in the Smokies have been like when one had only an animal path, unmaintained trail, compass, or part-time guide? The glorious technology of a good map makes it possible for people to be in and move through the woods, and I am grateful to those who made them.

▲▲▲

DESPITE THE ISOLATION of the Smokies, reports of the mountains' height and ruggedness had piqued the curiosity of botanists and geographers, who were beginning to conduct serious scientific studies of the mountains in the middle of the nineteenth century. The geographers focused on mapping the area, describing its most important features, and accurately measuring the altitude of the dominant peaks. Challenges lay in access to remote areas without roads and in using the instruments of the day, namely the cumbersome mercury barometer that was dependent on air pressure. Measurements from this instrument varied throughout the day and, of course, with changing weather.

In the summer of 1858, Thomas Lanier Clingman led a party of six to a number of the peaks in the Smokies. By this time Clingman was an explorer, scientist, and politician, holding one of the U.S. Senate seats for North Carolina. Clingman already had quite a reputation for exploring. Previously, he had been engaged in a contest with a former professor of his at the University of North Carolina, Elisha Mitchell, to determine the highest peak east of the Mississippi River. Mitchell and Clingman had both measured the mountain that was the winner, located in the Black Mountains of North Carolina. But while verifying earlier measurements, in 1857, Mitchell accidently fell from a cliff above a waterfall and drowned. Subsequently, his name was given to the mountain both Mitchell and Clingman had championed and where Mitchell lost his life. Mount Mitchell is 6,684 feet high.[1]

An Asheville resident, Clingman was also a great promoter of the western Carolina mountains. The group he led to the Smokies in 1858 included Samuel Leonidus Love, a prominent physician and political figure of Waynesville, North Carolina, and Samuel Botsford Buckley, a geologist and naturalist who became the state geologist of Texas after the Civil War.[2] This group traveled to the crest of the Smokies through Oconaluftee Valley, and Buckley conducted barometric measurements, though they would not prove accurate in the long run. He also named a number of peaks, including Mount LeConte and Mount Guyot. The former was named for one of the Le Conte brothers, either Professor Joseph Le Conte, who was a prominent geologist but did not work in the Smokies and seems never to have visited them, or his older brother John Le Conte, a physician and professor of chemistry, physics, and natural history. The story justifying John as the namesake is that he took comparative barometric readings from Waynesville when Buckley did so from the Smokies. Buckley named Mount Guyot for the eminent Swiss geologist Arnold Guyot, whom he knew and with whom he had previously explored other parts of the southern Appalachians—though not the Smokies—in 1856.[3]

By 1859, Guyot himself was prepared to explore the Smokies, which he described as the "master chain of the Appalachian System."[4] With funding from the Smithsonian Institution and planning support from Clingman, Guyot spent the summer traversing the entire fifty-mile crest of the Smokies and taking more accurate measurements and making more systematic records and maps than had ever been done previously.[5] Guyot was a lifelong friend of paleontologist Louis Agassiz, who discovered the effects of Ice Age glaciation in the northern hemisphere. He had followed Agassiz to the United States once his employer, the Academy of Neuchâtel, closed because of war. Guyot's talents were soon recognized, and by 1854 he was chair of physical geography at Princeton University. He launched a study of the Appalachian chain in 1848 and turned his attention to the southern section in 1856, spending three additional summer vacations on this project: in 1858, 1859, and 1860.[6]

Clingman arranged for Robert Collins to serve as Guyot's guide for the 1859 expedition and, beforehand, to clear a six-mile horse trail of sorts to the highest peak, then called Smoky Dome by mountain folk. Cherokees knew the place as Kuwahi, "the Mulberry Place." This was the mountain under which the legendary White Bear of the Cherokees had his council house. No doubt by this time Collins was well known as the mountain guide of choice on the North Carolina side. During what Guyot described as "the remarkable rainy season" between late June and early August, he and Collins, along with one or more of Collins's sons, "camped out twenty nights, spending a night at every one of the highest summits, so as to have observations at the most favorable hours. The ridge of the Smoky Mountains I ran over from beginning to end, viz: to the great gap through which the Little Tennessee comes out of the mountains."[7] Historian Paul M. Fink insightfully imagined the immense difficulty and achievement of Guyot's work:

Arnold Henry Guyot.

COURTESY OF PRINCETON UNIVERSITY LIBRARY, N.J.

> To one who has pushed his way through the jungle-thick vegetation of the more remote parts of the Smokies, even in this late day (1938) when trails of a sort exist, there can be no more striking illustration of the zeal that actuated this great explorer than a mental picture of him, with but a single companion, struggling up the steep, trackless, laurel-tangled slopes of Smoky, burdened with supplies for a week or more, and handicapped still further by a bulky, fragile barometer, that must be carefully protected from any rude contact that might wreck beyond repair its delicate mechanism. But though laboring under such difficulties, so painstaking was Guyot with his observations and subsequent calculations that the figures he cites for the various points in the Smokies seldom vary as much as a score of feet from the latest altitudes announced by the United States Geological Survey.[8]

Though a number of his names were later changed, Guyot named the triad of peaks around Smoky Dome: Mount Buckley, Clingmans Dome, and Mount Love. The first was to honor the efforts by Samuel Buckley the year before, a return compliment. The last was to recognize Col. Robert G. A. Love, who "kindly loaned" him the horse that was the first to ascend Clingman's Dome by way of Collins's path. And, of course, the dome, the highest peak in the park, was named for Clingman out of gratitude and acknowledgment of his previous exploring but also because Guyot claimed that that name was already in current use. Even though it appears that Buckley had first named Clingmans Dome after himself, in a letter to the *Asheville News* explaining his choices, Guyot said, "I must remark that in the whole valley of the Tuckasegee and Oconaluftee, I heard of but one name applied to the highest point, and it is that of Mount Clingman." Consequently, the highest peak in the park, at 6,643 feet, has carried Clingman's name though the tribal council of the Eastern Band of Cherokee Indians passed a resolution in July 2022 to return to the Cherokee name.[9]

Other mountains that retain Guyot's appellations are Luftee Knob, the Sawteeth, and Tricorner Knob. In addition, Guyot called the gap to the east of Indian Gap (where the original turnpike traversed the crest) New Gap, which was the basis for its current name, Newfound Gap. Also, Guyot recognized Collins's help by naming for him the peak whose name was later changed to Mount Kephart. This appellation honored twentieth-century writer and key park proponent Horace Kephart. Ironically, when Kephart learned that the mountain was to be named after him, in 1928, he wrote to the chairman of the nomenclature committee explaining that he would instead prefer the mountain at the head of Deep Creek to bear his name, because he had lived on Deep Creek and because Tennesseans were upset that a mountain they already knew to have a name that honored someone with Tennessee ties (Collins) should bear a North Carolinian's name. But Kephart's preference was not followed. To the contrary, *Kephart*'s preferred peak was named for Collins. Apparently, when someone names a mountain after you, you should not quibble about which one it is.[10]

Guyot was systematic and thoughtful in all areas of his work. He articulated a sensitive and reasonable philosophy for which names should prevail when multiple names for the same location were in use. Of course, this situation was much the case in the Smokies. He advised that "the name which appears the most natural or more euphonic" was the right choice. Further, he said, "When the choice lies between the name of a man and that of a name which is descriptive and characteristic, I should choose the latter." Finally, names used by residents should be accorded "priority," rather than those applied by scientists. These rules do seem sensible, so it is curious that the names of the key peaks of the park, some of which already had names, were indeed changed by scientists for their own memorialization. Even though Mount Guyot—the second highest peak in the park at 6,621 feet—was named the year *before* the Swiss geographer arrived in the Smokies and applied by fellow scientist Buckley, Guyot let the name stand. This peak had been formerly known as Balsam Cone and Balsam Pine; the Cherokees called it Sornook.[11]

After his return to Princeton, Guyot wrote a detailed manuscript about his work in the southern Appalachians, "Notes on the Geography of the Mountain District of Western North Carolina," which he sent to the superintendent of the Coast Survey in Washington, D.C., in 1863. However, it was never published and apparently was filed away in the library of the Coast and Geodetic Survey for many years.[12] It contained precise descriptions of the watersheds, ranges, and transportation routes in, around, and through the Smokies. For example, Guyot saw the Smoky Mountains as an "almost impervious barrier between Tennessee and the inside basins of North Carolina." As for the hard-won and vital Oconalufty Turnpike, he commented: "Only one tolerable road, or rather mule path, in this whole distance is found to cross from the great valley of Tennessee into the interior basins of North Carolina—and the road reaches its summit, the Road Gap, as it is called, at an elevation of not less than 5,271 feet. It connects Sevierville, Tennessee with Webster, Jackson Co., North Carolina, through the vallies of Little Pigeon and Occona Luftee, the last of which is the main northern tributary of the Tuckaseegee."[13]

Guyot also provided a scholarly view of the forests of the Smokies during this era, a place that was not affected by glaciation and had not yet seen commercial logging:

> The forests, which, with the exception of a few spots, cover almost the totality of that mountain region, are truly magnificent, especially near the foot of the hills where humus has been accumulated by action of the water. The trees there are from 80 feet and upwards, and 8 to 11 nay 12 feet in diameter are no great rarity. The Oak, the Chestnut, the tulip-tree, the wild cherry, over 60 ft. high, with beautiful straight stems, the Magnolias and the Hickory compose the bulk of these immense forests and cloth with a foliage of perfect beauty the Mountain slopes up to 5,000 and 6,000 ft. Beyond 6,000 ft. the dark Balsam fir or its allied species the Fraser pine crown with black caps all the summits which rise beyond that limit.[14]

Of the Oconaluftee River, he says, it "is mostly a wild mountain torrent. Its two main sources rise at the Road Gap in the Smoky Mt. and at the Luftee

Knob, in the corner formed by the Great Smoky and Balsam Mts. The whole basin is a bed of mountains which are the high spurs of the Great Smoky." The valley provides "beautiful and fertile though narrow flat bottoms."[15]

The report's conclusion, interestingly, highlighted the relevance of Guyot's work to Union strategy during the Civil War, which was, of course, ongoing by 1863. The roughness of the country and the limited access to it became considerations for the placement of troops:

> An Army settled in the large and fertile Valley of east Tennessee where it can be abundantly provided, can easily occupy by very moderate forces, all the mountainous region, and all its available passes, across the Blue Ridge, and thus keep as it were, the keys of the doors to each of all the Southern States just mentioned. It can thus threaten from within, every one of those States and their Capitals, keep at bay any opposing forces, in the low country, and prevent their being concentrated.— It cuts in two the Confederacy from east to west.[16]

And the final paragraph provides an excellent analysis: "In time should the rebellion be ever overcome in the lower country, the occupation of that mountain region will, to a great extent, prevent its leaders from the possibility of taking a refuge in it, and from thence indefinitely prolonging a defensive if not an offensive war."[17] Because the manuscript was stashed away, whether it influenced any of the actions of the Union troops cannot be known. However, some Confederates also recognized the military potential of the mountains and the importance of the passes. One of the leaders who reached the same conclusion was none other than Will Thomas. These early scientific explorations reveal, yet again, that the mountains and even Oconaluftee Valley in particular were of interest to international, national, and regional leaders, well worth study and professional attention.

Chapter 7

AN ISOLATED VALLEY IN WARTIME

A BIRACIAL CONFEDERATE FORCE

It's just a pull-off from Clingmans Dome Road now, but throughout the nineteenth century, Indian Gap was the overmountain pass where travelers, livestock drovers, and Confederate and Union soldiers would cross. Newfound Gap, 232 feet lower in elevation, was not in use then. Throughout summer these days, a handful of cars might be parked at the pull-off by folks hiking a section of the Appalachian Trail. Alternatively, the hikers might take Road Prong Trail to the Chimney Tops Trail, though this would be an unusual choice since the return would be all uphill, when one's energy may be dwindling and legs protesting.

That's what I do now, anyway. Almost as soon as I've left the clearing of the gap, the sunshine gives way to dappled shade along a rocky, four-foot-wide trail. The ethereal song of a veery transforms my pace from a rush to a deliberate saunter. I'm content to listen to the veery, accompanied by a junco and a red-eyed vireo, as long as possible. No one else is on this trail today. Looking at my feet and the path ahead, I cannot imagine that I'm traveling the critical infrastructure of the Smokies' settlers, the Oconalufty Turnpike that a committee of local men developed into a road of sorts. The labor would have been done by Cherokee, enslaved, and white men. It was already in place when Guyot came through; he had nothing good to say about it. But he did recognize its strategic value in the conflict that was brewing and became the Civil War. So did Will Thomas. As an advocate for western North Carolina and the Lufty Cherokees, Thomas conceived that guarding it for the Confederacy was an appropriate role for Oconaluftee Valley residents. This task could keep enlistees to the Thomas Legion close to home so that they could farm and protect their families. Of course, the plan did not fully succeed, but it did work to a degree.

GIVEN THAT NEITHER the Cherokees nor the white farm families in the Oconaluftee Valley depended on slave labor and that North Carolina as a state was slow to secede from the Union, involvement in the Civil War by the area's residents might be expected to have been minimal. However, both fighting-age men and the entire civilian population were dramatically affected by the conflict throughout and long after the war years. After much public debate and a state convention, North Carolina seceded from the Union on May 20, 1861, eleventh to do so among the southern states. President Abraham Lincoln's call to raise troops against the Confederates who had attacked Fort Sumter in South Carolina served as a tipping point for many who, though they did not view the slave economy as something for them to fight for individually, were offended by the idea that Lincoln would raise troops of southerners in the states that had not seceded to fight against their regional neighbors.[1]

EARLY CONFEDERATE ENLISTEES

Local views of the Confederacy divided the community to some extent and are obliquely referenced in the minutes of the Lufty Baptist Church in the fall of 1861. The September minutes stated, "Fellowship not found for a peculiar cause," a singular instance of the breakdown of community harmony in the official church record. In October, the church did not meet for "certain causes," so presumably the situation had not improved over a month. It is intriguing to speculate where the dividing lines may have fallen in the community. One wonders if the more affluent families who were slave owners may have been more in favor of secession than those who were not. According to the 1860 census, John Mingus enslaved two individuals, and the two Enloe households in the valley enslaved a total of eight persons. Of course, the Jackson County residents who enslaved the most people were William Holland Thomas, who owned thirty-eight, and J. B. Love, who owned forty-nine, but they did not attend the Lufty church. In his study of western Carolina slave owners, historian John Inscoe presented evidence that non-slave-owning whites believed strongly in property rights, held racist views, and were unsettled by the idea of free Black people, thinking that it was better for them to be enslaved than not, even though in the mountain communities they posed little security threat because of their small numbers.[2] Nonetheless, the church did remain open during most of the war; pastors Richard Evans and W. H. Conner held services.[3]

A few Oconaluftee men volunteered for the Confederate forces before secession. Both Hamilton T. Mingus, the son of Dr. John and Polly (Enloe) Mingus, and Thomas Enloe, the grandson of Abraham and Sarah Enloe and son of Scroop and Sarah Ann Enloe, volunteered their service on April 27, 1861, traveling a few miles east to Webster, North Carolina, to join different regiments. Two of Abraham and Sarah's sons and another grandson volunteered soon thereafter. Benjamin M. (Mattison) Enloe, age fifty-three, and his brother John's son, Benjamin F. Enloe, age twenty-four, enrolled a couple of weeks later on May 15 at Edneyville, and William A. "Bill" Enloe, brother to Benjamin M., enlisted as a captain late in the summer on August 31. Joseph A. Collins, son of Robert and Elizabeth (Beck) Collins, enlisted on May 30 in the same company and regiment as Matt Enloe.[4]

An August letter from twenty-one-year-old Hamilton stationed in Asheville to his brother Abraham Mingus, who was back at home, suggests his enthusiasm for the cause:

ASHEVILLE, N.C. AUGUST 23, 1861

Dear Brother.

I have the opertunity of droping you a line and I cannot fail to imbrace it. We are still in Asheville, thought [*sic*] we do not know how soon orders may come for us to march.

Several of the boys are sick, Cogdille is very bad off, with the fever. We have plenty to eat and carpet in the house, all sleep in rooms on blankets. The offiers are clever, Jim Love has Cogdills office., as 2nd Lt. If we stay here any lenth of time, I shall need some clothes.

Some thinks very likely we will be stationed here for several months. News arrives here this morning that N.C. went for secession.

I sent my [pay] home by W.A. Enloe. Also he paid me five dollars in money. There is three Companys stationed here., Jackson, Macon and John Woodfews Company. We get our washing done for 10 cents per garment. The people are very generous, Andy is very clever to the boys. If we leave here I will write to you and let you know, where we go to and how we are doing. I am in good health.

We have to lay down and write on our blankets.

Yours affectionat

Brother, H. T. Mingus[5]

Tragically, several of these volunteers exited the ranks quite early. Hamilton became ill in November and was admitted to Chimborazo Hospital in Richmond, Virginia. He was later transferred to Petersburg, Virginia, and died on January 11, 1862; it is not clear that he saw combat. The older Benjamin Enloe, Benjamin M., was discharged "for disability" about six months later, on June 6, dying about a year later. Thomas Enloe, a twenty-three-year-old private, was killed at the Battle of Mechanicsville, Virginia, on June 26, 1862; local historian Carl Lambert claimed that his tongue was shot off. Captain Bill Enloe engaged in battle at Cumberland Gap under Gen. Braxton Bragg in May 1862 but was "quite sick on way to command" on February 1, 1863, and resigned because of a disability on April 20 of that year.[6]

THE THOMAS LEGION

One prominent citizen of the region, Will Thomas, supported the Confederate cause from the start. By 1860, he was fifty-four years old, a successful entrepreneur, a state senator, a slave-owning farmer, and the agent of the Lufty Indians. Thomas favored secession in the North Carolina Senate, where he was serving his seventh consecutive term, as well as at the state convention, where the vote for secession was held. Thomas believed that, once the war was over, western North Carolina would become the center of the new Confederate nation and an economic hub with increased tourism and industry due to its central location. After the vote, he returned to the area and began creating infantry companies of Cherokees, which were first named the Junaluska Zouaves in honor of the late warrior hero of Horseshoe Bend. Envisioned as a home guard, these men began improvements to the Oconalufty Turnpike, because Thomas recognized that this road would be key to transporting goods and men over the mountains during the conflict. Even though the North Carolina Cherokees had no stake in the conflict, Thomas saw that they would have to participate to retain their legal, but uncertain, status in the region. Of course, the Cherokees' agreements were with the federal government, so association with the Confederacy endangered their status and further delayed annual payments for their loss of land and other assets during the removal. At first, Thomas attempted to negotiate citizenship in the state as a condition of Cherokee service, but when the governor rejected this idea, Thomas persuaded the Cherokees to volunteer anyway, largely on the basis of their trust in him as their adviser. Also, in postwar interviews with anthropologist James Mooney, Thomas claimed that Gen. Kirby Smith hoped to enroll the eastern Cherokees for his command and sent a representative to them early in 1862 to persuade them to join. Thomas realized that if he allowed Kirby to enlist the Cherokees, they would soon be moved far from their homes and families and from his protection, so he conceived of enlisting the Cherokee companies himself as a local defense, especially guarding the mountain passes. Consequently, recruiting began in the spring of 1862.[7] On April 9, 120 Cherokees and 12 whites enlisted at Quallatown as the North Carolina Cherokee Battalion and Thomas's Highland Rangers, respectively. Thomas had already received orders for them to report to Knoxville; they left a few days later on April 15. Despite this immediate departure, Thomas worked continuously to keep the Cherokee and white soldiers close to home. He understood their tenuous ideological commitment to the cause, the real need for their labor at home, and their well-founded concern for the safety of their families, livestock, and homes.[8]

Just a day after the companies' departure, the Confederate Congress passed the conscription law requiring all able-bodied men between eighteen and thirty-four to serve in the military for at least three years. No doubt, this law compelled many Oconaluftee Valley men to enlist in the Thomas Legion, the enlarged version of the early white and Cherokee companies. The conscription law was deeply resented by the mountain families who had few enslaved people to leave behind to maintain farm operations and who had already volunteered in proportionally large numbers. Resentment was further fueled by the exemption of white farmers who owned more than twenty slaves and could purchase a substitute for $300. Non-slave owners who had the money could also purchase a substitute. No doubt, conscription was an important reason that July 17, 1862, was such a big enlistment day for the legion in Quallatown. On that day at least twelve Oconaluftee Valley men enlisted, including Aseph T. Enloe (the son of Benjamin Mattison Enloe and his second wife, Mary Jaynes); brothers Sevier S. Enloe and John T. Enloe (sons of Abraham and Sarah Enloe); John Collins (the son of Robert Collins and Elizabeth

Beck); Ephraim S. Conner (the son of Joel S. Conner and Katherine Mingus); Benjamin Carver (the son of Israel Carver and Mary Bradley); brothers James Holland Jr. and Osborn Bradley (sons of James Holland Bradley and Martha Grant); and brothers William, John, Stephen, and Samuel Carson Beck (all sons of Samuel and Cynthia Beck). All were placed into Company F of the Infantry Regiment of the legion, under Thomas's command until the end of 1862.[9] Interestingly, future principal Cherokee chief Nimrod Jarrett Smith joined Walker's Battalion, the second regiment of the legion, but on September 1, he was transferred to Cherokee Company A, serving as first sergeant.[10]

By September 27, 1862, when the enlarged and combined forces of the Thomas Legion mustered at Knoxville, it had two regiments. The Infantry Regiment of eleven companies was led by Thomas, who gained the rank of colonel by election of the men, and by Lt. Col. James R. Love II, a nephew of Thomas's wife. The second regiment, Walker's Battalion, was composed of five infantry companies, three cavalry companies, and one artillery company, led by Lt. Col. William C. Walker. In December 1862, however, the cavalry companies were transferred out of the Thomas Legion.[11]

Several theatrical moments followed the arrival of the original Cherokee companies into Knoxville. These Cherokee volunteers under Thomas's command made their way to Knoxville in the spring of 1862 via Webster and Franklin, North Carolina, attracting additional recruits as they went. Enola, a chief, and Ayunini, a conjuror, are reputed to have served as sergeants of the companies, though service records do not confirm their presence.[12] From Sweetwater, Tennessee, the Cherokees took the Tennessee and Georgia Railroad into the city, where they marched in formation down Gay Street, one of the central city streets, on their route to a camp north of town. Captain James W. Terrell, a longtime friend and business associate of Thomas, recalled that they "seemed to be the object of a grand curiosity, a large crowd followed or passed on the sidewalks all the way from the depot."[13] The troops once again drew a crowd when a Cherokee-language service was held at the First Presbyterian Church on Sunday, led by Unaguskie, the grandson of Yonaguska, and included both a sermon and music, all conveyed in Cherokee without translation. Soon the companies moved farther out of town, to Strawberry Plains, to guard the railroad bridge over the Holston River. Throughout their encampment in the Knoxville area, the Cherokees were objects of great interest, attracting visitors to their camp to watch their ball games, put on as diversions during some uneventful days. The Cherokees also experienced several diseases as they adapted to camp life: camp fever (epidemic typhus), measles, and mumps, which resulted in several deaths.[14]

In September, one of the most consequential battles occurred for the Cherokees, establishing their reputation among Union troops as fearsome warriors. They were led toward Cumberland Gap to watch for federal troops who might be moving south. At Baptist Gap, the Cherokees were ambushed and responded swiftly and effectively to drive off the Union forces. Unfortunately, Lieutenant Astoogatogeh, a grandson of famed warrior Gul'kalaski, was killed during the battle, inflaming the Cherokees, who retaliated by scalping several of the wounded and dead Union soldiers. This incident embarrassed Thomas, who had worked steadily to ensure whites of the Cherokees' "civilized nature." Apologies were made and the scalps were returned to the surviving Union troops. Captain Terrell later claimed that the Cherokees scalped defeated Union soldiers throughout the war, but records do not exist to confirm this report. Nonetheless, much contemporary newspaper coverage of the event sealed the Cherokees' reputation as fierce, certainly, and brutal, whether or not that characterization was deserved. In addition, they were recognized as excellent fighters and exceptionally talented trackers of deserters, criminals, and bushwhackers, which were loosely organized Union companies that terrorized and plundered mountain families and, when they met them, Confederate troops. Until the fall of 1863, for roughly a year, the Thomas Legion, including its Cherokee and white companies, camped at Strawberry Plains and guarded roads and railroad bridges from attack by small groups of Union loyalists in Tennessee who made repeated attempts to shut down the transport and communication lines in East Tennessee. However, the loyalists had fleeting support from the Union command, so the bridges that they burned were soon rebuilt and many of their leaders were brought into custody and sent to Tuscaloosa, Alabama, as prisoners of war.[15]

Understanding that many men from East Tennessee and western North Carolina were reluctant to pick up arms against the Union but were willing to serve as home guards and skilled craftsmen, Thomas recruited "miners and sappers" to enable these men to comply with conscription and help the war effort less directly than as soldiers. The idea was for these men to build roads and bridges and to serve as masons, carpenters, blacksmiths, and gunsmiths for the Confederacy. Unfortunately, once Alfred E. Jackson was promoted to brigadier general of the brigade that included the legion, he ordered the miners and sappers to take up arms alongside the rest of the soldiers, a decision that led to a number of early desertions among men who felt coerced to fight against their will.[16]

Even so, Thomas succeeded in assigning some men to detachments that worked in this capacity. It seems that one instance where the miners and sappers were at work was in building a fort to protect Alum Cave, a source of saltpeter for gunpowder. Thomas also repeatedly made a strategic argument for the detachments guarding the mountain passes. In a letter of November 22, 1862, to Governor Zebulon Vance, Thomas explained his thinking: "As long as we can hold the Country encircled by the Blue Ridge and Cumberland mountains . . . we have the heart of the South. The loss of this country larger than England and France is the loss of the Southern Confederacy and we sink under a despotism."[17] Service records of a number of Company F recruits indicate that they were on detached service for several consecutive months in the Smoky Mountains under Colonel Thomas's order. As a civilian volunteer at age fifty-six, Robert Collins, the well-known guide of the North Carolina Smokies and toll keeper of the Oconalufty Turnpike, led a group of these men in work to improve the turnpike, construct Fort Harry, and build a road up to the cave. Although there is some dispute about the size and design of the fort, it was built just below the bluff; using today's landmarks, it was positioned on the north side of Newfound Gap Road one-half mile north of the first tunnel after the Chimney Tops parking area, in the V between the Chimney Tops and Mount LeConte at 3,300 feet in elevation. Some sources have described it as a log fort of 100 feet by 100 feet, with a palisade of two rows of pointed logs on the perimeter. Aden Carver, the younger brother of Benjamin Carver, a private in Company F, was just sixteen years old at this time and too young to enlist, so he was tasked with supplying the fort with cornmeal ground at the original Mingus Mill ten miles down the North Carolina side of Oconaluftee Valley. He made regular trips to the fort on this mission.[18]

Living conditions in the fort were primitive. The barracks were damp, unheated, and crowded; with 300 men stationed in a small area, they had to sleep in three shifts and share bunks. Cooking was done over an open fire, and water was retrieved from a box spring inside the palisade. Consequently, many men suffered from pneumonia while stationed at Fort Harry. Unfortunately, Collins himself caught pneumonia at the fort and died there on April 9, 1863. Robert's eighteen-year-old son, Kimsey, had enlisted as a private in the Thomas Legion, Company F, just three months earlier. His service records show that he was on detached service in the Smokies in March and April, so he may have been stationed at Fort Harry when his father fell ill. After Robert's death, his body was carried over the mountain to be buried in the old Beck cemetery in Oconaluftee, now near the Tow String horse camp. Perhaps his son was able to organize this trip and accompany his father's body to his final resting place. Thus the life of one of the most renowned Oconaluftee mountain guides ended.[19]

Also, it seems possible that Benjamin Carver died of the same illness contracted in the same way as Robert Collins; his pay records note that he was on detached service in January and February 1863, present with the company in Tennessee in March and April, but dead by May 24, 1863. In December of that year, his widow, Narcissus, filed a claim for him with the state auditor; they had been married less than a year when he died, and his son, Benjamin, was born that same, sad year. The location of his grave is unknown, but it might have been in a cemetery nearby, the Fort Harry Confederate Burial Ground, said to include the graves of thirty-nine soldiers and one hundred Cherokee civilians. This cemetery has long been marked by a large three-by-four-foot stone, roughly in the shape of an upright arrowhead, placed along Road Prong Trail, which follows the old turnpike on the Tennessee side. Though no headstones exist, author Pete Prince attempted to locate the graves by dowsing in the 1980s.[20]

OCONALUFTEE CONFEDERATES AT FREDERICKSBURG

Meanwhile, Oconaluftee Confederates in other regiments were seeing battle action in Virginia. Benjamin F. Enloe and Joseph Collins served in the Twenty-Fifth North Carolina Infantry Regiment. This regiment spent the winter of 1862 in South Carolina but moved into Virginia and Maryland in June, fighting at Antietam, Malvern Hill, and Fredericksburg in the late summer and fall of that year. Though Antietam was inconclusive, Malvern Hill was a Union victory. Consequently, the Confederate victory at Fredericksburg, December 11–13, 1862, was reassuring to the company despite the thousands of casualties suffered there on both sides.[21] In a letter to his uncle Dr. John Mingus, Benjamin described the Union charge on Marye's Heights in that battle. In this charge, massive Union forces were disadvantaged by the Confederates' strong position behind a stone wall along a hillside:

VA. DEC. 18, 1862

Mr. John Mingus,

Dear Uncle,

It is with great pleasure that I avail my self to drop you a few lines to let you no that I am still in the land of the living yet, hopeing these few lines may safely come to hand and find you all well and doing well. I have had good health ever since I first come in service. I have had good health all the time, with the exception of a bout, two weeks.

> I way only 100.80 pounds. I hand any thing of much interest to right at this time.
>
> Suppose you have herd of the fight that we had at Fredricksburg Va. It was the hardest fight that we have ever had yet. The Yanks charged on us all right deep.
>
> While our lines was only 4 reg. deep. There was one Yanky Regt. That had twelve hundred in it. And there was only 300 of them escaped, we have taken 33 thousands stands of armes and rations and half of ammunition powder from them. It was a hard fight seen to witness. I hant any more of interest, to right—right. To me as soon as the lines comes to hand. Brother, A. T. Enloe is at Richmond waiting on the sick. His health is not good, he was well the last I herd from him. They was all well at home, the last time I herd from them. I don't hardly ever here from them, I have wrote 4 letters to you and hant had no answer from you. I looks like you have all forgotten me, please tell Uncle Wesley that I want him to right to me with out fale.
>
> So I must come to a close, please right soon and give me all the news you can, Farewell friends and relations if we meet here on Earth no more I hope we met in haven.
>
> *B. F. Enloe*[22]

Pay records confirm that Benjamin F. served until late in the war. He was captured at the third battle of Petersburg on April 2, 1865, a decisive Union victory leading to the capture of Richmond, the Confederate capital, and Gen. Robert E. Lee's surrender a week later at Appomattox Court House, Virginia. After his capture, Benjamin F. was taken to Point Lookout, Maryland, as a prisoner of war. On June 12, 1865, he was paroled and required to take an oath of allegiance to the United States.[23]

Joseph Collins also continued to serve, though he was listed as sick during November and December 1862. No later pay records exist to determine if he took part in the siege of Petersburg; it is likely that he did not because Aden Carver placed him at Soco Creek in early 1865.[24]

LAWLESSNESS AT HOME

Tepid support for the Confederacy and the resentment over the conscription act caused the North Carolina highlands to become overwhelmed with deserters who "lived off the area, banded together for protection, and defied all attempts to return them to their commands," according to historian Noel Fisher.[25] Combined with continuing violence instigated by these deserters and by Union loyalists, the region became disordered and lawless. Civilians' daily lives were marked by threat of attack from desperate gangs and individuals who were hungry but also inclined to thievery and violence. By early 1863, Governor Vance estimated that 1,200 deserters were hiding in the Blue Ridge and Smoky Mountains.[26] Also, deprivation from lack of farm labor and from looting caused homesteaders to hide food, valuables, and livestock any place they could imagine. To protect provisions, families hid food in wells, between walls, under floorboards, above ceilings, under porches, on their persons (such as in bags and under long skirts), in caves, under logs, or buried in the ground.[27] A couple of anecdotes suggest the confusion of the times. In the spring of 1863, Bill Slate, the husband of Rebecca Mingus Slate, set out on a trip to Tennessee across Indian Gap to buy seed corn. But he never returned and was never again heard of. Relatives believed that he had been attacked and killed by bushwhackers. That same season, Carson Beck, who was on furlough from the Thomas Legion for sickness, nonetheless made a trip across the gap for salt. Salt, of course, was essential to the mountain families to maintain their livestock and to preserve food. On his return, he met bad weather and was forced to unload his cargo, hide it, and return for it the next day once the storm had passed.

By June, the Confederate assistant quartermaster general wrote that it was "impracticable" for him to collect the tax in kind from civilians in Cherokee, Macon, Jackson, and Haywood Counties because of the privation of the citizens.[28] This tax, enacted just a few months before, in April, directed 10 percent of each family's agricultural production to Confederate troops and was adopted, in part, because it was easier to collect than previously enacted taxes on luxury items and slaves. But when there was no harvest and nothing to eat, obviously the tax could not be paid. Conditions only worsened. The Cherokee families, especially, were starving throughout 1863 and 1864. In early 1864, Thomas wrote requests to Richmond for cornmeal and flour from the Confederate storehouses in South Carolina to be distributed to Cherokees. Eventually some was dispersed, though conditions remained dire. By May 1864, Margaret Love, the wife of a legion officer, wrote to the governor of North Carolina that the Cherokees were trying to survive by eating weeds and tree bark. There is no doubt that the security and food problems on the home front sapped morale among the troops, leading to more desertions.

THE THOMAS LEGION'S CAMPAIGN IN EAST TENNESSEE

During the winter and spring of 1863, the companies of the Thomas Legion were scattered around East Tennessee guarding bridges, railroad depots, and other key locations. In June, Union colonel William P. Sanders launched a campaign to control East Tennessee. He approached Knoxville indirectly by traveling west and south of the city, then turning north to attack the critical railroad bridge at Strawberry Plains. At that moment, however, most of Jackson's command, including the majority of the Thomas Legion, was well north of this location, expecting incursions from Virginia. After a skirmish with the Confederates at the Strawberry Plains bridge, the Union forces burned the bridge; seized stores of food, salt, ammunition, and guns (though later they had to be abandoned); and captured about 137 enlisted men. These men were primarily from the Thomas Legion. Perhaps because the Union had no way to transport or guard the prisoners, they were paroled by a Union colonel, sent home, and told not to fight any more. Understanding that the men were fatigued and that some were actually ill, Thomas accepted the parole once he learned of it. For example, typhoid had spread among the troops; Osborn Bradley had died of it on April 4, 1863, just a couple of months before. But Jackson disagreed with Thomas and demanded that the men return to their companies, an order that a portion of the parolees complied with but that others, feeling tricked, did not. Jackson took offense from Thomas at this turn of events and had him arrested for disobedience. After a while, these charges were set aside in the face of continued skirmish activity in East Tennessee. Even so, this incident aggravated an antipathy between Jackson and Thomas that had existed since Jackson's nixing of the "troops" of miners and sappers.

On September 1, 1863, the Union occupied Knoxville, which pushed the Confederate troops both north and east to defend the region and to prevent additional incursions from Virginia. The next day, Thomas, who was stationed again at Strawberry Plains, was ordered to take the two Cherokee companies to the mountains and protect the passes along the Tennessee–North Carolina border. While en route, he was pursued and attacked by Union forces but not captured. He returned to his headquarters in Quallatown, and the Cherokee troops camped at Soco Creek as well as Balsam Gap, a few miles east. This order effectively split the legion apart and reassigned the command of the white soldiers, the majority of the troops, to Col. James R. Love. Major William W. Stringfield, a standout junior officer, remained to serve with Love throughout a fall chase of Union troops around East Tennessee. A few

Cherokees seem to have remained with these companies, though almost all were under Thomas's direct command.[29] For example, Joe Welch, also known as Willogeskik and originally assigned to Cherokee Company A, became a prisoner of war after the third battle of Winchester on September 19, 1864, and was sent to Point Lookout, Maryland, as a prisoner of war, so he must have remained with the white companies after the split. Love, Stringfield, and Lt. Col. William C. Walker led Thomas Legion soldiers on successful Confederate skirmishes at Limestone, Telford Station, Greeneville, and Henderson Mill, Tennessee, at one point capturing 350 troops who were sent by train to Richmond as prisoners of war.[30]

WAVERING LOYALTIES AND DESERTIONS

Regardless of these successes, desertions continued for an array of reasons. Some soldiers changed sides. In September 1863, enough men and boys to comprise six companies from North Carolina's southwest counties joined Union forces in East Tennessee; they became the Second North Carolina Mounted Infantry of the Union.[31] Also, the highlanders were aware of the precarious existence of their families back home. As North Carolina enlistees, they wanted to serve in their home state and to be commanded by a North Carolinian such as Thomas, rather than by Jackson, a Tennessean. Finally, resentment over the Conscription Act persisted. During this period, more than 350 men in the Legion went absent without leave.[32] Some of the deserters were Oconaluftee soldiers. Asoph Hughes, son of Rafe and Elizabeth Hughes, enlisted in April 1863 and spent time on detachment in the Smoky Mountains that spring, but by October 20 he was listed as absent without leave. By January 1863 he was declared a deserter, and in April 1864 he was back on the receipt roll of Walker's Battalion of the Thomas Legion. Although one source stated that he did not return to his widow, Mary Nations, and eight children after the war, a family story states that he fell ill while on furlough from the legion and died at home. He has a headstone in the Hughes Cemetery.[33] Three additional Bradley cousins, brothers Andrew Jackson, William, and Thomas, as well as James and Osborn's half brother, Wilson, had enlisted in the legion the previous March and were present for the string of conflicts in East Tennessee, along with James, who had joined in 1862.[34] All but Andrew Jackson were in Company F of the first regiment of the Thomas Legion; Andrew Jackson was enlisted in Company K. The pay records of the Bradley cousins in Company F show that they went absent without leave and then deserted in mid-October, immediately after the skirmish at Greeneville. James and

Wilson returned to their companies at some point because they participated in the 1864 campaign in the Shenandoah Valley. William did not return; at the end of the war, according to Confederate records, he took an oath of allegiance to the United States in Knoxville, Tennessee. Thomas seems not to have returned either, but the Confederate records do not establish where he went after he deserted.[35] Further, Union service records suggest that William, Thomas, and James enlisted in the Union's Second North Carolina Mounted Infantry. However, the records are vexingly inconclusive because the Knoxville enlistment dates for these three men were recorded as October 6, 1863, before they were reported as Confederate deserters. Even so, if these sets of records refer to the same individuals, they do show that James, though he enlisted in the Union company, "false mustered" and did not serve, which would be consistent with his return to the Thomas Legion. The Union records show that William was detailed as an orderly at a regimental hospital from December 1864. By the spring he became one of Col. George Kirk's raiders and died in Boone, North Carolina, on April 4, 1865, of typhoid pneumonia; however, this account cannot be true if he appeared in Knoxville at the war's end to take an oath of allegiance. The records for Thomas do not present as much confusion; he was detailed at a hospital as a wood chopper in the winter of 1864 and then guarded a forage train the next year.[36] Although the actual service of these men remains a mystery, the combined records do reveal a fluidity in commitment among a share of mountain soldiers.

COLONEL THOMAS'S MOUNTAIN STRATEGY

During the fall of 1863, the Cherokee companies focused on three tasks: improving the turnpike, seeking deserters and compelling them to rejoin their companies, and suppressing looting and raiding by Union bushwhackers crossing the border from Tennessee and from active North Carolina Tories. Thomas was given authority to recruit two additional Cherokee companies for these tasks, but they were inadequate given the massive area that they were to police. Thomas's superior at this point, Brig. Gen. Robert B. Vance, the governor's brother and the commander of the Department of Western North Carolina, favored arresting deserters and sending them to Asheville, rather than collecting them back into their companies. He also determined that the North Carolina troops should become more offensive and harass, if not directly attack, Union troops just over the border. Consequently, in early December 1863, Thomas moved about half his troops to Gatlinburg and set up camp, evidently preparing to stay the winter, because the men built huts and some brought their wives. Once the Cherokees were in place, the Tennessee home guard captured and imprisoned a Thomas scout; in retaliation, Thomas took 200 men to Sevierville to free the scout, which he did while also briefly arresting sixty home guards and seizing their guns and ammunition. Keeping the arms and ammunition, Thomas's men returned to camp in Gatlinburg, but the foray aroused the ire of Union brigadier general Samuel D. Sturgis, who sent a party of 200 men, guided by Union loyalists, to retaliate. Cherokee lookouts sounded the alarm of the Union soldiers' approach in time for them to engage in a one-hour volley and then withdraw back into the mountains and all the way to Quallatown. The Union troops captured one prisoner and recovered the arms and ammunition just seized, as well as several horses. The "prized souvenir," though, was Thomas's hat, left behind in haste.[37]

The new year began with a watershed event for the Thomas Legion and for Thomas personally. On January 3, 1864, Lt. Col. William C. Walker, commander of half of the legion, the regiment called Walker's Battalion, was roused from his sickbed at home in Cherokee County by Union raiders, shot, and killed. The brutality and boldness of the attack stunned the Confederates and made it plain to all how serious the threat of bushwhackers had become in western North Carolina. Thomas acknowledged the event as a warning and immediately hired a twenty-man "Life Guard" of Cherokee warriors for his personal protection. These civilians protected him until the end of the war. Even though his life had been threatened before, this murder was taken seriously.[38]

Despite this undeniable sign that the region needed better Confederate policing, the larger war caused General Vance once again to order Thomas with about 125 Cherokees over the crest of the Smokies and into Tennessee. He was accompanied by Lt. Col. James Henry of the Fourteenth North Carolina Battalion and about 375 cavalrymen. The planned action was intended to block Gen. Ambrose Burnside of the Union from communicating with federal forces to the north. The poor condition of the road and the frigid winter weather made the crossing especially difficult. According to North Carolina historian John Preston Arthur, the artillery had to be dismantled to transport it downhill:

> When the artillery got to the top, following the rough road Col. Thomas had constructed, it had a hard time getting down the other side. The cannon were dismounted and dragged over the bare rocks to the bottom, while the wheels and axles of the carriages were taken apart, divided among the men and so carried to the foot of the mountain, when

Aden Carver on Road Prong Trail, 1937.

GREAT SMOKY MOUNTAINS NATIONAL PARK ARCHIVES, TOWNSEND, TENN.

> they were reassembled. The guns were not tied to hollow logs, as in Napoleon's passage of the Alps, but were dragged naked as they were down the steep mountain side.[39]

Nonetheless, the Cherokees completed the ordeal and made camp, once again, in Gatlinburg on January 12. Half of Henry's men settled in Wear's Cove, with orders to join Vance as backup in a day, and Vance took the other half of Henry's men to Sevierville. There he overwhelmed and confiscated a large Union supply train, a great achievement for the general. Vance moved to the planned rendezvous point, but Henry and his half of the cavalry troops did not appear until a day later; the reasons for his delay have not been confirmed. News of the seizure reached Union command quickly, and a company was sent out to retake the supplies. Vance and his portion of Henry's men were surprised by an attack the next morning, January 14, in part because the general failed to post lookouts. He and fifty of Henry's men were captured, as were the supply wagons. Subsequently, Vance became a Union prisoner in Virginia for the remainder of the war. With this undesirable outcome, both Henry and Thomas were viewed as at fault for disobeying orders, and some accounts say that they were charged and senior officers demanded a trial, but if charges were filed, they were later dropped. This calamity hurt Thomas's reputation with key politicians, Congressman Allen T. Davidson and, of course, Governor Vance, the general's brother.[40]

Thomas and the Cherokees returned to North Carolina, probably repeating the arduous hauling of wagons and artillery over mountain, and camped in Deep Creek by January 22. They resumed their efforts to patrol Cherokee, Clay, Jackson, and Macon Counties. Federal raids over the state line continued, and in early 1864, fifteen Cherokees were captured and taken to Knoxville, where they were bribed to betray Thomas. While captive, they cooperated with their Union hosts but did not comply with the requests in the long run. Thomas was too respected by the Cherokees to be betrayed. Upon release, most of the captives returned home to serve again in the legion. However, a few did defect and joined the Union for the remainder of the conflict. After the war ended, they were ostracized when they tried to return home.[41]

Another continuing activity of Thomas's men was to collect deserters and reunite them with their companies. The colonel's willingness to accept deserters back into the fold was ill regarded by other officers; in time their disapproval manifested itself in numerous complaints to the Confederate secretary of war, James Seddon. Also, Thomas did not comply with the command of Col. John B. Palmer, General Vance's replacement. In September 1864, Thomas was arrested and sent to Goldsboro, North Carolina, for a court-martial. He was found guilty in October, but Thomas refused to accept this ruling and went to Richmond to appeal to the president. Meanwhile, Brig. Gen. James G. Martin was appointed to command the Western District of North Carolina, supplanting Palmer, on September 16, 1864. Martin was an accomplished veteran of the Mexican War who was forced to relinquish a more active Confederate command during the Civil War because of limiting effects of an amputated arm. From his headquarters at Morganton, Martin was asked to weigh in on the Thomas controversy by General Lee and President Jefferson Davis. He provided the rationale for reversing the court-martial: "Col. Thomas certainly is no military man but many allowances are to be made for him. He has heretofore had but ten waggons [*sic*] in his whole command and only very recently no [quarter]master or commissary, no designated point from whence to draw his supplies . . . and the troops in my district have not been paid since December 1863. At this time I deem it inadvisable to make any more changes and trust those already made may be deemed satisfactory."[42] With this opinion,

Thomas was allowed once again to return to his position in the legion, and within a few weeks, he was authorized to recruit three companies, one as engineers, and allow absentees to return.[43]

OCONALUFTEE SOLDIERS FIGHT IN THE VIRGINIA CAMPAIGN

When Thomas and the Cherokee companies went into the mountains during the fall and winter of 1863–64, the rest of the legion, under the command of Love and Stringfield, went to Whitesburg, Tennessee, where they lived on very short rations. In late April, they fearlessly defended Carter's Depot, Tennessee, from a Union attack of three cavalry regiments, a success that showed their mettle to the Confederate leadership and sent them north to Saltville, Virginia, to guard a salt quarry. Hoping to improve the situation in the mountains, Thomas wrote to General Bragg, with support from Governor Vance, asking to have the legion reunited and returned to western North Carolina, and the decision was made to do so. However, a communication delay and a round of new attacks in Virginia pulled the soldiers into the Shenandoah Valley, where they became part of a long campaign during the spring, summer, and fall of 1864. In early June, the legion companies fought valiantly at Piedmont, holding a weak gap in the Confederate line. Nonetheless, the Union forces prevailed; 1,000 Confederates were taken prisoner and 1,600 were killed or wounded. In the legion, 12 were killed, 21 wounded, and 42 captured. Only 300 men of the legion remained ready for battle. While following the Union troops west toward West Virginia, the surviving legion visited the grave of the revered general Stonewall Jackson in Lexington, an inspiring moment, and were met with heartwarming public support from citizens. Next came the Battle of Monacacy in Maryland, a Confederate win, but the legion did not participate and was fresh to lead the subsequent march east to the outskirts of Washington, D.C., in early July. Even so, the legion's Company F was recognized for its accuracy with firearms and for its fierceness; it acquired the nickname of Conley's Sharp Shooters after Lt. Robert T. Conley. Because Confederate troops were outnumbered, they withdrew from Washington into Virginia for six weeks of marching and countermarching against the Union throughout the state. On September 19, Confederate forces engaged the Union for the third time at Winchester, also known as the Battle of Opequon.[44]

This battle ended in defeat for the Confederates and cost the legion seventy-five men, killed, wounded, or captured. Cherokee Joe Welch, or Willogeskik, was captured and sent to Maryland as a prisoner of war. At least one Oconaluftee Valley resident, William Beck, was severely wounded at this battle. A private in Conley's Sharp Shooters Company F, he had enlisted with his three brothers in July 1862. His brother John had likely been killed in the summer at Cool Spring, though definitive service records are missing. The whereabouts of Stephen and Samuel Carson are also uncertain. The last record for Steven placed him on sick furlough in December 1863, and Carson endured a period of illness in early 1863 but reenlisted in February 1864. So Carson may have been with his brother on that fateful day. At enlistment, William was the thirty-three-year-old father of six children, and his wife, Rachel, was pregnant with the seventh. Records show that after the battle William was taken to Baker Mansion, a field hospital, where he stayed for two weeks, suffering from a gunshot wound that had caused a compound fracture of the tibia and fibula of one leg. The leg became gangrenous, which led to William's death on October 26, five weeks after the battle. He was buried at Stonewall Cemetery in Winchester, Virginia.[45]

By this time Thomas had been arrested pending court-martial in North Carolina, so on September 30, Love ordered Stringfield to Asheville to take over command of the Cherokee companies. He settled at the Quallatown headquarters while about 400 men guarded a 150-mile line in the mountains from Murphy to Asheville. Love remained with the remnant of the legion in Virginia, which included fewer than sixty men following an October battle at Cedar Creek, also a Confederate loss. On November 17, 1864, Love and fewer than one hundred men were at last able to leave Virginia to reunite the legion in western North Carolina in early December. Though they had lost three-quarters of the men who entered Virginia the previous spring, at this great price they had earned a distinguished record of service.[46]

UNION RAIDS AT HOME

Because of "too much confusion in the land, the cold weather and the excessive rain," as the minutes note, Lufty Baptist Church did not meet regularly during the fall of 1864 and winter of 1865.[47] Indeed, not only did dangers and problems with deserters continue, but the mountain community experienced its most direct involvement with the war that February. On February 4, 1865, Col. George W. Kirk, one of the most feared, despised, and effective Union raiders, led 600 men into western North Carolina via Newport, looted Waynesville, burned Colonel Love's home there, and freed prisoners from a jail. On the return, Conley's Sharp Shooters ambushed Kirk along the Soco Gap Road, so the Union companies retraced their steps to Waynesville and set out across Balsam Gap on February 6. Once again, Kirk met Thomas Legion troops, this time at Wilmot, as he and his men encountered Stringfield and about 300 Confederates, both Cherokee and white soldiers, in the encounter that became known as the Battle of Soco Creek. Incensed that Kirk was invading their home, the legion fought fiercely for an hour but ran out of ammunition and was outnumbered two to one. Consequently, Stringfield was forced to withdraw toward Quallatown, while Kirk's raiders followed the Oconaluftee River to the turnpike and up and over the crest into Tennessee.[48]

As they swept back into Tennessee, the raiders looted and terrorized. Florence Conner Gass, who was seven at the time, later recalled her parents' home being ransacked. Aden Carver remembered shooting at Smokemont (then Bradleytown) and said, "I remember about Kirk. . . . Kirk's men were foraging and stealing as they went. Only the old Indians were at home. The younger ones were with Col. Thomas [actually Major Stringfield]. These old Indians were carried off by Kirk and some of them shot." Indeed, at least one old Cherokee man was forced to flee with Kirk; when he became unable to continue, he was shot and left. Confederates soon found the man, cared for him until his death, and buried him in a shallow grave. The place where he was buried is called Indian Grave Flats in his honor.[49] Fort Harry, also on the route, was burned by Kirk's men during their dash back into Union-held East Tennessee. Afterward, usable remains from the camp were salvaged by Bradleytown residents, including a partially burned wagon.[50] Cheering Kirk's success, the Knoxville paper reported that for booty he brought back "three rebel flags, more than twenty prisoners, 150 horses, and killed more rebels than he captured," though these claims and numbers seem questionable.[51] Even though Kirk was ambushed and hotly pursued on his return trip, the daring and deep penetration of Union forces into western North Carolina signaled the region's vulnerability to all.

The spring brought more incursions into western North Carolina, but no more large raids occurred in Oconaluftee. Even after the truce between Generals Robert E. Lee and Ulysses Grant at Appomattox Court House on April 9, 1865, attacks, lootings, sackings, and skirmishes took place in Salisbury, Boone, Asheville, and Waynesville. Companies of the legion were scattered throughout the area guarding towns and fending off attacks, often effectively. Most famously, Conley's Sharp Shooters skirmished with Union colonel William C. Bartlett as late as May 6 and forced his company to retreat to Waynesville. Lieutenant Robert T. Conley claimed to have fired the last shot and killed the last Union soldier in the war, though the assertion can extend only to North Carolina, not the war as a whole. Colonel Thomas, attempting

Veterans of the Thomas Legion taken at the New Orleans Reunion of Confederate Veterans, 1903. (*Front row, left to right*) Usai, Kimson Saunook, Jesse Ross, Jesse Reed, Sevier Skitty. Back row, Bird Saconita, Dave Owle, Col. W. W. Stringfield, Suyeta Owle, Jim Cag, Wesley Crowe, Jessan, Lt. Calvin Cagle.

COURTESY OF THE MUSEUM OF THE CHEROKEE INDIAN ARCHIVES, CHEROKEE, N.C.

to intimidate Union forces in Waynesville, had his Cherokee companies light nighttime bonfires around the perimeter of the town, just before a surrender negotiation the following day, on May 7. On that day, General Martin, Colonel Love, and Colonel Thomas accepted surrender terms from Bartlett but only after Thomas had made a show of force by arriving with his Life Guard of twenty dressed in war paint and demanding that Bartlett surrender. Martin accepted Bartlett's terms, which were surrender and immediate parole after the troops and officers handed over their arms. On May 9, the Civil War ended in North Carolina. Because they were civilians, the members of Thomas's Life Guard were allowed to keep their personal rifles, though this story was exaggerated subsequently by Thomas to claim that all of the legion were allowed to do so, which was not true.[52] Nonetheless, the exploits of the Thomas Legion are extraordinary in that both Cherokee and white soldiers served together for years, though not always in fully integrated companies.

That fact suggests that full measures of mutual respect and acceptance must have been present among both groups. A reunion photograph taken in 1903 of Lieutenant Colonel Stringfield with eleven Cherokee veterans shows the pride among these survivors of the Thomas Legion.

Though a backwater, the valley was ensnared by the war, affecting residents at home and placing the men of the community in harm's way in their service to the Confederacy. By the end of the war, living conditions in Oconaluftee Valley, as in all of western North Carolina, were poor. The farms had no draft animals, seed, or livestock.[53] Resident Edd Conner, who was a child at the time, reported as an adult that food and clothing were very scarce and that the roads were "muddy quagmires, making travel impossible."[54] Most every mountain family of Oconaluftee lost one or more enlisted man to the war, either as a casualty or by illness. Some were taken prisoner and released only after the surrender. The many Cherokees who enlisted suffered equally during the war, and their families probably suffered more than the whites from deprivation. During the spring of 1865, after months of canceled meetings, the Lufty Baptist Church held a spring revival that was well attended and included a baptism ceremony in the Oconaluftee River.[55] This ritual of rebirth signaled a new era for the community, with entirely new opportunities and challenges.

Chapter 8

SEPARATE REALITIES

RACE AND LAND OWNERSHIP

▲▲▲

One of the best-known historical structures of the valley, and even of the national park, is Mingus Mill. A sign for it appears shortly after I exit the Oconaluftee Visitor Center and head up Newfound Gap Road toward the crest of the ridge. I take a left and park. I've been there all seasons, and it's usually busy. It is this summer day. The mill building and race are the main attractions, and they merit the stop. Today the building is open. Attendants are grinding corn and giving tours, explaining the works. The process is relatively straightforward, but the mill's design is ingenious. I understand why the building has been rebuilt, reconditioned, and maintained so well for so long. My favorite detail: the initials of the builder, Sion T. Early, etched into the outside wall, just below the peak of the roof. He was proud of his work.

So much is known about this place. Its story is documented, published, and advertised, appreciated. It represents a big achievement by a prosperous family and one that served the community, the kind of history that's recognized, accessible, and official—appropriately so.

Without a sign, on the opposite side of the parking lot, and up a steep path, I find a cemetery in a rectangle of land. Few folks join me here. On the Smokemont 7.5 quadrangle map of 2016, the location is named the Enloe African Cemetery. Because the vegetation is trimmed, I can count at least eight mounded gravesites. Some have fieldstones to mark the head and foot, though none is engraved. Who were the people interred here? No one knows for sure. Very likely they were people owned as slaves by the Mingus and Enloe families; this was their land. Some of these people may have supplied labor to build the mill, but their initials are not etched anywhere. Neither their work nor their lives are memorialized. Perhaps the absence of a sign protects a vulnerable place—though I've recently read that a marker is planned. In any case, the site tells me that I cannot provide a satisfactory account of them. I must be grateful that a memory of them can be read from the land itself.

Absences, limitations, and unanswerable questions obstruct the pursuit of an inclusive history of the valley—especially for those who did not own land and were not white. I have searched records for hints, but I cannot learn much, most times, about their lives. I must accept that I cannot construct a truly equitable history even if I try, even if I include every mystifying detail I discover. Often the details do not fit together. Consequently, I share the names and accounts that I do know. Doing so, I hope, will acknowledge—and cause me to remember—the story's incompleteness.

▲ ▲ ▲

TO THE FEW TOURISTS who visited Oconaluftee Valley in the years following the Civil War, the scars of the struggle may not have been immediately visible. In letters and published accounts, the travelers described a distinctive mountain community set in a lush, fertile landscape. Wilbur G. Zeigler and Ben S. Grosscup characterized the scene in *Heart of the Alleghanies*, a travel narrative published in 1883: "The waters of the Ocona Lufta, even at its mouth in Tuckasege river, are of singular purity, and through some portions of its course, from racing over a moss-lined bed, appear clear emerald green. Above the Indian town the valley grows narrow, and prosperous farmers live along its banks. The forests are rich in cherry and walnut trees, and all necessary water power is afforded by the river. Joel Conner's is a pleasant place to stop."[1]

Nonetheless, Oconaluftee families did suffer gravely from the war. By the end, nearly every family had lost someone, and most endured privations of war or direct losses from bushwhacker and deserter raids. Edd Conner, a grandson of Ephraim and Sophia Mingus, was born during the war. Later in life he recalled the Reconstruction period as "close time's for all to live" when families had to rebuild homes and farm buildings, recover from or endure physical injuries and hardships caused by the war, cope with hunger and

Mingus Mill.

GREAT SMOKY MOUNTAINS NATIONAL PARK ARCHIVES, TOWNSEND, TENN.

Enloe Enslaved Cemetery.

GREAT SMOKY MOUNTAINS NATIONAL PARK ARCHIVES, TOWNSEND, TENN.

privation, manage without goods from outside merchants, and work tirelessly to "drive poverty from their door's." Conner described farmers working all day and then making and repairing shoes by "pine-torch held by some member of the family until mid-night or after" and using maple sprigs for the task.[2]

In a few seasons, white mountain families rebounded and the community rebuilt and expanded. The lives of their few emancipated slaves are far harder to trace; some seem to have stayed for a while, and a very few of these prospered; some left, and of these people not much is known. Recovery was far slower for the Cherokees both within the township and in the Qualla Boundary. In the 1870s, Oconalufty Township, including Big Cove and Bird Town, was a community of families connected by marriage, longtime familiarity, neighborly bartering of goods and services for farm and construction labor, and shared faith. By 1880, it contained 68 households or farms and 186 families, 85 of them Cherokee, and 6 Black, in addition to 1 mixed-race couple.[3] Some big families saw their children leave the area while others married, stayed, and grew even larger with more and more complex connections to one another. Some new families moved in. A couple of these had the means to buy bottomland. For instance, several Queen brothers bought land from North Carolina to establish homes in Oconaluftee Valley, one of which was a large home where Smokemont is today; others bought upslope on rockier, steeper tracts; and some scraped by as farmhands, sharecroppers, or squatters.

Residents' circumstances varied considerably. The oldest and most established white families, like the Enloes and Minguses, owned the most fertile land and largest farms on the floor of the valley. Now in their third and fourth generations in the valley, these families were prosperous, had built comfortable homes, and had some access to larger population centers when they took livestock and the surplus harvest to market. Zeigler noted these in his travels: "Fine farms of rich black soil lay on the either side between the river and the environing mountains, which grew higher, steeper, wilder and closer together as we advanced. The farm houses were large, looked old fashioned in their simple style of architecture, ancient with their gray, unpainted exteriors, but homelike and cheerful surrounded by their large, blossoming apple orchards."[4]

Other white families, such as the Conners, Becks, Bradleys, and Carvers, were also well established but placed a bit higher up the valley along the river's terraces. These upslope families made do with marginal land and an abundance of resourcefulness, optimism, and hard work. Over time they gained a level of comfort and affluence as they purchased additional land tracts, brought in good harvests, and cultivated multiple sources of income through beekeeping, orchards, livestock, and handcrafts. New families, the McMahans, Treadways, Parkers, and Matthewses, also moved in and pursued this model.

Because there are few diaries and letters from this period, the picture of family life is episodic and omits many. The white male heads of the prosperous households were literate, but few women, poorer white, Black, or Cherokee people could read or write. Consequently, little information about the lives of women and freed slaves exists. This situation differs somewhat for the Cherokees, whose stories are chronicled from the point of view of a traveler, a government official, or, later, Cherokee ethnologist James Mooney. Among all the mountain families, some names and dates are available in records, but they supply little insight into individuals' struggles and joys. A travel account by Rebecca Harding Davis published in *Lippincott's Magazine* in 1875 includes a bit of detail of women's home life. She visited the home of a Colonel P., whom she identified as the only white farmer in Qualla, the Cherokee homestead:

> Colonel P's mansion is a huddle of log-built rooms, chunked with mud, squatted in the middle of cornfields which his wife has helped to plough. She weaves on a heavy homemade loom the clothes of the household, waits on her husband and sons at table, and eats herself with the servants, white and black. She is a shrewd, clean-minded just woman, bony and gray-haired, dressed, like her cook, in brown linsey, with a yellow handkerchief knotted about her neck. Her comfortless house was as clean as a Shaker's, and her table bountifully spread. It was not the custom of wives to join in the conversation of their husbands and other men.[5]

Still farther upslope were the "branch-water people" who tended rock-rich land that they may not have owned.[6] From year to year their lives were precarious. To make ends meet, they might have hired out as laborers to their more prosperous neighbors. Toward the end of the century, they might have left the valley periodically to work building railroads, on logging teams, or in timber mills. Davis also provided a glimpse into the situation of the poorer mountain people who "live in unlighted log huts, split into halves by an open passageway, and swarming with children, who lived on hominy and corn-bread, with a chance opossum now and then as a relish." She explained,

> They were not cumbered with dishes, knives, forks, beds or any other impedimenta of civilization: they slept in hollow logs or in a hole filled

> with straw under loose boards of the floor. In these villages we found thoroughbred men and women, clothed in homespun of their own making, reading their old shelves of standard books: they were cheerful and gay, full of shrewd common sense and feeling, but utterly ignorant of all the comforts which have grown into necessities to people in cities, and of all current changes in the modern world of art, literature, or society: in fact, almost unconscious that there was such a world. Among the mountain-woodsmen we found other men and women who had never learned the use of a glass window, or a cup and saucer, and manifestly never learned to keep themselves clean; yet they were of honorable, devout habits of mind, and bore themselves with exceptional tact and delicacy of feeling and the dignity and repose of manner of Indians.[7]

Yes, there was the road, the Oconalufty Turnpike. It linked Sevierville, Tennessee, with the valley and other areas of Swain and Jackson Counties in western North Carolina. Shortly after the end of the war, in October 1865, former Confederate colonel Will Thomas led the effort to remove the barricades that his men had placed to block the road to slow and frustrate Union soldiers and renegades. His goal was to make it usable for wagons quickly, presuming the resumption of overmountain traffic and trade.[8] But its condition was miserable. When millwright Sion Thomas Early and John McMahan, who was helping him, needed to bring tools and equipment over the state line to work on a new mill on the Minguses' property, the "road was so rough that it was necessary in some places to jack the wagon up with poles in order to get it over boulders and other obstructions, in other places it was necessary to cut logs and chain them to the wagon to act as a brake when going down steep grades."[9] On this trip the men were also tracked by a panther that abandoned them as potential prey only after hours of stalking and emitting three bloodcurdling screams from a perch above their evening campfire.

So the valley, while not entirely isolated, remained remote and untamed until late in the nineteenth century. The white, Black, and Cherokee residents lived as neighbors throughout the era, but they faced different challenges, a fact that separates their stories. White farm families concentrated on cultivating their farms and shoring up their economic security while enhancing, when they could, their community with a school and permanent church building. Emancipated slaves either stayed as paid tradespeople or laborers or left to seek livelihoods elsewhere. The Lufty Cherokees faced another round of existential challenges in the forms of smallpox and flu epidemics, multiple changes to their legal status in regard to the federal government and to North Carolina, complex and consequential internal politics, and lawsuits for the land that Will Thomas had bought for them but was in jeopardy because of his business and personal debts after the war ended. Their story follows that of the formerly enslaved people and white mountain families.

In 1871, Swain County was formed from parts of the existing Jackson and Haywood Counties, and the valley was assigned to this new county whose county seat became Charleston, today's Bryson City. Jackson Beck, the son of John and Jane Beck, told a telling riddle of the changing county lines in the nineteenth century. Though born in Haywood County in 1821 on a farm about a mile below today's Smokemont at the mouth of Beck's Branch, he was reared in Jackson County and lived the last decades of his life in Swain County—not because he had moved but because Oconaluftee Valley was shifted from one county to another twice during his lifetime as the number of North Carolina counties, along with its population, increased.[10] The new Swain County soon established public schools supported by property taxes at the rate of twenty-five cents per one-hundred-dollar value.

AFRICAN AMERICANS IN THE VALLEY AFTER THE CIVIL WAR

The 1860 census shows that just a couple of households using the Oconalufty Township post office had slaves. These households were in the vicinity of today's Mingus Mill and the Oconaluftee Visitor Center. The John and Polly Mingus family enslaved two people, an eighteen-year-old male and a ten-year-old female. The Wesley M. and Malinda Enloe family enslaved seven people, ranging in age from five to fifty-five years of age, with five being male and two female. Other families in Qualla, Webster, and the rest of Jackson County (but not within Oconalufty Township) owned more slaves. In Qualla, these families were the Gibbs, Hyatt, and W. W. Enloe families. In Webster, they were the Sherrill and Coleman families. About forty-six households owned slaves in all of Jackson County. Most notably, William Holland Thomas, who lived in Whittier, owned thirty-eight, and James B. Love, a prominent land owner and a business associate and future brother-in-law of Thomas's, owned forty-nine. A total of 268 people were enslaved in Jackson County in 1860.[11]

After emancipation, it is difficult to trace the lives of those who had been enslaved, and the information that can be located through public sources does not provide a satisfying account of their lives. Following individuals across subsequent census records, from the slave schedule of 1860, where they are not listed by name, to the 1870, 1880, and 1900 censuses, where everyone is listed by name, is challenging. In most cases, definite connections cannot be made. For example, the seven individuals enslaved on Wesley Enloe's farm in 1860 do not appear to be present in 1870. At that time two Black people "work[ed] on the farm," Nancy Hyatt, a thirty-five-year-old Black woman, and Chrisenberry, also known as Berry, a fourteen-year-old boy. According to a statement by Berry that his daughter Dora Elvira Howell submitted to *The Heritage of Swain County, North Carolina*, Berry was taken to the Enloe farm by his mother and given to Wesley Enloe, but it is not clear if Nancy Hyatt was his mother. Family accounts establish that Berry had been born on Ute Hyatt's farm in Marble, North Carolina, in 1855. The ages of Berry and Nancy do not match those of the people listed on the 1860 slave schedule as enslaved by Wesley Enloe. It is not known where the seven went. Perhaps they left the state; perhaps they moved elsewhere in Jackson County or even in North Carolina. But without names, finding a family or an individual by means of only ages and gender is impossible, especially given the changes in households, names, changes in relationships that may occur over a decade, the possibility of mistakes in the census records themselves, and the variability of how individuals' names were recorded. However, occasionally the lives of those who had been enslaved can be traced. The 1880 census lists a Black household immediately after Wesley and Malinda's that is surely that of Chrisenberry "Berry," or C. H. Howell. Later records reveal his full name to be Chrisenberry Napoleon Haynes Howell. Berry was then living with his wife, Sarah, and five other people, most probably in a cabin on the Enloes' property and working for them; no further record of Nancy Hyatt can be found. Berry and Sarah stayed in the area all their lives and prospered, according to property records and Elvira Howell's article.[12] Even so, among the fifteen Black people who were enslaved by or worked for the Enloes between 1860 and 1880, only two can be reliably identified in later years.

Similarly, neither of the two people on the Mingus farm in 1860 seems to be there in 1870, though a Black male, David Mingus, age thirty-five, was present. Further, the 1880 census lists a separate Mingus household headed by Dancie Mingus, Black and age thirty-one, and Sarah Mingus, white and age twenty-eight, which included five "mulatto" children.[13] None of these people can be identified in the 1900 census at all, alas. Unless the records are mistaken, it seems unlikely that David and Dancie were the same person, given the younger age of Dancie in 1880. Sarah's identity remains a mystery as well. It seems quite possible that some of the members of this family are buried in the small "slave" cemetery located near Mingus Mill. The graves there are unmarked but identifiable as at least eight in number. Perhaps surviving family members moved away once the ownership of the Mingus farm passed to the Floyd family in the 1890s. Making family ties clear is challenged further by the lack of census records for 1890.[14]

One Black Mingus family member whose story can be told is Charles Mingus. The 1880 census shows that Clarinda, twenty-three, a white granddaughter of Dr. John Mingus, lived in the household along with her son Charles, age five. Clarinda was the daughter of Abram Mingus; he is listed on her death certificate as her father, but a mother's name is not included.[15] Her son Charles is listed as white in the census, but he is probably the son of David Mingus, the Black man who had been on the Mingus property in 1870. Because Abram Mingus was the enumerator for the 1880 census, it seems reasonable that he would accurately list his own household, though perhaps he did not want to designate Charles as mulatto.

The young Charles was to have a very different life than seemed likely. He left Swain County and enlisted in the U.S. Army in Knoxville, Tennessee, on December 30, 1897. He had a long career serving in the Twenty-Fourth Infantry, traveling to the Philippines, and achieving the rank of sergeant. In 1914, he received an honorable discharge. While Charles was living in Nogales, Arizona, his first wife, Harriet Philips, gave birth to the youngest of his three children, Charles Jr., in 1922. The son and his two older sisters, Vivian and Grace, were raised in Watts, a city in Los Angeles County, California, and in 1923, Charles Sr. married Mamie Carson. Charles Sr. died in 1951 and is buried in the Los Angeles National Cemetery, but his son, whose musical talent was evident from an early age, had become a renowned double bassist and jazz musician by the middle of the twentieth century.[16] The unexpected connections between a remote valley and a jazz legend show the choices Black people made to gain livelihoods and shape their own destinies.

Some connections among people who were enslaved in the Qualla Township and remained after emancipation are also possible. For example, in 1860, E. G. Hyatt enslaved two people, a fifteen-year-old male and a twelve-year-old female. These individuals seem very likely to be (or be related to) Henry and Eliza Hamilton, ages twenty-eight and twenty-six, respectively, listed in the 1870 census. The likelihood of their connection is enhanced because their household is listed between that of E. G. Hyatt, their previous owner, and his brother A. E. Hyatt. But the next census, for 1880, does not include them. Similarly, in the 1900 census, a Black couple, Anthony and Eliza Lowrey, lived in Qualla; Anthony is sixty-five and working as a farm laborer. But Eliza's age is marked as "unknown," making it impossible to guess more about her history. It seems likely that she was close in age to Anthony, which would

Charles Mingus (Jr.) performing at the Village Gate Nightclub, New York City, 1978.

KEYSTONE PRESS/ALAMY STOCK PHOTO.

mean that she may have been enslaved.[17] Unfortunately, the Lowreys cannot be identified a decade later.

Similarly, a Woodfin family headed by Nick (forty and Indian) and Lucy (forty-one and Black), as well as four of their eight children by 1870, may have been connected to the eleven people enslaved by John Gibbs of Qualla. In the 1870 census, they are listed just below the Gibbs household, which had owned slaves; however, Woodfin is the surname of two prominent Buncombe County slaveholding households, so it was equally possible that after emancipation the couple returned to Qualla because of Nick's Cherokee heritage. By 1880, Tabitha, a daughter, age twenty, was keeping house for a younger sister, two younger brothers, and a baby of her own. By 1897, only Nick, now age seventy, and Thad, one of the brothers in Tabitha's home in 1880, appear to be in Qualla; both Nick and Thad are on the Indian census rolls for 1894. Thad was the head of a household of five, and Nick lived alone. None of the other members continued to live in Qualla Township.[18]

The 1880 census lists seven Black and mulatto households in Ocona Lufty Township (as it was listed), Bird Town, and Big Cove, which are all in Swain County. (The rest of the Qualla Boundary was in Jackson County by then and counted separately; further, the other sections were not inside Oconaluftee Valley but in other watersheds.) These were the families of Berry and Sarah Howell, Dancie and Sarah Mingus (both previously mentioned), Robert and Ellen White, Washington and Margaret Gibson, David and Caroline Johnson, Thomas and Margaret Mills, and Landon and Hannah Tompkins; all but the Howells had at least four children.[19]

The Johnson, Tompkins, and Mills families all farmed. Notably, they bought land together in 1876 and again in 1895. First they purchased over 200 acres along Adams Creek, a tributary of the Oconaluftee River in the Bird Town section of the Qualla Boundary and south of the national park, for $150; later they purchased fifty acres along Galbreath's Mill Creek, a tributary of the Tuckasegee River. Curiously, the three families and households do not appear on the 1900 census for Oconalufty Township, Qualla, or Swain County. Thomas Mills sold part of the Adams Creek property in 1890 and the Galbreath's Creek land in 1899.[20]

Berry Howell's biography in the *Heritage of Swain County* stated that he and Sarah lived and worked on the Enloe farm until he was forty years old, around 1897. He said that he and his wife liked to farm, and he was happy with and well treated by the Enloes. For example, when he had pneumonia, he said that Mrs. Enloe "took as much care for me as if I was white." (Of course, he may have had multiple reasons for this characterization, but it is the one he made to his daughter years later.) Berry bought a farm in Bird Town and three others during his life; he also worked on others' farms intermittently as well. He was a deacon of a Baptist church (but not the Lufty Baptist Church, which was white), raised fourteen children with his wife, Sarah (or Sallie) Howell, and also raised seven "orphan children of different folks." The Howell family appears on the 1900 census as still living and farming in Oconalufty Township as one household. According to property records (which don't entirely match Berry's account), the Howells purchased about fifty-three acres along Adams

Creek for one hundred dollars in January 1884. Notably, the deed states that C. H. already had a home on this land, which was owned by the couple W. P. and S. E. Hyde. A decade later, in 1894, the Howells bought sixty-five acres along Big Jacks Mill Creek, another tributary of the Oconaluftee River, from A. H. and M. E. Hayes, a husband and wife. In 1904, they purchased a seventy-five-acre farm in Sherrill Gap, west of today's Bryson City, for $560 and sold it in 1909, next purchasing sixty-five acres, excluding the mineral and mining rights, from J. H. and M. Teague, a husband and wife. The Howells also sold land in 1904 to a Teague, sixty-five acres for $300. By the second decade of the twentieth century, the sons of the family—Landon, Thomas, and John—and their wives, were purchasing land, in some cases subdivided lots from land that an older sibling already owned. These were located in Charleston Township, or the current Bryson City. In 1936, Berry and Sarah sold their daughter Dora Elvira a small plot of land for five dollars and "love and affection." It is likely she used this half-acre lot for her own home as a single woman. Berry died in 1938 at age eighty-two and Sarah in 1943 at age seventy-eight; they were buried in Watkins Cemetery in Bryson City.[21]

In addition, in 1900, the Powells, a Black family from Georgia with two households, had come to the Jackson County part of Quallatown. One was headed by Lizzie, a widow, and included seven children; the other was headed by William and included his wife, Sarah, two sons, one stepson, and one stepdaughter, both of whom were Johnsons. Perhaps Sarah Howell was an older daughter of William and Sarah's, but that cannot be confirmed. Members of the Powell family remained in the area, bought land and homes, and lived in Bryson City. They farmed, married, and were neighbors with other Black families in the area, including the Gibsons. For example, Julius Gibson and Lizzie Powell were married in 1910, but after she died, Julius married again, to Avoline Sallie Parrish. Anna Powell, Lizzie's daughter, married James Thomas. They lived in Bryson City and raised a family. Their descendants lived in the area throughout the twentieth century. A street in Bryson City is named Powell Street, likely after members of this family.[22]

A fascinating family story emerges from tracing the lives of Harrison Coleman and his wife, Mourning Emaline Gibson, through public records; it shows that white, Black, and Cherokee households after the Civil War were not always separate. Harrison Coleman was born in 1855 to Betty Coleman, who was enslaved by Mark Coleman of Webster in 1860. In 1875, Harrison married Mourning Gibson, the daughter of Washington and Angaline Gibson of Waynesville, North Carolina. Harrison long claimed that he was half Cherokee, and he applied for admission to the rolls repeatedly on behalf of

Chrisenberry "Berry" Napoleon Haynes Howell on his old horse Nan.

FROM THE COLLECTION OF ANN MILLER WOODFORD.

himself and his children. He claimed his father was Koh-soo-yoh-kee, or John Littlejohn, of Soco Creek, a full Cherokee. He was accepted on the Hester Roll of Eastern Cherokees in 1884 along with the three sons he had at the time. By 1900, Harrison and Mourning had nine children, who were listed as "mulatto" in the 1900 census, and they farmed on the Cherokee land that was assigned to them off Goose Creek Road, which was provided by the Eastern Band. Goose Creek is a tributary of Oconaluftee River in Bird Town, just a bit farther west than Adams Creek, where the Howells lived. Harrison died on January 1, 1923, and his death certificate listed him as Native American. As a widow, Mourning continued to farm. In 1927, Mourning, her oldest son, John Nicodemus Coleman, and her daughter Rhoda R. E. Thomas testified at length to Harrison's Cherokee ancestry to Fred A. Baker, the examiner of inheritance for the Baker Roll of 1928, which was intended to be the final roll for the Eastern Band and the one that would be used to determine land ownership if the federal policy of allotment of tribal lands were executed. The testimony included details of their lives as a mixed-race family. The family stated that although they lived on the Qualla Boundary and the children attended Cherokee school some of the time and also received some government payments, they did not always feel accepted into the tribe or welcome by authorities. Ultimately, Harrison's heirs were denied enrollment in the Eastern Band. The 1930 census shows that a daughter, Bertie, two sons, and two granddaughters were living with Mourning at the Goose Creek farm, though by 1940 Mourning had moved and was living with Bertie and her seven children in the Gibsontown neighborhood of Haywood County, outside Waynesville. Mourning lived until age eighty-four and died in February 1941. She is buried at the Gibsontown Cemetery in Haywood County along with many family members, both Colemans and Gibsons.[23]

Despite these instances of ethnically mixed households, for the most part, Oconalufty Township and Quallatown were not deeply integrated. No households of white and Cherokee married couples are listed in the 1880 census. One household, that of Jim and Soky Cheoa, a farmer and a wife, shows a marriage of a Cherokee man and a Black woman; they also appear in the 1870 census as a couple. In 1900, there were a few mixed families, but they were rare. Excluding a couple of homes with lodgers and the Cherokee Boarding School and the households of its staff, where Cherokee pupils lived with white teachers, cooks, and others, only 23 households had married couples of different ethnicities out of a total of 549 families. Of these 23, all were composed of white and Cherokee couples except the home of the Coleman family.[24]

These observations match those of Russell Thornton in his study of Cherokee populations, though he focused on later decades. He found that the North Carolina Cherokee population changed significantly from 1910 to 1930, "from 66.4 percent full bloods in 1910 to 38.7 percent in 1930. Also, in 1910, the North Carolina Cherokees had a higher proportion of full-bloods than the total American Indian population, but in 1930 they had a lower proportion."[25]

In 1900, North Carolina Cherokees of mixed blood were predominantly white and Cherokee (429 individuals, or 92 percent of mixed-blood Cherokee), but there were 38 (8 percent) triracial Cherokees (white-Black-Indian), and 2 (4 percent) Black-Indian Cherokees (presumably allowing some double counting across categories to account for a total larger than 100 percent).[26]

These accounts reveal that the formerly enslaved people of the valley pursued a range of strategies after the Civil War. The records that are available seem to be about those who were most successful in finding their footing as sharecroppers, independent farmers, and laborers, rather than those who may have drifted away from the valley to seek their futures in advance of the Great Migration of the twentieth century. Additionally, a few Black families moved into the area, but most of these people seem to have been drawn by family ties rather than by economic opportunity. Some of the sons of emancipated slaves did work as loggers and teamsters, but for the most part they took up these jobs because they were already living in the valley rather than coming in response to the need for these laborers.

Chapter 9

THE ESTABLISHED FAMILIES FLOURISH

FARM AND COMMUNITY UPGRADES

Try as they might, National Park Service interpreters of the Mountain Farm Museum on the south end of Oconaluftee Visitor Center have a hard time overcoming the nostalgia of the place. When I walk around it on a summer day, it is serenity embodied. Yes, chores, sometimes many of them, would have been part of every day for those who worked this land before the park. Note the many structures: main house, meat house, chicken house, apple house, corn crib, gear shed, woodshed, barn, blacksmith shop, springhouse, garden, and field. They suggest a litany of tasks that the Enloe family, servants, hired hands, and enslaved people would have had to do—all the time. It wasn't easy.

Even on the busiest days, when the place has tourists in every corner, a deceptive stillness pervades it. For me, this stillness is particularly rich at the barn. It is the only structure that is original to Wesley Enloe's farm. The barn is a wonder for its monumentality—grand, well made, form matching function. I enjoy the aesthetic of the weathered wood, gray in two distinct tones, the featherlike overhang of shingles at the peak of the roof, and the saddle-notched corners. I love walking through it, looking at the sleds and harnesses. My blood pressure and heart rate lower when I do. I have to check myself and remember that this barn was the scene of intense activity, particularly in the fall when livestock was driven to markets for sale, either in North Carolina or overhill in Tennessee. On their way, drovers would have stayed overnight and their animals would have been put up in the barn. Hay would have been stored in the massive loft all year. Though the barn seems an embodiment of idealized agrarianism, that dream is illusory. It's like visiting a botanical garden and not seeing all the effort that goes into its daily maintenance after hours by busy teams of workers, as if everything looks picture perfect all the time.

The barn and museum seem apart from our economy and our lives, but most of the pressures were not unlike what people face today: social hierarchies, workplace pressures, desirability of specialized skills, profits and losses, seasons, and deadlines. And perhaps there was little choice, no career advancement, and few regular paychecks. The barn marks economic success, and really it is only as typical as that success was, for a couple of families such as the Enloes.

▲▲▲

THE COMFORTABLE MINGUS FAMILY

A sign of rebound from the Civil War was a new wood-sided, two-story home that Dr. John Mingus built on his land between the Oconaluftee River and Raven Fork in 1877. The first Mingus home had been a log home closer to the river. The new home's location along the turnpike would have been a profitable one because livestock drivers could overnight there on the way to market. According to park archives, the new home was the "finest and most pretentious dwelling in the park."[1] This account, likely the prose of park historian H. C. Wilburn, continues with a detailed description:

> Certain it is that more decorative carpentry is in evidence here than in any other dwelling in the park. Full boxed eaves, with returns; arched window and door casements; arched entablature over the porch; and a decorative type of balustrade. On the inside artistic mantels and casement trim is of beaded and artistic design. Originally there were four large main rooms: two on the ground floor, and two up stairs, with spacious halls between. Later an "L" extension on the back was added. . . .
>
> All the framing, timbers, weatherboarding, inside finish and trim material was sawed out on a sash-saw mill located at the mouth of Mingus Creek, some few hundred yards distant. Heavy foundation timbers, corner posts and braces were used; all mortised, tenoned and securely

> pinned together. An improvised dry-kiln on the site seasoned the plank which was then hand dressed, tongue-and-grooved and beaded for the inside work.[2]

The home's deep front porch was framed by four two-story columns, and the second-floor balcony was cased with a decorative balustrade and, eventually, screened. A photograph of the home shows full-size brick chimneys on either side of the main home; a third reportedly existed, perhaps at the end of the L where the kitchen was situated. In addition, a two-story stone springhouse was near the home.

Abraham, often called Abram, helped his father build the home. They were aided by Sion Early as master carpenter and by sometime valley resident Aden Carver, who set the stone foundation and helped the family clear the land and fence it with walnut rails. Carver's pay was several medical consultations with Dr. John.[3] At this time, the Mingus household would have included John and his wife, Polly, who were seventy-eight and seventy years old, respectively, and Abram, who was unmarried and in his early fifties. Abram was also elected as school examiner and served as the census taker. As already mentioned, additional family members Clarinda and her son Charles were present as well and perhaps Lucinda Gaither, who was listed in the 1880 census as doing housework.[4]

After patriarch Dr. John died in April 1888, the surviving Mingus family remained in the new home. Polly lived another six years, dying in October 1894. The property was passed on to daughter Sarah Angeline Mingus and her husband, Rufus G. Floyd. By the 1900 census, their son John Leonidas "Lon" Floyd, forty-three, is listed as the head of the household and living with his wife, Callie (short for Calgonia), two daughters, two sons, and Abram Mingus, seventy-six, who was listed as a boarder in the home he helped build.[5] The house, the barn, and the original cabin, which was subsequently used as a smokehouse, stood until 1955, when the National Park Service tore them down.

The next postwar building project undertaken by the Mingus family remains to this day. In 1886, Dr. John decided to build a new turbine mill for corn and wheat, replacing an earlier overshot waterwheel mill design. Though small family-run mills were common on streams, this mill was to become a community hub. It was located centrally near the Mingus home but on the other side of the river and along Mingus Creek. John deeded ten acres to his son, Abram, and his grandson Lon Floyd for the mill. They supervised its construction, which was led, like that for the house, by Sion Early. In an interview conducted in the 1930s, Early said that he spent three months building the millhouse and was paid $600.[6] His initials, STE, are carved above the third-floor window just below the central eve of the mill and remain clearly visible. The W. J. Savage Company of Knoxville, Tennessee, installed the turbine, and it was a 13¼-inch vertical standard hydraulic-reaction turbine built by James Leffel and Company of Springfield, Ohio.

Mingus and Floyd also purchased a second turbine of the same size for another mill on Cooper Creek, west of Oconaluftee but owned by Uriah Cooper, Lon Floyd's father-in-law.[7] Mingus Mill ran continuously for the next forty-five years and was operated by hired millers. The building is plain but carefully constructed of yellow poplar lap siding over a substructure of dry-laid fieldstone piers and braced posts over the millrace at the rear.[8] The mill's wood race extends upslope alongside the creek about 200 feet and was made of oak planking and locust posts and crossbars. When the race meets the mill building, the water flows into a twenty-two-foot penstock and then into the turbine, which turns the millstones. This design was a great advance for the mountain families, but it was not technologically new in the 1880s. The design was completely established by the 1820s and widely used by the end of the nineteenth century. In addition to Early, a number of Oconaluftee residents worked on the structure. Once again Aden Carver was on the job, along with Bill Bradley, Nelson Sutton, Mell and Ellis Williams, who were Early's nephews, and Hall McDade, according to Early.[9]

For many years, the mill and a nearby store run by the Floyd family became workday gathering places for neighbors as they brought in their corn and wheat for grinding. The miller's toll was one-eighth of the finished product. Many twentieth-century residents of the valley recalled trips to the mill, usually hauling sacks of corn or wheat on horseback and returning with sacks of meal or flour.[10]

The Enloes' Perfectly Situated Farm and Home

For an example of the close nature of the community, one has only to note the connection between millwright Sion Early and the Enloe family. Sion married Sarah Thomas Enloe, a great-niece of Wesley and Malinda Enloe.[11] Wesley was the son of patriarch Abraham Enloe, who had built his large farm at the mouth of the valley, which came to be called Floyd Bottoms and now is the location of the Mountain Farm Museum. It is easy to imagine how Sion and Sarah may have met: Could Sarah, whose family lived outside the valley, have

Mingus Mill miller John Jones in front of Mingus home, 1937.

GREAT SMOKY MOUNTAINS NATIONAL PARK ARCHIVES, TOWNSEND, TENN.

been visiting her great-uncle's home and gone to the mill? Might Sarah and Sion have met at Lufty Baptist Church some Sunday at an after-service picnic? In any case, Sarah had cousins her age at the Enloe farm, and that fact explains why she might have been staying there. Sarah's cousins were daughters of Wesley Enloe and Malinda Lollace, who had married in 1847. This couple had eleven children, two of whom, Alice Minerva and Mary Malinda, were about the same age as Sarah and living at the farm in 1880.[12]

Because of its choice location, the Enloe place was also a stopover for travelers. In 1888, Eben Alexander, quite likely a Knoxville native who became a professor of Greek at the University of North Carolina, Chapel Hill, set out from Asheville for a hike (or tramp, as it was called then) through the Smokies for "Grand Scenery, Good Fishing, and Plenty of Solitude." He began in Asheville, passed through the Cherokee village of Yellow Hill, continued up the turnpike and on to Clingmans Dome, Cades Cove, and Chillhowee, where he left the current park land and subsequently visited Montvale Springs, Maryville, and Knoxville, Tennessee. In the early August account of his trip published in the *New York Evening Post*, Alexander recommended staying a night at Wesley Enloe's home and another at John McMahan's, seven miles uphill and "the last house on the road."[13]

Berry Howell was employed by the Enloes until the late 1890s and commented on the scale of the operation: "Mr. Enloe always had around three hundred acres of cultivation. Usually he would make around 300 bushels of wheat and always made from twelve to fifteen hundred bushels of corn. We would fatten and kill thirty hogs every year. Mr. Enloe would work ten work hands every day and feed them in crop time."[14]

It seems that most of Wesley and Malinda's children married and moved out of the valley in the final decade of the century. By 1900, Wesley was living only with his daughter Eliza (fifty), who was separated or divorced from her husband, David Manly Hyatt, his granddaughter Pearle (twenty), and his great-granddaughter Meta (four). Wesley's wife, Malinda, had died December 10, 1897. Wesley lived to be ninety-two and died on August 16, 1903. After his death, the property was sold by the heirs in 1905 to Lon Floyd, Dr. John Mingus's grandson and the owner of the mill and large Mingus farm.[15] At this time the Enloe farm became known as Floyd Bottoms. Despite the gradual departure of Wesley's immediate family from the valley, other members of the Enloe clan were still in the area. For example, Watson Enloe, a brother of Wesley's, lived in Tight Run, up Raven Fork, with his wife Mary Elizabeth. Their son Biney married Elmina C. Enloe (known as Clem) in 1872; they stayed on their land until the park forced them out in the early 1930s. Also, Wesley and

Wesley Enloe.

GREAT SMOKY MOUNTAINS NATIONAL PARK ARCHIVES, TOWNSEND, TENN.

Malinda's son Joseph, born in 1865, stayed in Oconaluftee and had a family with Lula Hayes Enloe. Lula was commissioned as postmaster in Oconaluftee in 1912 and held the job until 1915, when Marie Floyd took it over. Joseph and Lula moved to Tennessee by 1920 and are both buried there.[16]

Three Curiously Related Conner Families

The Conner name comes up everywhere in the history of the postwar valley, and it is tempting to think of the Conners as descendants of one early Conner couple, as are the Minguses and Enloes. However, the Conner families were not related through Conner ties. In fact, three distinct Conner families inhabited the valley as early as the late 1840s. Most Conners were related, but they were related on the maternal side of their families. Two of the three Conner-family wives were the children of Ephraim and Sophia Mingus, who had homesteaded on Big Cove early in the nineteenth century. (Ephraim was the older brother of Dr. John Mingus, the man who inherited the Mingus farm from parents Jacob and Sarah Mingus.) Two of Ephraim and Sophia's six daughters, Katherine and Mary Caroline, stayed in the valley and married into two different Conner families. Katherine Mingus married Joel Conner in 1841, and Mary Caroline Mingus married Edward Franklin Conner in the late 1840s.[17] The third Conner family was headed by the Reverend W. H. (William Henry) Conner.

Though all these families became intertwined, the Reverend Conner, or William Henry, seems to have been the first to arrive in Oconaluftee. He and his wife, Rachel Gibson, settled in the valley in the early 1840s. The Lufty Baptist Church records show that he was baptized in 1847 by Jacob Mingus. By 1858, he was licensed to preach and served as the supply pastor at a number of Baptist churches in Jackson, Macon, and Swain Counties, including Cherokee churches and Lufty Baptist Church.[18] A photograph of W. H. shows a calm face with a high forehead and lower face framed by a full white beard. The line of his mouth is straight, but his light eyes reveal warmth and kindness. In 1876, for $700, he purchased 300 acres from the heirs of Robert Collins, who had died during the Civil War. This purchase included the home and farm along Collins Creek of the deceased Smokies guide. The Reverend Conner and his wife had eight children between 1850 and 1873, but the two who were prominent in the community were "Dock" Franklin Conner, born in 1855, and Wiley Evans Conner, born in 1865. Dock grew to be a successful farmer who raised cattle and drove them to market in Knoxville. He had a large family with Margaret York, whom he married in 1876 at Bradleytown, later known as Smokemont. Wiley followed in his father's footsteps and became a preacher in 1892 and served a number of western North Carolina Baptist churches until he moved to Knoxville and was pastor of the Fourth Avenue Baptist Church.[19]

Journalist Vic Weals wrote about Dock's life and family in the *Knoxville Journal* in 1976. He explained how Dock's cattle business operated:

> His busiest years as a trader appear to have been when he was middle-aged and past. The farm on the Luftee was a collecting point for the yearlings he bought each spring, most on the North Carolina side in the counties of Haywood, Swain, Jackson and Macon. Each springtime,

> Dock and the late Good F. Ownby made the rounds of the families they'd been buying from down through the years. These mountain farmers would raise steers to yearlings, one of several head, in anticipation of the Conner-Ownby visit.
>
> Weighing was by guess, but it was said of them that they seldom missed an animal's weight by more than a very few pounds. They paid the farmer the most recent market price of which they were aware. They bought several head from a farmer on Deep Creek in one instance, and when they got home they learned that the market was significantly higher than the price they had paid him. So they returned to Deep Creek and paid the man the difference. It was a mountain way of doing business that enabled Dock to stay in business.
>
> When they had gathered enough cattle to make it worthwhile, they, meaning members of the Conner family, usually would start a drive back into the mountains, looking for good grazing in the river valleys, on the heads of creeks and on the ridge tops. The pounds that the cattle put on that summer, assuming that the market didn't go down drastically, represented a profit. Dock almost always sold off all his cattle in the fall. Sometimes he sent them east through Asheville to the market in Richmond, Virginia.
>
> Where the cattle had been grazing when it was time to take them out of the mountains often determined whether they would be driven north and west into Tennessee, or south and east through Carolina.[20]

Dock's father, the Reverend W. H. Conner, passed away following an accident on Deep Creek. The story goes that he was crossing Deep Creek in February with a wagon and turned over into the icy water. On many parts of Deep Creek, the banks are steep and challenging for someone with a horse-drawn wagon. It is possible that he was helping his son with the cattle operation in some way at the time. He caught pneumonia afterward and died on March 14, 1887. Lufty Baptist Church held a two-day memorial service honoring his memory. This event shows how central the church was to the white community; it was where aunts, uncles, in-laws, and cousins worshipped together. The service took place eight months later, in November, and began with a baptism in the river of two Mathis children and two Treadway sisters. The memorial service brought a number of former Lufty preachers back to the valley, including the Reverend Richard Evans, who had been W. H.'s friend and colleague throughout the Civil War period, the Reverend J. G. Corn, and the Reverend John Elder, both early prewar Lufty ministers.[21] Rachel, W. H.'s wife, had died two years before, in the summer of 1885, of unknown causes. They were buried together in a small cemetery along Oconaluftee River. Their graves lie side by side with a joint headstone shaped by two hearts on either end, inscribed with their names, dates, "Father" and "Mother," and "Gone from our homes, but not from our hearts." Two other graves in the cemetery are likely to be those of two children who did not survive into adulthood.

Joel Conner and Katherine Mingus Conner headed another Conner family living along the western side of the Oconaluftee River after the Civil War. They lived on land Joel had partly inherited from his parents, Samuel Conner and Nancy Swearingen Conner, and partly purchased from Joel's siblings, who had relocated to White Oak Flats (later Gatlinburg, Tennessee) in the late 1840s and early 1850s. This land included property previously owned by both John Hyde and Jacob Couches along Couches Creek, below Tow String Creek. Samuel had purchased this land in 1819 and 1834. Samuel and Nancy had been charter members of Lufty Baptist Church when it was first organized in 1836. But after Samuel died sometime before 1840, his widow and the other nine siblings moved to Tennessee, leaving Joel as the only child still in North Carolina.

Joel and Katherine had a family of nine children as well, who were born between 1843 and 1865. Their homeplace included a mill along the banks of Oconaluftee River. Several of their children married into other valley families as they grew up: Elmina married sons (consecutively) from the Bradley and Hughes families, Elizabeth married Taylor Hughes, Arbizena married a McMahan son, and John Henry married a Nations daughter. In addition, Florence Haseltine, also known as Tiny and Tina, was born in 1855 and married Horace Gass, a Sevierville, Tennessee, man who met the family through Joel's work as postmaster.[22]

Joel Conner provides a fine example of how families diversified their income in order to shore up their financial security. Before the Civil War, Joel received a contract from the U.S. Postal Service, along with Daniel Wesley Reagan, a prominent resident of White Oak Flats, to deliver the mail from Sevierville, Tennessee, to Cashiers Valley, North Carolina. The route of over ninety miles wound through the mountains and used the Oconaluftee Turnpike; it connected White Oak Flats, the Cherokee towns, Sylva, Cullowhee, and other North Carolina villages. Despite the route's many stream crossings, no bridges existed to speed the travel.[23] A round trip took about a week to complete on horseback, which is why authors Wilbur Zeigler and Ben S. Grosscup separated the behavior of the mailman from every other person they encountered on the road through the valley:

> The mail man, mounted on a cadaverous horse, with leather mailbags upon his saddle, is apt to meet the tourist; but, differing from the general run of the natives, he travels on time and is loath to stop and talk. Not so with the man who, with a bushel of meal over his shoulders, is coming on foot from the nearest "corn-cracker." At your halt for a few points in regard to your route, he will answer to the best of his ability; and then, if you feel so inclined, he will continue planted in the road and talk for an hour without once thinking of setting down his load.[24]

Of course, the identity of the busy postal carrier cannot be verified, but it might have been Joel. Or it might have been his son-in-law. At some point Horace Gass of Sevierville took over the Tennessee part of the route from Reagan. Presumably, when Horace brought the mail to Joel Conner's home, he met Florence Haseltine. They married in 1877. For a time, the newlyweds lived with Horace's family in Sevierville, but after he purchased land in Ravensford, the couple moved to a home there in 1888.[25] Horace eventually took over the whole route from his father- and brother-in-law, James Chambers. The post was officially assigned to him in 1897, and later the site of the "office" was moved to a new location, "Stonery," on the other side of the river at the Gass home. This Ravensford home had a large front porch and front room to accommodate the post office. Haseltine served as postmistress while her husband made deliveries. In time, their son, William Taylor Gass, was postmaster until the Stonery post office closed in 1919. Horace and Haseltine were deeply involved in the life of the community. They were both members of Lufty Baptist Church, and Horace was elected as clerk, deacon, and representative of the church in congregational conventions. Horace also served as sheriff of Ravensford for a time. Even after Horace died in 1907, Haseltine remained in the park until 1937, and she died in November 1938. Horace is buried in the Chambers Cemetery near the home of Joel and Kate Conner, while Haseltine was buried in the Thomas Memorial Cemetery outside Cherokee, North Carolina.[26]

Katherine "Kate" Mingus Conner's younger sister, Mary Caroline, born in 1826, married yet another Conner from an unrelated family: Edward Franklin Conner, who was born in Cleveland County, North Carolina. How or where they met is a mystery. But this branch of the Mingus family did not fare well after the Civil War. Edward Franklin reportedly died in 1864 while returning from service, and his wife, Mary, died in 1867 at age forty-one. They left five or six children ranging in age from four to twenty. The oldest was Margaret Clarinda Conner, and the youngest by far was Edward Clarence Conner, called Edd. Little is known about the lives of the other children, but it seems that they did not stay in the Oconaluftee Valley area long after their mother's death necessitated the dispersion of the family. However, Edd grew up in and around Oconaluftee and, because of his distinctive personality, is remembered as one of the valley's storied characters.[27] His tale follows in the next chapter.

Tightly Knit Becks and Bradleys

By the 1870s, the families of the early white settlers were in their third and later generations. Like many during the nineteenth century, these rural families often grew very large. Mothers might have had a child every year or so for twenty years. Or mothers might have died in childbirth or shortly after, leaving their husbands to marry again. Widowers would have needed an adult female to raise the young children of the first wife and run the home while the husband farmed and brought in income from a trade or labor. Often, second and third wives were younger than their husbands and so bore a number of children as well, creating large families of half sisters and brothers who lived together in one cabin or in a compound of homes on adjacent tracts of land. Children of these large families also grew up and married young, in their late teens and early twenties; they would also have plenty of children, and when five, or six, or ten children in a family had that many children of their own, then many, many cousins resulted. Further, in a valley dominated by just a few families, the ties between families were multiple and complex. And it was not unheard of for cousins to marry.

The Beck family was one of the oldest of the valley, and it became one of the largest after the Civil War. The patriarch was John Beck, who died at age eighty-four in 1861; his wife, Jane, died at the same age in 1869. They raised nine children on their farm near the mouth of Becks Branch.[28] One daughter, Elizabeth Beck (1809–1876), married famed guide Robert Collins and raised eleven children. Samuel Beck also stayed in the valley. He fathered seven children with Cynthia White. Their four sons, William, John, Stephen, and Samuel Carson, served in the Civil War.[29]

John and Jane's youngest child, Henry Jackson Beck, born in 1821, grew up to be deeply involved with the activities of Lufty Baptist Church throughout his life. He was ordained as a deacon in 1851 and subsequently served as clerk, moderator, and Sunday school superintendent. He is the preacher who officiated over the marriage of 400 Cherokee couples in a mass ceremony, legitimizing long-term relationships among mature couples and even grandparents at a time when it was desirable for them to follow Christian rituals. He was also a man of distinction in the larger community, holding the position of justice of the peace and superior court clerk. Despite these achievements, perhaps the most remarkable was his role as a father; he fathered twenty-two children with three successive wives.[30]

The dates from the Henry Beck family genealogy suggest a history of trauma, resilience, and longevity. Henry's first wife was Jane Morrow Sims, and they married in 1843, when he was twenty-two and she was sixteen. They had nine children during the twenty-six years of their marriage until Jane died, along with her infant, at age forty-two in childbirth.[31] At this point, her youngest surviving child was four years old and her oldest was eighteen. Less than four months after Jane's death, Henry married Mary Elmira Haynes, who was twenty-eight. They had seven children during the eleven years of their marriage. Sadly, Mary also died in childbirth at age thirty-nine in 1880. The newborn child, Rufus Haynes Beck, survived. Mary's oldest child was not yet ten when she died. Three months later, Henry married Harriett Farmer, twenty-seven, and they had five children. The youngest child of this marriage, Sarah "Sallie," was born in 1889 when Henry was sixty-eight years old. Henry died at the age of seventy-eight in July 1900, and Harriett lived until June 1913, dying at age sixty. All told, Henry's twenty-one surviving children were born over a period of forty-four years.[32]

An undated but late nineteenth-century Beck family photograph shows Henry and Harriett surrounded by a crowd of more than fifty of their kin. Another indication of the size of the family and the depth of its family ties in the community comes from a look at the two Beck cemeteries. The "Old Beck Cemetery" is relatively small, with twenty-five graves, including that of Jane Morrow Beck, Henry's first wife, and of Robert and Elizabeth (Beck) Collins. It is located above the confluence of Becks Branch and the Oconaluftee River and is also known as the Huskey Cemetery. The "New Beck Cemetery," situated below Becks Branch, holds about seventy graves and includes those of Henry Jackson Beck, his third wife, Harriett, and at least two graves of children from his first marriage, Elizabeth C. Conner and Jacob Henry Beck. Even though fifty of the grave markers in this cemetery are not inscribed, the tombstones that are engraved bear the names of many Lufty families: Ayers, Bradley, Conner, Jenkins, Kimsey, Maney, Queen, and Wilson, among others.[33]

The Bradley family, whose first farm in the valley was placed higher upslope than the Becks' but on the same east side of the river, also was large and became elaborately interrelated to neighboring families in Oconaluftee after the Civil War. The Bradleys first came to the valley in the early 1840s when the patriarch, Isaac, purchased 250 acres on the east side of what soon came to be known as Bradley Fork. At this time, Isaac's family was already large because he had children from two marriages, ten with his first wife, Anne Allison, and eight with his second, Sarah Coxley. A number of the children from his union with Anne, however, were already married and settled in Rutherford County, North Carolina, by the time the family moved to Oconaluftee, so only two sons from the first marriage, James Holland and Augustine, then about thirty-nine and twenty-nine years old, respectively, came to the Smokies. All but one of the children from the Isaac's second marriage to Sarah Coxley eventually came to Oconaluftee. All told, the second generation of Bradley children included six males and two females.[34]

Son James Holland had already begun the third generation. He arrived with his second wife, Martha Grant, and seven children, three of whom were from his first marriage. These third-generation children ranged in age from two years to their late twenties. Sadly, James Holland died in 1843, the same year that he bought his own farm in the valley. At that point, his widow, Martha Grant Bradley, would have had six children eleven years old or younger. At least two of these children lived in the valley most of their lives and died on farms along Tow String Creek, a tributary of the Oconaluftee that runs between Bradley and Raven Forks.[35]

As Isaac and second-wife Sarah's children married in the late 1830s and 1840s, the couple sold parts of their land to their children and their spouses. Son William J., who married Deborah Roberts, bought land adjacent to his parents, as did daughter Martha and her husband James Reagan and daughter Mary and her husband Israel Carver. The youngest son, Thomas, also bought land from his parents after his marriage to Mary Conner. His tract was likely the homestead because the deed required that he support his parents until their deaths in order to own the land outright.[36] Isaac died in 1855, but Sarah survived beyond 1860; she does not appear in the 1870 census, so presumably she died in that decade. Consequently, the second-generation Bradleys are the ones on the scene after the Civil War.

At least one of Isaac and Sarah's children initially moved out of the valley after marriage. This was their son Andrew Jackson; he married Mary Trentham in the late 1840s in Sevier County, Tennessee, and bought land along the Little Pigeon River. Before then, in 1839, Andrew served in Company F of the third Indian Removal Regiment of the North Carolina Militia, which was tasked with rounding up Cherokees before removal. At this time he likely met his future brother-in-law, Israel Carver, who served at the same time in

Company E. Israel must have met his future wife, Mary Bradley, Andrew's younger sister, this year because she and Israel married in 1839, a couple of years before the biggest group of the Bradley family moved to Oconaluftee.[37] So even before the postwar era, the Bradley family was large and spread over the ridge of the mountains in both Tennessee and North Carolina.

A number of Isaac and Sarah's grandsons served in the Civil War. By the time it was over, at least two, Benjamin Carver (Israel and Mary's son) and Osborn Bradley (James Holland and Martha Grant's son) had died. Other Civil War veterans, such as Andrew Jackson Bradley, James Holland Bradley Jr., and Thomas, came home to Oconaluftee. The family story goes that Andrew Jackson Bradley and his family were run off of the farm in Sevier County, Tennessee, during the war because of their Confederate sympathies. Ultimately, the land was turned over to the Trenthams, in-laws, who mostly stayed in Tennessee. At some point, Andrew Jackson, his wife, Mary Elvira, and their children came to Oconaluftee Valley, but it is not clear where Mary Elvira and the nine children she had by 1862 spent the war years, likely with family. Andrew Jackson served in the Thomas Legion of the Confederacy. After the war, in appreciation for his confederate service, Andrew Jackson "received a grant of 100 acres" from his Confederate commander, Col. William Holland Thomas. This land was on Tow String Creek. Eventually, other Bradley households occupied the Tow String area, including Andrew Jackson's older sister Keziah and her husband William Griffith. They had married in the mid-1830s and moved around from North Carolina, to Georgia, to Tennessee, and back, finally, to Tow String.[38]

By 1870, the Bradleys were a large, widespread family in the valley. The 1870 census lists eight separate households with the Bradley last name, including fifty individuals. The number increases to eighty-one if the in-law families of the Griffiths, Reagans, and Carvers are counted.[39] The relationships become quite complex through intermarriage of first and second cousins. For example, three of Keziah Bradley Griffith's daughters married cousins. Melissa Griffith married first cousin Zadock Bradley, Rebecca Griffith married half first cousin Morris Bradley, and Armintha Griffith married half second cousin William B. Bradley. Also, Andrew Jackson Bradley's son Andrew Jackson Bradley Jr. married Zilla Bradley, a first cousin. Another kind of complexity occurred when Sarah Caroline Bradley Reagan, a daughter of James Holland and Martha Grant Bradley, died in 1886 and her widower Richard Reason Reagan married her younger sister Martha Luesy Bradley Bohannon, who had been widowed by her own first husband six years before.[40] It seems fair to think that by the end of the nineteenth century, even if someone's last name was not Bradley, if the individual lived in Oconaluftee Valley, then that person was probably related to a Bradley somehow.

It would be easy to conceive of the typical household of the valley as that of a yeoman farmer, a wife, and their children with a focus on a self-contained homestead. Such families did exist, but they are not easy to research, and they did not have much of an influence on the community as a whole. The idealized small family farm concept does not account for the extended family landholdings and interrelationships between longstanding family groups such as those described in this chapter. These large, long-term families functioned like family enterprises with operations well beyond subsistence. They were resourceful and largely able to sustain themselves from their own harvests, but they raised and sold surplus crops and livestock outside of the valley. They ran grain and lumber mills, carried the mail, and preached at a church within the community. Their economic lives were multifaceted and expansive, rather than narrow and insular. This outlook may be why, at the end of the century, they were open to large-scale logging rather than opposed to the environmental ravages that it would bring.

Chapter 10

MIGRATORY LIVES

DEPARTURES, RETURNS, AND ARRIVALS

▲ ▲ ▲

It is fitting that the site of the Robert and Elizabeth Collins farm is now the park's largest picnic area. Robert was an early guide in the mountains, and his family's spacious log cabin offered hospitality to travelers. That tradition continued when his family sold the 300-acre farm to the Conner family after the Civil War. The Conners built their own sizable frame home and also put up visitors. One of Dock and Margaret's sons, Charlie, did some guide work, too.

Today, the Collins Creek Picnic Area boasts about 180 tables on cement pads with charcoal grills plus a seventy-seat pavilion, all arrayed under shady second-growth trees. I've never seen it even half full when I've visited. It's a pleasant place and offers a ready table and a level walk along the creek after a lunch or supper. Even though it's not one of the premier hikes in the park, the Quiet Walkway has most of the features that characterize a Smokies walk: copious wildflowers in the spring and early summer, a couple of log bridges crossing the creek, and several spots to sit a while on a big rock and become mesmerized (and refreshed) by the sound and glistening of the water.

Though some traditions continue, the place reminds me that the valley was not frozen in time. The residents adapted to changing circumstances as they had to. Robert died of pneumonia in 1863, so the family sold to the Conners. The Conners farmed but also worked as loggers and Civilian Conservation Corps (CCC) camp foremen. Similarly, the Mingus farm ultimately became a Floyd farm, and after Wesley Enloe died, his farm, too, was sold to the Floyds, becoming known as Floyd Bottoms. Some Bradley land was sold to the Queen family and then became the location of the Smokemont logging town. Though it's fair to say the valley was a stable community, it saw changes throughout the nineteenth century. Of course, some individuals led more itinerant lives than others, and those ranged from gumptiously migratory to desperately vagrant.

▲▲▲

THOUGH A NUMBER OF valley residents stayed put on their land throughout the nineteenth century, not everyone did, or could. Some were lured away in hopes of a brighter future elsewhere, and others were pushed to find employment and opportunity. Oconaluftee families felt the same strains and temptations as other southern citizens looking for ways to rebuild after the Civil War. It is an illusion to conceive of the valley as a Shangri-La, as can be observed by the relocations of some who went to nearby towns and cities, some who went to Tennessee, and one other who went across the Mississippi. Also, two of the most famous personalities of the valley were among those who did not just stay put all their lives but left and returned.

HUGHES SONS TAKE LEAVE

Asoph Hughes was the son of Rafe and Elizabeth Hughes, one of the first families to settle in the valley along Raven Fork at the foot of the ridge that carries their surname. Asoph served in the Thomas Legion during the Civil War but unfortunately died in 1865, in his forties, leaving his wife, Mary Nations Hughes, to raise eight children who were between infancy and age sixteen. Consequently, many of the children of this family needed to seek their fortunes outside of the valley; at least four of the sons did, and they traveled varying distances. The oldest son, Taylor, moved to the Camp Creek section of Jackson County and became a carpenter. William moved to Waynesville and also worked as a carpenter and later moved to Andrews, where he owned a general store. Thomas Irvin married an Enloe daughter and moved to Quallatown, then to Yellow Hill, where he clerked in the store of another valley descendent, D. K. Collins. Ultimately, he relocated to Bryson City and opened a store of his own, T. I. Hughes General Merchandise, later Clampitts Hardware Store. A fourth son, Asoph Hamilton (called Ham), who was less than a year old when his father died, married in his midtwenties and lived in the Conley Creek area of Swain County for a few years, where his wife's family was from. Seeking more opportunity out west, he and his wife left North Carolina in 1894 for Harrison, Arkansas, where it was possible to get a homestead from the federal government for free under the Southern Homestead Act. But the venture was poorly timed because of "low [crop] prices, erratic weather, and periodic boll worm infestation" in 1899. In response, the family returned the next year, but they moved to a farm west of Bryson City, Swain County, where Ham also worked as a carpenter like a couple of his brothers.[1]

EDD CONNER: ECCENTRIC CHARACTER OF THE VALLEY

As the youngest child of Edward Franklin and Mary Caroline Conner, who were both deceased by 1867, Edd was an orphan needing care. Initially, he was sent to Pigeon Forge, Tennessee, to live with his Aunt Betsy (Elizabeth) Mingus and her husband, Wilson Bradley. He may have stayed there for about two years. Edd was close in age to Wilson and Betsy's two youngest children, Lula and Sarah, so he had playmates. By 1870, Edd's oldest sister, Clarinda, had married William Aseph "Ace" Enloe, and he returned to North Carolina to live with them. On his return trip he spent a night at the home of Joel and Katherine Conner, his uncle and aunt, on Couches Creek, which he recalled in a memoir with details about the cold weather and his delight at seeing pierced-tin candle lamps for the first time. Most of the details available about his life are presented in his memoir, which was penned in the 1920s when he was in his sixties.[2] Edd settled in with his sister and her family at Stecoah Bottom, where they were renting from William Holland Thomas, the one-time Cherokee agent and Confederate colonel. Subsequently, the family settled in Big Cove adjacent to Cherokee families and relatively near his mother's childhood home. Edd spent most of his childhood there. He developed friendships with some of the nearby Cherokee children, such as Standing Turkey Wolfe, the son of Joe Wolfe, who owned the farm Ace Enloe rented early on in Big Cove. When he could, Edd attended school and church in Oconaluftee, though it was eight miles away from home. In all, he claimed to have attended five terms of school from age seven to sixteen. In his teen years he boarded with Dr. John and Polly Mingus, his great-uncle and aunt; this arrangement shortened the one-way distance to school to about two miles on the turnpike, a much easier daily trek than going home to his sister's. At that time, Miss Maggie Monteith was the schoolteacher; Abram Mingus had likely given up the teaching post once he was occupied with building a new house in the 1870s.[3]

At age seventeen, Edd was saved by Christ in Lufty Baptist Church at a revival on December 28, 1880. In his memoir, he credits the Reverend Henry Conner (no relation) for calling him to Christ that revival week, by saying, "Eddy, do, do, don't you wa, wa, want to ga, ga, get saved?"[4] Then he felt forever changed: "I raised my face to see if I could realy behold his cross and in that very act, of obedience, my Soul was just fluded, and filled with an inexpressible joy of light, love, and a wonderful peace, the audience was singing a hymn, of which the couris was like this; who will come and go with me? I am bound for the promiced land." Once the service ended, Horace Gass, a deacon, invited Edd to spend the night at his home on Couches Creek rather than make the long journey home. At some point, Edd wrote a poem about the conversion, describing his elation in the ninth and final verse:

And as the waves rolled on and on
Ore Lufty'es sparkling shoals
They seemed to give God perfect praise
For saving precious souls.[5]

This event figured greatly into his subsequent notoriety because Edd was nothing if not evangelical. His memoir describes many moments when he stopped his activities, whether he was walking along a road or in his home, because he was moved to kneel and pray. Once at age twenty-six, shortly after one of his brothers had been killed and the other had been injured in a mill accident outside the valley, he became overwhelmed with concern that they had not been saved. At the time he was hiking Becks Bald in search of his hogs. He had intended to round them up that day. But the spirit overcame him, and he "just kneeled down in the brush, asking Him, who giveth all to men liberaly and up braideth not; to bless my troubled heart with his love."[6] Feeling no relief, he resumed his walk but again and again knelt to pray, finally asking that his brothers and sisters find salvation with Jesus. Feeling consoled at last, he rose and wandered the mountains "shouting, and praising, 'God's precious Holy name,'" and he did so for so long a time that he scared all his hogs away. He concluded his tale by explaining that "instead of finding my hogs as I had pland that day I just found Jesus in the hog range, to my happy surprise, and

I judge that we scared all the hogs out of the woods as those old-time log-house revivals were not common in the hog range any-way!"[7] Sadly, when he returned to his sister's home late that night he learned that a telegram had arrived saying that his injured brother had died in the afternoon.

Edd's memoir also chronicles his struggles securing a livelihood throughout his adult life. At first, in the 1890s he seemed to be moving toward security as a farmer. He used the $300 he inherited from the sale of his parents' land to buy land, cattle, and hogs. His farm was in Otto, North Carolina, some fifty miles south of Oconaluftee Valley in Macon County, and he met Flora Guffey there and married her. They had five children, though two did not survive more than a couple of years. Records indicate that three, Katherine, Cassie, and Loretta, lived to adulthood. In June 1900, Edd fell from his horse and broke his thigh in several places and dislocated his hip. During his slow, difficult recovery, tensions arose between him and his wife, most likely because of the loss of work and income; this strain eventually ended their marriage, after an acrimonious period when Edd claimed that Flora and her friends falsely accused him of abusing his wife in order to force him off his farm. As he told it, at several points he nearly ended up in jail because of charges of abuse and abandonment, but in each case reasonable authorities freed him. To support himself and to help his children, he began a long period as a vagabond, wandering, usually on foot, though North and South Carolina, Georgia, Tennessee, and Virginia in search of work. He got seasonal and short-term jobs on farms, in sawmills, in textile mills, and with logging companies even though he walked with a marked limp and was weakened by his original injury. In spite of his travels, he was never long away from Oconaluftee Valley. He occasionally worked for John Mingus, his uncle, and lived alone sometimes at his sister's home in Big Cove.[8] Clarinda's family seems to have moved away about 1901,[9] and she died in 1917 in Judson, North Carolina.

Edd helped others with his cures for skin cancers, warts, moles, corns, tumors, and wens (or boils). Though his memoir does not divulge the precise remedy, others reported that he would peel a square of bark from a tree, place Bible verses inside, and replace the bark. The cure was supposed "perfected" once the bark healed over again.[10]

A telling story about Edd emphasizes his Christian faith. As a young man in his twenties, Edd planted three walnut trees to shade his sister's home. Two of the three grew; one flanked the door on the south side of the home and the other was set in the corner of the yard. By 1918, the trees were sizable and the land had been sold to Parsons Pulp and Lumber Company. On a trip to the old farm, Edd stopped by to see the trees and determined that he wanted to use the lumber from the one by the door for his casket, even though he was in good health and not expecting to die anytime soon. He spoke to the watchman, Mr. Lucus, about his idea, and was referred to Frank Blankenship, the general manager of the site. Once Edd explained that he had planted the tree thirty-four years before, Blankenship gave him the tree and, along with his son Lewis, even helped him cut it down, on November 12, 1919. Edd gathered a half bushel of walnuts as a thank-you gift for Blankenship and then got two Cherokee men to help him drag the trunk to the railroad, where it was taken to the Ravensford sawmill. Workers there met some difficulty sawing it into boards because spikes had been hammered into the tree, but eventually enough was salvaged to be delivered to Jim Ayers's mill shop in Oconaluftee, where it was made into a casket. Edd also made a walking cane from the tree. The resulting casket was fancy. The panels were of solid walnut with cherry molding and a face glass, and the wood was stained to highlight the color differences, with walnut for the panels and red cherry stain for the trim. Edd himself finished the interior with "white bleaching" and padding.[11]

Once the casket was done and a white painted coffin was constructed to encase it, Edd hired a tailor to make a "snow white sleeping suit." The jacket and pants were sewn from a length of bleached Irish linen costing $22.50. The pants were designed so that Edd's body could be easily dressed after death; buttons lined the outside seams. The outfit was completed with white underwear, shirt, collar, tie, socks, and gloves. When he was laid to rest, Edd explained that he would be an "emblem of purity," ready to meet his maker on Judgment Day.[12]

By the time the ensemble was complete, the fortieth anniversary of Edd's conversion to Christianity approached, so he arranged an evening service at Lufty Baptist Church to commemorate the event. On December 28, 1920, forty years to the day after he had been saved, he brought the casket and coffin to the church and set them down over the spot where he had kneeled years before. Dressed in his "burying garb," he asked that a photo be taken of himself with his coffin and casket, and it was subsequently published in newspapers. His message to the peopled gathered at the service was to show them how his conversion in that very place had been a "lasting power and spiritual influence for good" that they might also enjoy if they were saved.[13] Even though Edd was ready for eternity in 1920, he did not need his casket and suit for seventeen more years. On May 19, 1937, he died in Bryson City and was buried, as planned in suit, casket, and coffin, in the Bryson City Cemetery.

Edd Conner with his walnut casket.

GREAT SMOKY MOUNTAINS NATIONAL PARK ARCHIVES, TOWNSEND, TENN.

ADEN CARVER: THE QUINTESSENTIAL MOUNTAINEER

After the Civil War, Mary Bradley, a daughter of that large family, and Israel Carver had a growing family of their own. Israel had bought land adjacent to Mary's parents along Bradley Fork and began farming there in the late 1840s. Mary bore fifteen children between 1840 and 1862, and eleven survived to adulthood. Once the war ended, perhaps because Israel's family was in Tennessee, most of the children moved over the crest of the Smokies to Sevier County.[14] Son Aden, who was named the most typical mountaineer by the Great Smoky Mountains National Park during its fiftieth anniversary celebration, lived an episodic life in Tennessee and North Carolina—both in the Smokies and in its foothills.[15] He pursued a variety of trades to support his family. Instead of staying put, he went where he could find training and a livelihood.

After serving as a teenager in the home guard for the Thomas Legion, Aden met his wife, Martha Roberts, in Tennessee. They were married on April 14, 1869, by the Reverend William Henry Conner, in his home. But the newlyweds went back to Tennessee to begin their family, which grew to eleven children, including two sets of twins. Late in life, Aden stated in an interview that he learned the trade of being a millwright and carpenter in Sevier County, Tennessee. He helped build a mill at the head of Flat Creek, which is now near one of the fingers of Douglas Lake, also known as the Bird Community. He observed that the people there were heavy drinkers and law breakers, so he established a Baptist church that changed the flavor of the town. Even so, it seems that he left Flat Creek and lived elsewhere in Sevier County most of the time his family was there.[16] The 1880 census lists the family as living in Harrisburg, about four miles east of Sevierville; Aden's occupation is listed as a general laborer.[17] In total, Aden claimed that he lived in Tennessee twenty-six or twenty-seven years. Most of the children were born in Sevier County, but at least four were born in Swain County, so this family, like others, moved around. Aden came back to the Oconaluftee Valley on at least two occasions during his young adulthood to help Sion T. Early with the carpentry of the Mingus home in 1877 and again with the construction of the Mingus Mill in 1886. Oconalufty Baptist Church records state that both he and Martha were "dismissed by letter" to another church in November 1876 and once again in August 1881.[18] During some of the time when the Mingus home was being built they must have attended church there.

By the late 1880s, Aden's father, Israel, was in his eighties and ailing, so Aden returned to take care of his father or, perhaps more likely, his father's farm because his mother, Mary Bradley Carver, was still living. Aden continued on the farm until the old man died in 1890. By 1892, Aden had bought his father's one hundred acres on Bradley Fork from his mother and siblings as well as an additional adjacent one hundred acres. The latter property was purchased for twelve dollars.[19] Presumably, at this time, most of Aden and Martha's children would have moved to North Carolina as well, though some may have stayed in Tennessee with other Carver relatives. By 1900, Aden's mother, Mary, died at the home of Eliza Jane (Carver) and John Watson, her daughter and son-in-law, in Sevier County. She was buried among numerous family members in Oldham's Creek Cemetery, located in what is known today as the Boogertown Community of Sevier County. Aden carved her headstone.[20]

With his return to Oconaluftee to help his father, Aden had come home to the valley to live the rest of a long life. From the 1890s until after the end of World War II, he made his living farming, keeping bees and selling their honey, and growing an orchard, as well as, no doubt, doing odd carpentry jobs when called upon. The homestead was a one-story-and-loft cabin with many outbuildings and acres of cleared land. A great-granddaughter, Janice Carver Mooney, described the cabin as similar to the restored house at the Mountain Farm Museum with "a porch on both sides, the smaller one facing the stream of water. A large porch at the back facing what they always called the yard, which had some shade trees, snowball bushes, rose bushes, flowers, and things like that. And there was a fireplace in the two major rooms. There was two major rooms, the fireplaces were there, and there was an upstairs. And then the ell kitchen."[21] The kitchen was equipped with a stove for cooking.

Many of Aden and Martha's children and their families lived close by during these years, off and on, but some moved out of the Smokies entirely. Aden served as a deacon in the Lufty Baptist Church and was known for his work ethic, geniality, and skill as a storyteller and practical joker. Great-granddaughter Janice recalled how he let her believe that he had known the biblical Noah in answer to a fanciful childhood question. Actually, Aden knew his own younger brother named Noah, not the Old Testament figure, but he did not mind letting Janice think otherwise.[22] Aden and Martha provide an excellent example of the resourcefulness and flexibility that mountain families exercised to feed their children and gain a measure of comfort by middle age. They were never rich, and they always worked hard. But they had enough money, were always well fed, and owned their own land.

NEWCOMERS JOIN AND STRENGTHEN THE COMMUNITY

The Queens were one family who arrived in the valley after the Civil War and became major landowners on choice sites. Patriarch James Smith Queen helped his children buy land from the state, the Floyd family, the Conners, and others in the 1870s and 1880s. Eventually the Queens purchased the area known as Bradleytown. For a time, Beck's Bald, the mountain above Bradleytown to the northeast was known as Queen Mountain, so the size of this family's holdings was significant.[23] This location placed the family in the midst of the community, very close to the Lufty Baptist Church and, eventually to the school, once a separate building was constructed for it in the 1870s.

J. H. Queen was ordained to preach in Oconalufty Baptist Church in 1882 after several years' service as a deacon. In 1888, the congregation paid him forty dollars for his service with an additional eight dollars for a saddle. After four years, he moved on to another church, but other members of the Queen family remained.[24] Notably, Wilson Ensley Queen married Alice Bradley in 1892, after he was widowed by his first wife, Amanda Catherine Queen, and Alice was widowed by her first husband, J. F. Harvey. They raised the children from their first marriages at Smokemont, very near to the church where they were devoted members.[25]

As the nineteenth century ended, a number of new families moved into Oconaluftee. Together, new and established families donated land, raised the money, and constructed a new building for Lufty Baptist Church at its present location. The project took time to realize. Church records state than in 1880 M. Treadway, F. M. Barton, H. J. Beck, W. H. Conner, William Alexander, and J. H. Queen formed a building committee.[26] Two years later, H. J. Beck and J. L. (James Leander) Queen jointly donated about four acres of land, two each, carved from property along their shared boundary line. This land was donated "for the use of Public School and Public Worship to the School committee in Dist. No. 16 & other Successors in office and the Deacons of the Baptist Church. To have and to hold from us and him and assigns so long as it is used for that purpose otherwise the land is to refer back to the said Beck & Queen or heirs."[27] In the deed, J. L. Queen reserved "the liberty of cultivating the cleared land in the said boundary" even after the land transfer, so perhaps he had crops already in the field and wanted to continue planting there. Also, in the passage describing the tract's boundaries, the deed states that a school building already sat on this tract, but it is not clear whether a church building did. It seems that the precise site of the new church was not immediately decided. One source says that H. J. Beck suggested placing the church near the graveyard in his field, but this site was rejected.[28] How the current hillside site was chosen remains a mystery. Nonetheless, by January 1896, deacons J. R. Kinsey, J. H. Queen, and William Jenkins formed a committee to "take subscriptions elect means and materials for and contract and superintend the building of a church house upon the platt of land deeded to said church for church purposes."[29] Also on this date, twelve benefactors signed up to donate cash, lumber, and "work or trade." A total of ninety-eight dollars was pledged. Only ten dollars came in the form of cash, five dollars each from J. Treadway and J. H. Conner. Ten contributors pledged work or trade, and two donated lumber. The cash "subscriptions" were due the first of June and the lumber was due the first of July, while trade and work were due when it was called for. With this plan, the committee constructed a log church at the present site of the church that year.

The log church building of 1896 was replaced around 1910 with the frame building that now stands. In 1906, Wilson Ensley Queen donated an additional acre of land to the church deacons. The deed states that he did so

> in consideration of the love and affection he has for the Lufty Baptist Church and other valuable considerations to him paid by the said deacons the receipt of which is hereby acknowledged have bargained and sold and by these presents doth bargain sell and convey to the said deacons of the Lufty Baptist Church and their successors in office a certain piece or parcel of land in Swain County and in Oconalufty Township . . . containing one acre more or less. To have and to hold the aforesaid tract and all privileges and appurtenances thereto. And the said W. E. Queen further gives to the Deacons of the Baptist Church a privilege to cut fire wood for the use of the Baptist Church but they are not to cut any Board trees or other valuable timber. The fire wood for the church to be cut on the ridge next to Becks line and the said W. E. Queen.[30]

It seems that the permission to cut firewood was for wood from Wilson Queen's land, not from the acre covered by the deed. Perhaps this extra acre and privilege to cut firewood were intended to replace the loss of use caused by J. L. Queen's reservation to cultivate the cleared land mentioned in the deed of 1882.

As the eventful nineteenth century came to a close, the valley continued to experience an increase in population. Between 1880 and 1900, the number of white families more than doubled in Oconalufty Township, according to census records. In 1880, about 75 white families are listed in the census; by 1900, 135 families are.[31] New families came into the area and settled. These included McMahans, who had the farm and informal inn highest up the turnpike, as well as the Treadways, Lamberts, and Parkers up Tow String Road. Mountain and Cherokee families developed ties and intermarried, establishing strong relationships between the neighboring communities. In his old age, Thomas Irvin Hughes recalled this period "as a time of great neighborliness."[32] The first two decades of the twentieth century saw an even greater influx of people as logging came into the valley. But the three and a half decades between the Civil War and the advent of logging were the years when the Oconaluftee community took shape as a distinctive place, a home of independent and resourceful people united by faith, neighborly collaboration, and family. These are the years that many descendants of Oconaluftee find most compelling because valley residents had their own culture, with their own characters and legends. The valley was never entirely isolated, but it was removed from many of the forces of change and industrialization that would arrive in the 1900s. There is good reason to be a bit nostalgic about these years. Yes, there were hardships and tragedy, but the families had autonomy and opportunity to build and improve their own farms and, in some cases, their fortunes.

Chapter 11

QUALLA'S LONG STRUGGLE FOR SECURITY

THE EASTERN BAND IS ESTABLISHED

▲▲▲

Early summer is the perfect season to drive on the Blue Ridge Parkway. The air is clean and life seems easy. Heading north from Newfound Gap Road, the first overlook is Oconaluftee River Overlook. I cannot see either the river or Raven Fork, which is the closer stream, directly from the pull-off. The forest has rebounded since the name was attached; it must have once been visible, and in a different season some of it may be. I crossed the river a ways back when I entered the parkway.

At the overlook, a hazy mid-distance green vista of the valley and mountains stretches just beyond the ferns and rhododendrons at the edge of a bluff. Ahead is Mount Stand Watie at 3,961 feet elevation, with Newton Bald just behind it, even higher, at 5,000 feet. To the left, with two antennae at 4,600 feet, is Mount Noble, which lies on the park boundary. To the right, Mount Clark rises to 3,854 feet. Along with the overlook's, these names have a curious sort of significance and reflect the decision making of the park's 1930s–40s nomenclature committees. First of all, the "bald" is not really a natural bald at all; its peak has regrown. It was named after a Newton family who lived in its vicinity, somewhat west of the valley. The two mountains in the center and to the right are named after prominent Cherokees, but not members of the Eastern Band. Stand Watie was one of the small number of Cherokees who signed the Treaty of New Echota, which doomed the nation to the Trail of Tears. During the Civil War, he was principal chief of the Cherokee Nation out west and was promoted to the rank of brigadier general in the Confederacy for his fierce leadership of Cherokee troops in Arkansas, Missouri, and Oklahoma. He was the only Native American to reach the rank of general in the Confederacy. Mount Clark celebrates the achievements of Watie's grandson Joseph James Clark. Clark, also a member of the Cherokee Nation, served with distinction in World War II as an aviator for the U.S. Navy, rising to the rank of admiral. Then he commanded the Seventh Fleet during the Korean War and was highly decorated for many achievements. Yes, Watie and Clark were prominent Cherokees, but they were hardly hometown heroes of the Eastern Band. Even so, these infelicities do not mar the glorious view.

Furthermore, they make the reality of the Cherokee Central School complex—mostly obstructed from view by vegetation and just a short distance below—even more poignant. It sits on the land known as the Ravensford Tract, which was the site of the logging town of the same name. In the 1910s and 1920s, a large two-story school stood on this site to educate the children of the loggers. After decades of requests and negotiations, the land was traded back to the Eastern Band from the National Park Service in late 2003 for a larger tract going to the park along the parkway. It exemplifies the success of the Eastern Band's long game to remain on ancestral land and secure the community with a stable and prosperous future.

▲ ▲ ▲

AFTER THE CIVIL WAR ENDED, the Lufty Cherokees in North Carolina were surviving—but in distressed conditions. They had endured the same dangers and privations as the white families during the war, but their hunger and impoverishment were significantly more severe, no doubt because the war entirely disrupted their agriculture and their involvement in the market economy of western North Carolina. They simply had less in the beginning and much less at the end of the war. Another destabilizing factor was that William Holland Thomas—their longtime advocate, former Confederate commander, principal adviser, and liaison to county, state, and federal officials—was no longer capable of protecting their interests. In the last year of the war, he began to experience episodes of mental instability, and after the end, it became clear to his family, business associates, government officials, and Cherokee leaders that he would not be able to continue in the strategic role that he had once played. This change led to years of legal disputes about the land that the Cherokees inhabited in Quallatown, which was mostly adjacent to the white Oconalufty Township community, although some Cherokee land holdings were intermingled with white tracts and some remained in the Snowbird area, about forty miles west. Thomas's decline also ushered in an era of factionalism and contested eastern Cherokee leadership. Consequently, the Reconstruction period for the Lufty Cherokees was marked by multiple social, financial, and legal challenges. They faced these challenges with the benefit of assistance from government agents, lawyers, and white teachers and missionaries, as well as with their own growing numbers of educated and capable leaders, but the motivations and agendas of the outside individuals and groups were never as transparent, long-lived, or clearly benevolent as Thomas's had been. Unfortunately, on occasion, even Cherokee leaders' incentives were self-serving. During this period the Lufty Cherokees traced a precarious arc from a vulnerable remnant of the Cherokee Nation to an established and nationally recognized tribe, the Eastern Band of the Cherokee Indian.

An immediate crisis at war's end was a smallpox epidemic among the Lufty Cherokees. The disease was brought back to Qualla by a returning Cherokee soldier who had fought for the Union and had been located at an infected camp near Knoxville. Though he died shortly after his arrival home, the telltale pustules were not immediately noticed and many in the community attended his funeral. A week later, Thomas recognized the disease on mourners. In November 1865, he asked Dr. John Mingus for an ounce of asafetida, which is a mixture of castor oil, garlic, and camphor worn about the neck, and "at least two gallons purified whiskey" to share as preventatives. When the disease spread, Thomas brought in a doctor from Sevier County, Tennessee, but his vaccine failed and many Cherokees also distrusted him and his instructions for care. They resorted to cold river plunges to treat the fever. This traditional remedy resulted in death; about 125 smallpox victims passed away, a significant proportion of the population. The episode set a somber tone for the remainder of the decade.[1]

The year 1866 included other significant events. On February 19, the general assembly of North Carolina granted the Cherokees permanent residency in the counties where they now lived. But it did not grant them standing as citizens of the state. This act secured the Cherokee payment of federal money from before the war; however, the state proposed to the federal government that only the interest on the funds be paid. George W. Bushyhead, a Cherokee headman in Macon County who had risen to prominence, was granted state funds to take the request for payment to Washington, D.C., which he did in

March. Amid a number of complicating factors—federal recriminations for the Lufty Cherokees' support for the Confederacy, postwar upheaval, and internal division over whether the eastern Cherokees should migrate west and join the Cherokee Nation—the payment issue remained unresolved. Bushyhead contended that 800 Cherokees wanted to go west, though few who lived in Qualla were interested. For more than two years, no funds were released to alleviate the suffering of the Lufty Cherokees.[2]

In early March 1866, another recovery effort got underway. Will Thomas and Abraham Mingus signed an agreement to build a mill that could grind both corn and wheat on land owned by Thomas inside Qualla. Mingus would oversee the mill's construction, including the acquisition of a set of burrstones, but the two would share expenses and proceeds. It is interesting to note that this mill project preceded the construction of the turbine mill on Mingus Creek by two decades. However, whether this mill in Qualla was actually built remains uncertain because it does not appear on a map dated 1876, though three other mills are indicated, one in Big Cove at the farm of Chitolski (Falling Blossom) and two others on Soco Creek. No doubt other small mills dotted the area to serve farms in other parts of the community. Thomas's Qualla tannery also continued after the Civil War. The original store remained open, too, but was signed over to James Terrell, Thomas's longtime business partner, in 1874.[3]

Even as some glimmers of progress emerged, fate created additional problems for the Cherokees. Though Thomas was actively trying to reestablish his businesses in order to bring in funds to pay debts, he was soon impaired by violent mental breakdowns and failing physical health. In March 1867, he was declared insane and committed to the state asylum, Dix Hill in Raleigh. The cause was likely late-stage syphilis, diagnosed some years later and acknowledged as the cause of his death in 1893. After a month's stay in the hospital, he returned home for a time. Years of intermittent lucidity and insanity followed; at turns he threatened family members and worked selflessly to buoy up the Lufty Cherokees. But he entered a period of decline with multiple hospital stays. The Cherokees' interests were directly affected by this personal tragedy because Thomas's businesses and financial matters were elaborately intertwined with theirs. For years, serving as their agent, he had bought land for them in his name in order to secure their geographical home. For a variety of reasons, it was easier for Thomas to hold the land in trust for the Lufty Cherokees and to pay tax on it for them. He extended them loans to pay taxes, sold items on account in his stores, and supported them in innumerable ways.

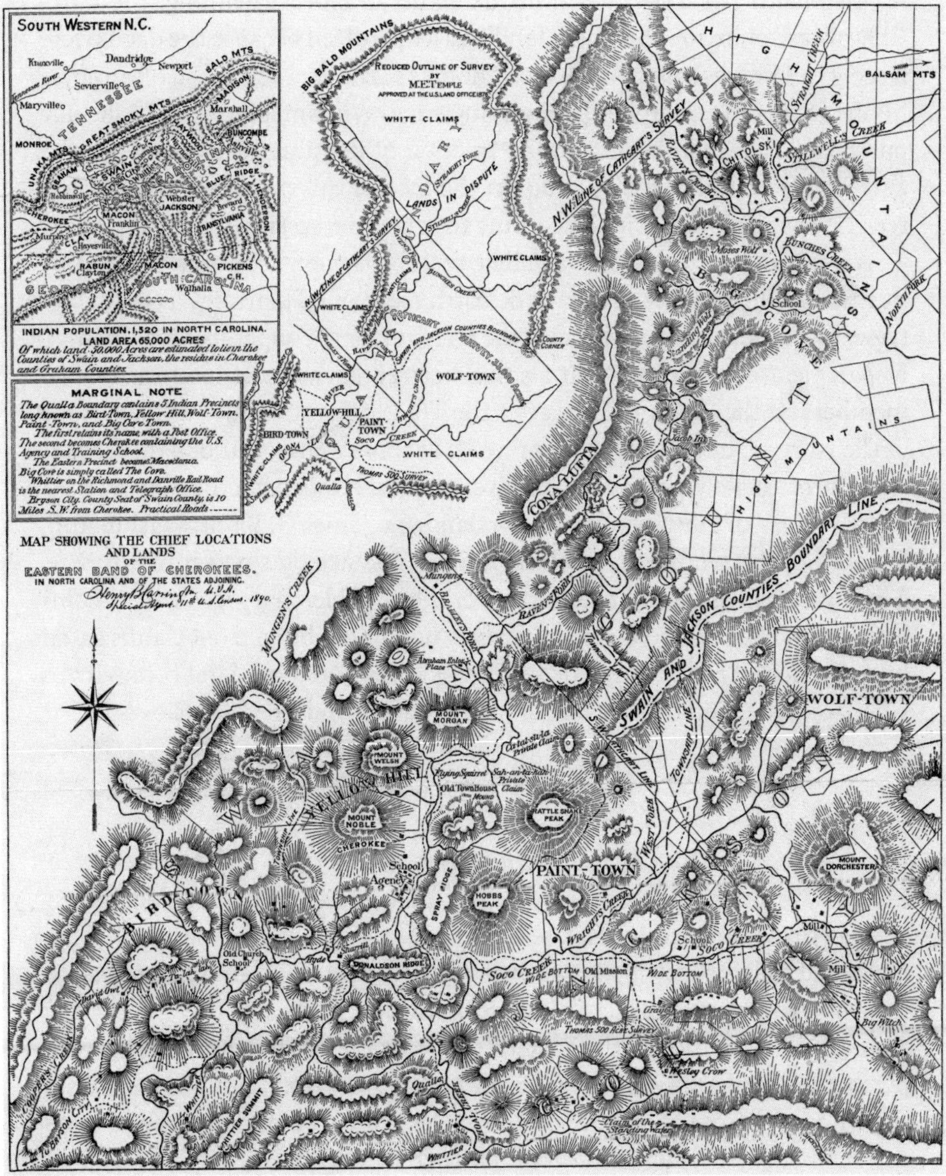

Henry B. Carrington, *Map Showing the Chief Locations and Lands of the Eastern Band of Cherokees*, 1890.

WILSON SPECIAL COLLECTIONS LIBRARY, UNIVERSITY OF NORTH CAROLINA AT CHAPEL HILL.

As his health failed just when his debts became overwhelming, the Lufty Cherokees' tenure on their own land was jeopardized because the deeds were largely in Thomas's name. Much of Thomas's land was auctioned off to cover his debts, and the Cherokee land was included. William Johnston of Asheville purchased the Cherokee land for a fraction of its value at this time, but he agreed to sell it back for $30,000. In the face of this predicament, Thomas resigned as agent (or "chief" according to some sources) in 1867.[4]

A year later, Congress responded to the payment requests pressed by Bushyhead. It formally recognized North Carolina Cherokees as a distinct tribe, like other tribes, and placed the tribe under the supervision of the U.S. Department of the Interior. It also authorized payment of interest to tribe members on the funds granted after the Trail of Tears. Finally, in 1869, some of the North Carolina Cherokees received about twenty-four dollars per person. Unfortunately, these payments were reduced from what they should have been because of graft by Silas H. Swetland and James G. Blunt, Washington, D.C., attorneys who distributed the money and acted as power of attorney. Through an illegal and brazen scheme, they double-charged for their commission and left $6,000 in claims entirely unpaid. As he paid out claims based on a revision of the Mullay Roll of Cherokees of 1848, Swetland counted 730 Cherokees in Qualla and 912 in Graham, Macon, and Cherokee Counties.[5]

A DECADE OF DRAMATIC CHANGE

Amid intense internal factionalism among the North Carolina Cherokees, Salonita, a fullblood Cherokee, was the first principal chief elected under the Cherokee constitution in late 1870. Also in 1870, the Eastern Band of the Cherokee Indians (EBCI) was authorized by Congress as an official tribe to bring suit in federal court against agents who had defrauded them, including Thomas. So even though the Eastern Cherokees held Thomas in high regard personally, they were compelled to file suit against him in order to separate their finances from his and to establish clear title to their land. In the same action, they sued Thomas's business partner, James Terrell, as well as William Johnston, Thomas's main creditor and the man who had purchased the land. At the trial for this suit, Thomas supported the Cherokees' claim to his own detriment. His loyalty was subsequently acknowledged and returned when the EBCI recognized Thomas's children and grandchildren as members of the tribe. The suit was decided in 1874 after the trial and arbitration. As a result, the Cherokees owed about $7,200 to Thomas for payment for Qualla Boundary land, a sum significantly reduced from the actual debt because of the delay and the suit itself. They were also allowed to purchase land south of Qualla known as the Cheoah Boundary, land that Thomas had lost as well, from both Terrell and Johnston. The cash for all these transactions arrived in March 1875; it was the principal and remaining interest from the government fund created in 1848 after the Trail of Tears. Additionally, the Reverend William C. McCarthy, a Baptist who served honorably as the federal Cherokee agent at this time, paid back taxes to the state. So at last the Qualla Boundary was legally the home of the Eastern Band of Cherokee Indians.[6] White squatters still remained on Cherokee land, and laxness in getting all the titles filed in the county office made it possible for whites to continue to homestead and cut timber on Cherokee land for years, no small problems to impoverished Cherokees trying to make ends meet. A U.S. census agent observed that the state had been complicit in the Cherokees' land problems, criticizing it in a long but pointed nineteenth-century sentence: "The looseness with which, for a small fee, the state of North Carolina permits entries upon lands known to fall within the territory embraced in the deeds by Mr. Thomas adds its uncertainty to aggravate the unrest which is everywhere visible among this people as to what they really own in consideration of the money with which they parted, they rightfully expecting valid and permanent titles."[7]

Though the Cherokees were wards of the federal government, they were able to vote as North Carolina citizens at this time. (Such ironies and inconsistencies mark the postwar era.) Most Cherokees were content to keep a low profile in state politics, following decades of advice from Thomas that they "project a positive yet unobtrusive image."[8] But in the years following the Civil War, many white citizens were concerned that the Cherokees could swing an election and usher in Republican officeholders. They presumed that the Cherokees would vote Republican because of the influence of federal agents and other white outsiders. So when Swain County was created from Jackson County in 1871, the line was drawn to split the Qualla Boundary between the two counties, thereby lessening any effect that Cherokees might have on subsequent elections.[9]

Once the question of the Cherokee land was addressed, issues of education and general welfare again became prominent. During his short but benevolent service as the federal agent, the Reverend McCarthy focused on schools. He established four day schools in Qualla at Yellow Hill, Bird Town, Big Cove, and the Echota Mission, as well as a boarding school to the south in Cheoah. McCarthy observed the children's poverty and need of clothing, so he requested money to help with these necessities as well as funding for a model farm that would serve as practical education and help prepare students to run their families' farms. Unfortunately, the secretary of the interior was not persuaded to support McCarthy's suggestions and dismissed him in 1876.[10]

During a tour of western North Carolina in 1874, writer Rebecca Harding Davis observed the Cherokees' keen desire for their children to have access to education. "All that they want of white men is schools," Davis quoted the preacher Inoli, "an intelligent old man of sixty."[11] The Cherokees she met reported that they could not keep white teachers long because of the remoteness of the area; for them, this was the major obstacle to maintaining the schools from year to year. Davis observed a number of households, ranging from ones that were basic and dirty with despondent adults to others that were neatly kept and adequately but plainly provisioned with owners hard at work in their gardens. She saw the same range in circumstances, education, and outlook among the Cherokees as she did among the white mountain families. Although her standards were those of the dominant white culture, she declared that the Cherokees were capable of more than their present circumstances permitted them to achieve:

> They were neither vicious nor vulgar in a single instance. On the contrary, they were grave, thoughtful, self-possessed: the vacancy in the face arose from lack of subject for thought, not of the ability to think. We visited, however, several huts belonging to Indians who could read and write in Cherokee, and even that small degree of education told in clean floors and neat flannel dresses; the iron pot and wooden spoons were still the table furniture, but a little shelf on the wall with half a dozen cups and saucers of white stoneware, kept for show in beautiful glistening condition, hinted at a latent aesthetic taste, just as plainly as would Indian cabinets laden with priceless bric-a-brac elsewhere. Packed away in these huts were always dress-suits of cloth and bright woolen stuff for state occasions, including always a high hat for the men and hoop-skirts for the women.[12]

Davis also met the Principal Chief Sowenosgeh, who perhaps was Salonita at his farm, and refuted a stereotypical concept of him. "He was neither drunk nor meditating on past glories of his race, according to our usual notions of a chief, but barefooted and clad in patched trousers, hard at work digging, as were his two sons. He was a short, powerfully-built old man, with a keen shrewd eye, which instantly measured his guests and held them at proper distance from himself."[13] The impression of her long article is that the Cherokees needed government aid to recover from the war and to build up essential social services such as schools. But the people, both individually and collectively, were willing and eager for work and advancement.

Davis's account ends with an appeal to churches to support schools in Qualla and for "some strong and kindly men and women" to recognize her call and come to teach the Indians.[14] Despite these pleas for investment in Cherokee education, by 1879, the secretary of the interior allowed the schools to close and instead sent only select students to nearby academies and colleges, using the tribe's common fund to pay the expense. A couple of years later, the Quakers did respond to Davis's call for schools and proposed a ten-year plan for them. Barnabus C. Hobbs, representing the Western Yearly Meeting of Indiana, bought thirty-nine acres from Chief Longblanket and reopened day schools in the boundary in 1881. By 1884, Henry Spray became the superintendent; he had previously headed the Quaker school in Maryville, Tennessee. He oversaw the construction of a large boarding school at Yellow Hill with a model farm—as McCarthy had envisioned. Day schools with one or two teachers and about thirty-three students attending each of them were opened in Big Cove, Bird Town, and Soco. Unfortunately, Spray was accused of encouraging the Cherokees to vote Republican in the election of 1884, and this rumor resulted in strong white opposition both to Spray and the schools. Under the subsequent Democratic administration of President Grover Cleveland, federal oversight of the schools was intensified. As a result, the day schools were closed in 1886, though the training school continued into the twentieth century.[15]

Regardless of the politics that eventually drove the Quakers away from their sponsorship of the Cherokee schools, during their years of oversight, much was accomplished, particularly at the Yellow Hill site, which developed into the Cherokee training school under the administration of Spray, his wife, two additional white teachers, and nine employees, three of whom were Cherokee. Settled on fifty acres of land along the Oconaluftee River, it "winds the bright current of the river."[16] In 1890, it consisted of four frame houses and seven outbuildings, including a barn, and accommodated about eighty-four resident students and twenty-four day students. Despite its success, the training school functioned on a modest budget of $12,000 a year and needed additional funding to house more students and to improve its water system. Instruction focused on "industrial work," which included "farming, fruit culture, gardening, grazing stock, and some shop work," as well as housekeeping, sewing, and needlework for the girls. All scholars took "their turn in laundering, cooking, and housework, so that all learn to make bread and qualify themselves for all kitchen duty."[17] The school cultivated about 125 acres of land (presumably most of which was not school property) and brought in "50 bushels of wheat, 500 bushels of corn, 75 bushels of oats, 600 pumpkins, 10 tons of hay, and 50 pounds of butter" in a year. The students also cared for "33 swine and 150 domestic fowls, 5 horses and 56 cattle, including 25 milch cows."[18] They followed a daily schedule that began at 5:00 A.M. and concluded at 8:30 P.M. but made time for recreation and music in the form of a boys' brass band. A huge mulberry tree formed the bandstand as musicians sat in the tree to perform "Dixie," "Yankee Doodle," and "Way Down upon the Suwanee River."[19] The civility and respect of the Society of Friends can be seen in a U.S. census agent's description of how the school approached religious teaching: "Religious instruction is largely a matter of precept and example, without catechismal or other straight forms for the inculcation of principles of right and duty."[20] This forbearance seems a particularly judicious move, given the strong Baptist and Methodist presence in the area as well as the traditional beliefs of many Cherokees.

CHEROKEE IDENTITY GAINS ATTENTION

By 1880, the Cherokee population had shifted somewhat since the end of the Civil War. The population of Quallatown had increased by almost 100 individuals to 825 since 1869, but that of Macon and Cherokee Counties had declined by more than half to 389.[21] This decline was the result of many non-Qualla Cherokees moving west to join the Cherokee Nation and of others moving into the boundary. Though the Cherokees had begun to consolidate as a community in Quallatown and establish it as their tribal center, trespassers still resided on their land. Their continued presence made it difficult for the tribe to pay taxes on the common lands that were occupied by the trespassers. Selling timber out of the Oconaluftee watershed was viewed as the best way to raise the necessary public funds. In addition, lawsuits against settlers and the state for failing to meet the terms of the 1874 arbitration were pursued as remedies.[22]

By this point Nimrod Smith (Tsaladihi) had been elected principal chief and established the seat of the Eastern Band in Yellow Hill. Smith was already distinguished in the community. He had served as a sergeant in the Thomas Legion and as a secretary in 1868 of the Cheoah Council, a group that had pushed for federal payments to support the Cherokees after the war. He was a striking figure, one-quarter Cherokee, six foot, four inches tall, and wore a distinctive handlebar moustache.[23]

On a tour of western North Carolina in the early 1880s, Wilbur Zeigler and

Ben Grosscup visited Chief Smith at his "comfortable house of four rooms" near "a frame building used for a school-house, meeting-house, and council-house." The authors' description of the encounter suggests that Smith fulfilled all their expectations of an informed and dutiful chief:

> We found Chief Smith in his residence, writing at a table covered with books, pamphlets, letters, and manuscripts. The room is neatly papered and comfortably furnished. The chief received us with cordiality. He was dressed in white starched shirt, with collar and cuffs, Prince Albert coat, well-fitting pantaloons, and calf-skin boots shining like ebony. He is more than six feet tall, straight as a plumb line, and rather slender. His features are rough and prominent. His forehead is full but not high, and his thick, black hair, combed to perfect smoothness, hung down behind large protruding ears, almost to the coat collar. He has a deep, full-toned voice, and earnest, impressive manner. His wife is a white woman, and his daughters, bright, intelligent girls, have been well educated. One of them was operating a sewing-machine, another writing for her father.[24]

Zeigler and Grosscup's article summarized the structure of the tribe's government and yearly pay for the chief and assistant chief ($500 and $250, respectively). The elected chief had veto power over a council of three executive advisers and two delegates per every one hundred tribe members, but he could act only with council approval.[25] Smith served as principal chief for eleven years, until 1891. Although Smith became discredited in the late 1880s for political corruption, disputes with the tribal council, and personal immorality (for instance, drunkenness, brawling, and adultery), he saw the tribe through a roller coaster of federal and state court rulings.[26] These included such critical issues as the legal status of the Eastern Band, the legality of its constitution, the North Carolina citizenship of the Cherokees, and whether individuals or the Eastern Band could use state courts. By the end of the decade, the North Carolina General Assembly recognized the Eastern Band as a corporate body that could sue and be sued in state courts over property matters. The significance of incorporation cannot be overstated, giving the Eastern Band self-governance and determination via its tribal council. Incorporation provided immediate and long-term protection from federal policies that tried to force assimilation and the dissolution of the Qualla Boundary. It also enabled the Eastern Band to develop its own economy through tourism, a market for traditional crafts, and logging contracts.[27]

Chief Nimrod Jarrett Smith.

COURTESY OF NATIONAL ANTHROPOLOGICAL ARCHIVES, SMITHSONIAN INSTITUTION, INV.01759200.

The 1880s marked the decade when Cherokee culture, rather than just its land, earned new attention from white society as significant and worth preserving. First came wealthy artifact collectors, and after them, the scholarly and sympathetic ethnologist James Mooney arrived. In 1881, the Valentine family of Richmond, Virginia, began to excavate mounds within Qualla Boundary as well as at other sites in Swain County. The family was headed by Mann S. Valentine, who owned a health tonic business, Valentine's Meat Juice, made from pure beef juice. He was also an avid artifact collector. While the father attended business in Richmond, his sons Benjamin B. and Edward P.

Valentine conducted and oversaw the excavations in North Carolina. They continued work for several years.[28]

The two Qualla mounds were the Sawnooke Mound (called the Sawnooth Mound by the Valentines) and the Bird Town Mound. Mann Valentine wrote a report about the former, describing the size and location of the mound as well as the artifacts and human remains excavated from it.[29] Because Cherokees buried their dead in mounds and in the floors of their earthen homes, it was not unusual that grave sites were found within the mounds. As amateurs, the Valentines collected everything they uncovered in the mounds and transported their finds back to Richmond. Many of these items remain today in The Valentine, a museum founded by Mann and his brother, a successful sculptor. For years the museum display included skeletons with their associated objects in glass-covered cases. Today, human remains would not be removed from mounds even by professional archaeologists without the involvement and approval of the EBCI, much less displayed, but the practice among collectors was far less respectful and constrained by regulation in the late nineteenth century. Despite this repulsive aspect of the Valentines' work in Qualla, the existing accounts of it offer interesting information about the community at that time. For example, Mann's report provides a narrative description of the Sawnooke Mound, with internal references to attached diagrams:

> On the east bank of the Oconee Luftee River, a mile above the village of Yellow Hill, Swain Co. N.C. was found standing alone with no other similar object in proximity, a large artificial structure of earth. The structure was elliptical in form, having its greatest diameter at right angles to the river. It was flat on the top from which the sides sloped downward at an angle of 45 degrees, and then gradually spread itself down, out into the level ground. The greatest vertical section of the mound . . . was 130 ft, and the least vertical section . . . 100 ft, is equal to the greatest and least diameter of the base. The greatest diameter of the top . . . was 56 ft. and the least diameter of top . . . was 36 ft. height of mound . . . eleven feet. The original lines of the structure had evidently been changed. Not only by the plough and rains moved the earth from the sides downward, and spread the earth further out, but previously to this the apex had with evident intent, had been cut off and pushed down towards the base. . . .
>
> The valley of the Oconee Luftee here had been for some time in cultivation—(the mound included) there was no longer any appearance

> of the old stumps of trees usually left in the clearing. Quite a large number of fragments of primitive pottery were strewed over this estate. In examination of the neighborhood there were found at the bottom of a ridge about 300 yards from the earth structure—what appeared to be two excavations.[30]

Given what is known about the smallpox epidemic after the Civil War, a local story about this mound has a ring of truth for today's reader that Mann, arrogantly, decided to discount:

> Tradition says that there been an Indian habitation on the top of this structure, that the Ind. Whose house it was having gone east, returned with the small pox from him his family took the disease and they having all died with it were buried in this mound. The inquiry very naturally, therefore, was made of us, if we were looking for smallpox—Having little faith in Ind. Tradition, we do not know that we felt much concern about the small pox story.[31]

The mound, located about 300 feet from the river, had a number of clay and ash layers with twenty-six graves and artifacts throughout, including beaded necklaces around the necks of skeletons, pottery, carved pipes, bones from deer and bear, bear teeth, deer horn, and shell pins and breastplates, as well as stone and iron hand tools. The mound occupied part of a farm owned by Posey Saunooke, who was about fifty-five years old when the excavation occurred and a member of the tribal council. He seems to have been a son of Chief Stillwell Saunooke. Mann Valentine noted that the current owner was "highly respected and near of intelligence [and] has some white blood in him."[32] Unlike writers Davis and Zeigler and Grosscup, Valentine harbored some prejudice against the Cherokees.

The Valentine sons, not their father, were clearly in charge of the Bird Town Mound excavation, which was located 300 yards from the Oconaluftee River's north bank on the farm of Jim Keg, a Cherokee, and adjacent to today's Aquoni Road.[33] The sons' supervisory role can be inferred from several letters sent by the brothers to their father. On July 18, 1883, Edward described the beginning of its excavation:

> Dear father We have just started on the Birdtown mound having procured the assistance of 6 Indians. It will make the most complete job of this that we have ever made. The mound is 100 ft. × 93 ft and about 7 ft

> high. Nothing found yet as we are making a circular trench around it. We are well and getting along as fast as could be expected among such slow people. We took a photograph this morning of the Indians & will take others during the progress of the work. Bob Hyatt will [illegible] carry us through the western counties. We did not get horses as we expected since we were able to get a buggy [illegible] and good [illegible] for 75 cts per day.[34]

In this mound the brothers found pottery, a clay pipe, and three graves. As word spread that the Valentines were purchasing relics, local artisans made a number of fakes to sell to them. Embarrassment from being taken in by this scheme eventually caused the family to decamp and return to Richmond.[35] The artifacts remain in The Valentine Museum today.

The next individual who arrived to investigate the Cherokees, James Mooney, took a far more serious and sensitive interest in the Eastern Band and created a legacy that has become the foundation of the United States' understanding of the history and culture of the Cherokees. Mooney had had a childhood interest in Native Americans. Through personal determination as well as considerable independent research, in a key first meeting he impressed John Wesley Powell, the founder of the Bureau of Ethnology, a part of the Smithsonian Institution. At that time Mooney lacked two important criteria for professional anthropologists: gentleman status and formal anthropological education, but the favorable impression he made at his meeting with Powell gave him a path toward acquiring these. In 1885, Mooney, at age twenty-four, joined the bureau as a volunteer and began working on a comprehensive list of tribal names and synonyms to determine how many tribes existed and where they lived. That first summer he was called to sit in on interviews of Native Americans who were visiting Washington. Led by a professional bureau ethnologist, the interviewers inquired about each tribe's culture. One of these visitors was Chief Nimrod J. Smith, who was in the capital lobbying on behalf of the Eastern Cherokees.[36]

Mooney's interest in the Cherokees began with the vocabulary and grammar of their language. When additional meetings with Smith took place the following year, he broadened his focus to mythology and material culture, and by this time Mooney was himself an official staff ethnologist for the bureau. Because Mooney was assigned to work on a linguistic study of Iroquoian languages, of which Cherokee was part, he gained permission from Powell to conduct three summers of field research in North Carolina beginning in 1887. After each season of fieldwork, Mooney returned to the bureau to organize the material he had collected and write about his experiences and about the Eastern Band's storehouse of traditional knowledge.[37]

In his first published work about the tribe, *Sacred Formulas of the Cherokee*, Mooney described how he got to know shamans of the Eastern Band and persuaded them to share their knowledge. He began this process by collecting plants with the help of hired Cherokee assistants. When these people hesitated to explain the incantations that accompanied the use of herbal remedies, Mooney turned to making the acquaintance of elders and tribal shamans who had the authority to decide whether and what they should share with the white government ethnologist via the help of hired Cherokee interpreters. Altogether, Mooney met with at least six shamans, and included almost 600 formulas from them in his book.[38] They comprised a cadre of full-blood tribal members who held positions of respect in the tribe. In some cases they were ill or deceased and their pages of cures, charms, and spells were prized by their children as family heirlooms. Ultimately, the descendants and living shamans gave him manuscripts containing medical treatments based on the use of native plants and spoken formulas, as well as a vast array of information about Cherokee beliefs and religion, mythology and history, cultural ceremonies, games, and dances.[39]

The first shaman to become an informant for Mooney was Ayunini, or Swimmer, a man who had served with Colonel Thomas in the Civil War. Mooney enticed Ayunini to tell him Cherokee stories but could not get him to sing the accompanying songs because Ayunini had paying customers for these. For example, the performance of a song could bring as much as five dollars from an eager hunter who would need this aid to kill bear or deer. Further, Ayunini was reluctant to share because he did not want to risk his reputation among other shamans. But Mooney suggested that Ayunini was wrong to hold back when Mooney was also paying for information, and the ethnologist explained that he could easily seek the same information from others. Mooney also reassured Ayunini that his goal was only to preserve the songs and the knowledge of the Cherokees once the old shamans had died. These appeals to the shaman's "professional pride" were effective.[40] A few days later, Ayunini brought Mooney

> a small day-book of about 240 pages . . . about half-filled with writing in Cherokee characters. Here were prayers, songs, and prescriptions for the cure of all kinds of diseases—for chills, rheumatism, frostbites, wounds, bad dreams, and witchery; love charms, to gain the affections of a woman or to cause her to hate a detested rival; fishing charms,

> hunting charms—including the songs without which none could ever know how to kill any game; prayers to make the corn grow, to frighten away storms, and to drive off witches; prayers for long life, for safety among strangers, for acquiring influence in council and success in the ball play. There were prayers to the Long Man, the Ancient White, the Great Whirlwind, the Yellow Rattlesnake, and to a hundred other gods of the Cherokee pantheon. It was in fact an Indian ritual and pharmacopoeia.[41]

Certainly, by today's standards, Mooney's coercive tactics seem unethical, though no doubt many are grateful that he succeeded in preserving and publishing these key documents of Cherokee culture. Mooney also persuaded the heirs of deceased shamans to sell (for extremely modest prices) their fathers' original documents, often providing the means for copies of the formulas to be made by the heirs or by a Cherokee translator. Such was the case of Gatigwanasti, whose manuscript was held by his son Wilnoti after the father's death. At first, Wilnoti was reluctant to give the crumbling pages to Mooney because of their sentimental value and because he did not want them ever to fall into the hands of rival shaman Ayunini. After considering the matter for a year, Wilnoti eventually was persuaded to sell the manuscript when Mooney returned in 1888. Mooney offered an explanation to him and others that had then become satisfying enough:

> By the time the Indians had had several months to talk over the matter and the idea had gradually dawned upon them that instead of taking their knowledge away from them and locking it up in a box, the intention was to preserve it to the world and pay them for it at the same time. In addition the writer took every opportunity to impress upon them the fact that he was acquainted with the secret knowledge of other tribes and perhaps could give them as much as they gave.[42]

So in time Mooney won over a number of elders who made much traditional Cherokee lore and culture available to him and, eventually, to the public. The original manuscripts were transported to the bureau and stored there for use by the government and scholars. These informed several publications: Mooney's *Myths of the Cherokee*, published in 1900, which included a history of the tribe (James Terrell and Will Thomas were interviewed); *The Swimmer Manuscript: Cherokee Sacred Formulas and Medicinal Prescriptions*, begun by Mooney and completed by Frans M. Olbrechts and published in 1932; and a record of the council of Wolf Town by Inoli, which was later published by Anna Gritts Kilpatrick and Jack Frederick Kilpatrick and which provided glimpses into the civic traditions of the Cherokees before the Civil War.[43]

Mooney's work with the Cherokees also helped to develop community leaders. His two primary assistants, James Blythe and Will West Long (Wili Westi), both became important individuals in the Eastern Band. Blythe became the first federal Cherokee agent who was actually a Cherokee, and Long became a leading scholar on the Cherokees and a learned and generous informant and collaborator for future ethnological studies of the Cherokees authored by Mooney and his subsequent coauthor Olbrechts and by Frank Speck and Leonard Broom for their work on *Cherokee Dance and Drama*.[44]

While in North Carolina, Mooney observed the Cherokees' living conditions and was concerned for their health. He noticed that

> the door of the Cherokee log cabin is always open, excepting at night and on the coldest days in winter, while the Indian is seldom in the house during his waking hours unless necessity compels him. As most of their cabins are still built in the old Indian style, without windows, the open door furnishes the only means by which light is admitted to the interior, although when closed the fire on the hearth helps to make amends for the deficiency. On the other hand, no precautions are taken to guard against cold, dampness, or sudden draft. During the greater part of the year whole families sleep outside upon the ground, rolled up in an old blanket. The Cherokee is careless of exposure and utterly indifferent to the simplest rules of hygiene.[45]

Mooney largely dismissed Cherokee medical practice as an ineffective "empiric development of the fetich idea."[46] But he also noted that much Western medicine was based on "the same idea of correspondences," such as the notion of the hair of the dog curing its bite. Mooney realized that the Eastern Cherokees were suffering from tuberculosis and trachoma, leading to a high death rate and resulting in population declines. He notified authorities at the Office of Indian Affairs of the alarming conditions. In response, a team was sent to Qualla to instruct Cherokees on strategies of preventive medicine. The Cherokee diet was simple: cornmeal dumplings, bean bread, chestnut bread, hominy, and gruel, as well as fish and meats from local wildlife such as squirrel and turkey. Sweeping dietary restrictions applied to sick or ill individuals because of "connections with the disease spirit." So someone who had rheumatism would not eat the leg meat of any animal because the disease resides in limbs. Also, lye, salt, and hot foods were always denied to those with an illness.[47]

During his second season, Mooney brought a camera and took several iconic photographs of the Cherokees of the era, including images of Ayunini and other informants such as Catawba-Killer; John Ax, who described the construction of a mound to Mooney; his wife, Annie Ax; a Cherokee woman named Walini; and Ayâsta, who was Will West Long's mother. She was knowledgeable about native plants as well as the formulas of her deceased first husband, Gahuni. Mooney's few photos of the Wolf Town ball players, scenes from the ball play, Cherokee houses, and landscapes also capture the details of Qualla at the end of the century.[48] Throughout his time in North Carolina, Mooney purchased Cherokee artifacts and crafts and gathered medicinal plant specimens, which he then took back to the Smithsonian.[49] Together these comprise an important visual and material record of key individuals and community life. Through insights shared by Ayunini, Mooney also gained information on the purposes and uses of the earthen Indian mounds both in Qualla and throughout the Southeast. Ayunini explained that the mounds were the sites of town council houses and the locus of the sacred fire for each town. These served as ceremonial sources for all fires throughout villages and also played a role for community events such as ball games and annual ceremonies like the green corn dance.[50]

No doubt, Mooney's sincerity and perseverance impressed the Cherokees he met. He learned to speak and read the language, an effort that required considerable time and study. He devoted months to fieldwork and observation of the Cherokees in many social and interpersonal settings. He exhibited an interest in and respect for individuals. And he did the same for cultural traditions that many whites felt should be discouraged, such as the Cherokee ball play, because they preserved beliefs and traditions that were neither white nor Christian. Mooney accorded the Cherokees respect as people living their lives, rather than mere objects of study, and if Mooney did not personally agree with cultural practices, he did not question their relevance and value to the Cherokees, as can be seen in his lengthy preface to the *Sacred Formulas*, where he framed traditions as a religion with purposes not entirely different from those of Christianity:

> The Indian is essentially religious and contemplative, and it might almost be said that every act of his life is regulated and determined by his religious belief. It matters not that some may call this superstition. The difference is only relative. The religion of to-day has developed from

> the cruder superstitions of yesterday, and Christianity itself is but an outgrowth and enlargement of the beliefs and ceremonies which have been preserved by the Indian in their more ancient form. When we are willing to admit that the Indian has a religion which he holds sacred, even though it be different from our own, we can then admire the consistency of the theory, the particularity of the ceremonial and the beauty of the expression. So far from being a jumble of crudities, there is a wonderful completeness about the whole system which is not surpassed even by the ceremonial religions of the East. It is evident from a study of these formulas that the Cherokee Indian was a polytheist and that the spirit world was to him only a shadowy counterpart of this. All his prayers were for temporal and tangible blessings—for health, for long life, for success in the chase, in fishing, in war and in love, for good corps, for protection and for revenge. He had no Great Spirit, no happy hunting ground, no heaven, no hell, and consequently death had for him no terrors and he awaited the inevitable end with no anxiety as to the future. He was careful not to violate the rights of his tribesman or to do injury to his feelings, but there is nothing to show that he had any idea whatever of what is called morality in the abstract.[51]

Though his career led him to focus on the Indians of the Great Plains after 1900, Mooney had become, among anthropologists, the leading authority on the Cherokees at the time of his death in 1921.[52] His scholarship and that of his protégés provided indispensable sources about the Eastern Band and all Cherokees late in the nineteenth century. Mooney arrived just in time. The living shamans were old and the manuscripts of the deceased ones were at risk of becoming lost. Ayunini died in 1899, but he was the longest-surviving informant. Gatigwanasti, whose manuscripts Mooney described as "the most valuable of the whole," had already died by Mooney's first summer, and his papers were acquired through his son.[53] The work of a third shaman, Gahuni, came from his widow; the shaman had died thirty years before. Inoli died in 1885, two years before Mooney arrived, and his surviving daughter decided to share her extensive set of documents. Tsiskwa (Bird) was sick during Money's second season of fieldwork and could only be interviewed indirectly because of the taboo against meeting strangers or allowing them to enter a sick individual's home.[54] It cannot be known what would have become of all these manuscripts and the lore they contained without Mooney; surely some if not all would have survived for the Cherokees, if not for the larger society. But just as surely, Mooney's first fieldwork project, conducted while he was still in his twenties, was highly consequential. Like the partnership of Yonaguska and Will Thomas, the connections between the Cherokee shamans and Mooney seem serendipitous in retrospect, like chance encounters that preserved a culture.

THE CATHCART TIMBER DEAL BRINGS LOGGING INTO THE VALLEY

In the last decade of the century, the Cherokees of Qualla Boundary, now the Eastern Band, continued to face persistent and deeply intertwined issues about their legal status, their leadership, and their land. Despite previous court rulings, the Cherokees' autonomy, North Carolina citizenship, and status as wards of the federal government remained in question. Any issue that arose was an occasion to rehash this complex matter. It was not clear who had the authority to make decisions, and when the Cherokees attempted to act autonomously, they were met with federal and state obstacles, obstacles erected from authorities who dealt with them inconsistently and were themselves inconstant in their attention. These governance problems might not have been so critical, except that the Cherokees faced immediate threats to their land, which they had worked for years to consolidate and call their own. They also faced social issues of providing education and preventive health care to their members, but though these issues were significant, they were overshadowed by the land disputes. Altogether, a context of vulnerability existed, and it arrested progress for the EBCI.

After Nimrod Smith failed in his reelection bid, Stillwell Saunooke replaced him as principal chief. The new chief, agent Blythe, and the tribal council decided to take immediate action to respond to land issues, particularly to Cherokee land being sold at auction for nonpayment of taxes. The problem was money. It was aggravated by squatters. Agent Blythe investigated land violations and shockingly reported that fifty-six white families occupied and farmed "6,000 acres, most of it good land," within the Qualla Boundary.[55] Considering that only 20,000 acres of the 65,000 in the boundary were arable or tillable, the squatters occupied about 30 percent of land suitable for farming. Because much of Qualla was communally held and on steep terrain, because squatters still occupied significant plots and logged illegally from them, and because tribal revenue was limited to federal funds that could be used only for education, there was no way to keep up with annual property

Ayunini (Swimmer) with family members in front of their cabin.

COURTESY OF NATIONAL ANTHROPOLOGICAL ARCHIVES, SMITHSONIAN INSTITUTION, INV.06212100.

taxes. What the Cherokees did have was timber, vast acres of desirable mature hardwood. So without consulting the Office of Indian Affairs, the chief and council decided to offer the timber of the Cathcart Tract for sale.

The Cathcart Tract comprised 33,000 acres within a rectangular boundary and included the watersheds of Soco Creek and the Oconaluftee River. The name comes from William Cathcart, who had been deeded the land at the end of the eighteenth century. A century later, of course, many individuals, both Cherokee and white, had bought land and settled parts of this tract. Ephraim and Sophia Mingus's old farm in Big Cove, later that of Clarinda Conner and Aseph Enloe, lay within the Cathcart Tract as well as a good portion of the Qualla Boundary, including Ravensford and Wolf Town. Even so, many acres were not owned by individuals and were also not under cultivation. They remained untouched hardwood forest owned communally by the Cherokees. These were the areas from which the Cherokees sought to sell timber.[56] But

James Mooney.

COURTESY OF NATIONAL ANTHROPOLOGICAL ARCHIVES, SMITHSONIAN INSTITUTION, INV.02862900.

when the Indian Office said that only enough to pay back taxes could be cut, the deal became the object of federal lawsuits about the Department of Interior's standing to control the Eastern Band's actions.

At about the same time, the commissioner of Indian Affairs, Thomas J. Morgan, decided to end its long-standing practice of contracting with religious denominations for the management of Indian schools. The Quakers had done an excellent job of establishing schools in the Qualla Boundary over the last decade, but they dropped out when the scandal with Nimrod Smith arose. Their superintendent, Henry Spray, was dismissed because he was viewed as a troublemaker who might lead the Cherokees astray and, worse, encourage them to vote for Republicans. So Commissioner Morgan appointed a government employee from New York as the superintendent and simultaneously abolished the office of the federal agent to the Cherokees in Qualla. That was the position held by James Blythe, who was a student of Spray's and an interpreter for Mooney. The new superintendent, Andrew Spencer, was paid an additional stipend to manage all the issues that had previously been the purview of the agent. In one action, then, Morgan fired Spray and his protégé Blythe, who was the first Cherokee to hold the office of federal agent. This was quite a blow to the tribe's autonomy and leadership. Spencer was the first of three federally appointed superintendents who worked to maintain something close to the quality of the Quakers' program. They began sending promising older students to out-of-state Indian boarding schools such as the Carlisle Indian Industrial School in Pennsylvania, Hampton Institute in Virginia, and Haskell Institute in Kansas, a strategy that was not successful in terms of completed degrees or apparent benefits to the community.[57]

When the federally sponsored tribal attorney George Smathers learned of the loss of land from tax arrears along with the proposed timber sale, he intervened for the tribe with the Office of Indian Affairs and managed to gain approval for the sale from President Benjamin Harrison in early 1892. The approval came with conditions that caused trouble down the road. Nonetheless, in preparation for the sale, in the spring of that year, P. W. Mitchell and M. C. Felmet appraised the timber along with the help of several Cherokee axe men to mark the trees. One of these Cherokees was David Blythe, James's younger brother.[58] In addition to the timber appraisal, T. C. Bowen, a civil engineer and surveyor, resurveyed several remote parts of the Qualla Boundary to correct mistakes in the acreage held by the tribe that were presumed to overstate the size and result in higher taxes than were justified. Bowen's survey led to a new tax assessment of Jackson County land and saved 30 percent for the Cherokees.[59]

The appraisers' report provided attractive details on the quantity and quality of desirable trees within the Cathcart Tract. It included estimates for poplar, oak, chestnut, and birch along Soco Creek and its tributaries as well as along the Oconaluftee that totaled more than 10 million feet of timber trees. Along Soco Creek and its tributaries, the appraisers measured a portion of the timber and estimated the rest. They noted that "the above lots of timber are all accessible and easy to handle, and is the finest lot of hard-wood timber that we have ever seen." Because of time and budget constraints, they provided an "approximated estimate of timber on Ocona Lufty River and its tributaries," whose 5 million feet of accessible timber was about half poplar, with the balance in chestnut and oak, some maple and ash, and less walnut.

The distance Oconaluftee timber would have to travel was a bit farther to the nearest railroad station at Whittier, between eight to seventeen miles away. In addition, two to four times more timber was available from Oconaluftee, but it was "hard of access" and included "hemlock, white pine, different species of oak, and considerable cherry."[60]

When the timber was first advertised in June 1892, no bids were made, probably because the president had said that the cutting would have to be limited to what was necessary for the Cherokees to pay back taxes, and that condition dampened the enthusiasm of lumber outfits that wanted to maximize profits. Once the limit was removed, the first bidder was a W. C. Smith from New York City, who contracted to log the timber for $15,000. Perhaps he was merely a speculator who planned to resell the contract. As an army captain who visited the Qualla Boundary in 1893 observed, this offer amounted to less than 50 cents an acre over fifteen years of cutting for timber that he felt was "worth many times the price to be paid."[61] Clearly, the federal government had reason to be concerned about the Cherokees being swindled. Smith abandoned the deal and was replaced by David L. Boyd of Newport, Tennessee, though the contract between him and the Eastern Band had been signed while the Smith contract was still pending. The Boyd contract, signed in 1893, recognized that the Department of Interior would have to authorize it, which could take time. The price and time period were the same as in Smith's offer.[62]

During the same years, the tribe continued to resolve the longstanding title disputes and squatter problems. Aided by the legal assistance of Smathers, in early 1894, the Cherokees reached an agreement with "several white tenants and claimants within the boundary." These people would "vacate" for $24,552, collectively.[63] Further, the Cherokees could purchase land held by the descendants of James Love that had long been in dispute. Love had been a prominent citizen of western North Carolina and a business partner and relative by marriage of Will Thomas. He owned 33,000 acres adjacent to the boundary on the northeast side, but confusion about it had existed for years because it had once been mistakenly surveyed as part of the Qualla Boundary. According to the agreement, this land could be purchased for $1.25 per acre. Congress appropriated the necessary funds in August and the agreement went through.[64]

The Cherokees' mixed status as North Carolina citizens and wards of the federal government became the heart of the legal battle surrounding the timber sale. Multiple court rulings and appeals ensued, ending in 1897 with a decision by the Fourth Circuit Court of Appeals in Richmond, which said that, in fact, the Eastern Cherokees were not North Carolina citizens but a tribe under the supervision of the federal government. An appeal of this decision to the Supreme Court was dropped when the Department of Interior accepted Boyd's contract. By then, Boyd had sold the contract to Harry M. Dickson and William T. Mason for $25,000. But it was Boyd's $15,000 plus a little interest that the Eastern Band received. Logging was now allowed to commence legally, though cutting may have already begun unofficially. Following Boyd's contract, Dickson and Mason had until September 28, 1908, to log the designated parts of the tract, leaving intact any trees on cultivated land or farms. But they continued past this deadline, and the Eastern Band brought suit in November 1908 to stop the logging, claiming that 4 to 5 million feet of lumber at a value of $10,000 had been removed from the tract after the deadline. The issue eventually went to the U.S. circuit court in the western district of North Carolina for a hearing in September 1909. At this hearing, the judge decided that denying Dickson and Mason the right to remove all the lumber they had already cut amounted to a forfeiture of the original contract, and because "forfeitures are not favored by the law," the defendants had the right to remove fallen timber for "a reasonable amount of time."[65] No additional trees were to be cut. A twenty-first-century reader of the transcript is forced to wonder whether the basis of the decision might have been sheer favoritism for white interests. The judge acknowledged the details of the contract, which the defendants did not observe, but decided in their favor even though the logging period had ended. One consolation to the Cherokees was that by the time this suit was decided, the Eastern Band had already sold land, not just timber, to another company that would log the Straight Fork and Raven Fork areas for the next decade.[66]

On the plus side, the Cherokees needed the proceeds, modest as they were, from the timber sale, but the Eastern Band's return to a murky legal status had to be discouraging. With their citizenship under question, their voting privileges were subsequently challenged and then denied in 1900, even though the Eastern Band functioned under a corporate state charter, paid state taxes, and followed state laws. By the way, their voting rights were not restored by federal law until 1930 and not allowed in practice until 1945, when Cherokee veterans returning from World War II forced county registrars to permit actual voting. More ominously, in the first decade of the twentieth century, the federal government began to consider whether the Eastern Band's land should be allotted, in keeping with the Dawes Severalty Act of 1887, a process underway in the Cherokee Nation and other tribes. But because the Qualla Boundary was owned jointly under a tribal corporation, allotment ultimately did not go forward.[67] The prospect of allotment being carried out caused unease and internal division during the roughly forty years that it was national policy. The process necessitated a new EBCI roll to determine who would be eligible to receive land and enjoy such other rights and benefits as voting in Cherokee elections and attending Cherokee schools. Predictably, this roll, known as the Baker Roll, included many more people than previous rolls, and the tribal council challenged it to exclude those whose connections seemed thin.[68]

In any case, once commercial logging began, the Oconaluftee Valley was forever changed. Roads were improved; access to markets and education improved, too, though slowly. Moreover, the scale of humans' impact on the land was now apparent, impossible to miss. The Cherokees' timber sale ushered in a new era of industrialization that would transform homesteads into logging towns and sites, increasing population and heightening the dangers of fire, erosion, land degradation, and logging accidents. It was the beginning of a new era for all of Oconaluftee's residents.

A few more events marked the last decade of the nineteenth century in Qualla. In 1893, both Will Thomas and Nimrod Smith died, ending their many years of oversight and influence. Three years later, an influenza epidemic—called grippe in those days—struck the Cherokees and resulted in the death of over 150 individuals, nearly 10 percent of the tribe.[69] Perhaps they suffered so badly because, as Mooney and traveler Virginia Young both noticed, the Cherokees were prone to consumption and of small stature.[70] By the end of the century, more Cherokees could read and write English, though still only a minority, and, paradoxically, the Cherokee ball games had become more common as expressions of traditional culture.

What is most striking, however, about accounts of the Eastern Band written by white travelers, journalists, and government officials toward the end of the century is that they said that the homes, farms, food, and well-being of the Cherokees were very similar to, if not a bit better than, those of their white neighbors. A travelogue written by Young in 1894 noted that Indian "huts" were "nothing different from the homes of poor white people. There was even the usual tangle of sunflowers, zinnias, dahlias and morning glories . . . [as well as] extensive apple orchards" with sweet, flavorful fruit from overwintering.[71] The U.S. census special agent Thomas Donaldson similarly noted that "wages are very low in the mountains of North Carolina, but the cost of living is small, and the Cherokees earn as much and live as well as the white people about them."[72] Also, Cherokee hospitality seems identical to that

Nancy George Bradley works on a basket in front of her home, 1940.
Note the child in the window.

GREAT SMOKY MOUNTAINS NATIONAL PARK ARCHIVES, TOWNSEND, TENN.

Cherokee man plowing a field with his oxen, 1936.

GREAT SMOKY MOUNTAINS NATIONAL PARK ARCHIVES, TOWNSEND, TENN.

offered by white mountain families such as the Enloes and the Minguses. When Donaldson visited Chitolski, "a Cherokee of means and influence," at his farm in Big Cove, the experience mirrors ones recorded about white Oconaluftee farmers:

> His home is a new and spacious block house, very comfortable, with the usual piazza in front. Upon accepting an invitation to dine, the water was turned upon the wheel of the mill close by, and fresh meal was soon served in the shape of a hot "corndodger." "Long sweetening" of honey or molasses gave a peculiar sanction to a cup of good coffee, and this, with bacon and greens, supplemented with peaches grown on the farm, made a most excellent meal. . . . Chitolski's house is said to be one of the best in the country, and very few houses of the white people upon Indian lands or lands adjacent approach it in comfort.[73]

Additional cordial visits took place at the farms of Big Witch, a 105-year-old man; councilman Wesley Crow; Vice Principal Chief John Going Welch; and the Reverend John Bird. The agent's report included detailed descriptions of such public buildings as schools, meetinghouses, and churches (often used interchangeably), as well as fences, farms, and roads. These were evaluated as just as good as and sometimes better than those in neighboring white settlements. Roads and bridges were challenging everywhere:

> All roads which border the numerous creeks are subject to rapid overflow in the rainy season or after heavy summer showers, and the streams become impassable. Simple bridges of hewn logs, often of great size, and guarded by hand rails, supply pedestrians the means of communication between the various settlements until the waters subside. In deep cuts, or where the Ocona Lufta river is thus crossed, substantial trestles or supports have been erected on each shore and in the stream, as no single tree would span the distance. Numerous short cuts or foot trails wind among the mountains and over very steep divides. . . . Wagon trails for hauling timber to single cabins or hamlets are not infrequent.[74]

Like white residents, most Cherokees were farmers and "domestic and industrious" in their efforts. A few worked as skilled tradesmen as blacksmiths, cobblers, and harness makers, wagon makers, and carpenters. The traditional crafts of basket making and pottery were practiced widely but not yet commercially.[75] The human and natural resources for commercial development were in place. With the turn of the century, the Eastern Band would face external challenges, particularly in defending its communal land against allotment. But its tribal council provided a new measure of self-determination that would help it develop ways of sustaining itself economically and defending itself from outside interests. Most of all, the identity of the Lufty Cherokees had been solidified into the Eastern Band.

Chapter 12

FROM BIRDSONG TO TRAIN WHISTLE

THE INDUSTRIAL AGE REACHES THE MOUNTAINS

▲ ▲ ▲

One lazy July evening, the specter of the Industrial Age emerges from the cement bridge at the Smokemont Loop trailhead in Smokemont Campground. Closed to auto traffic, with a gate and multiple road signs, the sixty-foot span shows how close the area was to development. In fact, the area was not close to development; it was developed! Once the site was the middle of a logging town. Today, the bridge is a quaint reminder of that era and a suggestion of the city that Smokemont likely would have become had the national park not been established. This was a bridge built for heavy vehicles, not just the occasional automobile, certainly not for hikers. Swain County invested in its construction expecting many years of use.

Happily, today it is for foot traffic only. I've seen it overgrown with saplings, wildflowers, and all manner of plants. Tire wear suggests that it is occasionally used by park service vehicles, but not very often. For the most part it provides a safe crossing over Bradley Fork and leads to a path along a former logging road—an easy after-supper stroll for campers. Second-growth trees abound on the banks and all around. Looking over the parapet midway across, I see wild turkeys poking along the creek side. They are oblivious to me and other humans. On my return, I notice the relief installed in the left-hand abutment by the bridge's makers: "Designed and built by Luten Bridge Co, Knoxville, Tenn. 1921." Says a lot.

▲▲▲

THE TURN OF THE CENTURY brought sweeping changes to Oconaluftee Valley, changes that would transform both the land and the community. The causes of change—logging and railroads—had been approaching for a couple of decades. Locals already understood that the timber on and surrounding their land was valuable. They had used the trees around them for years to build their homes, barns, fences, wagons, plows, and furniture. During their off-seasons, farmers had long practiced selective logging, taking the more valuable large cherry, ash, and black walnut trees and selling them to nearby western North Carolina mills. They could snake out single trees with a team of horses or oxen, cut them at one of the local mills, and then haul them out by wagon on the Oconalufty Turnpike.[1]

A sawmill had stood at the mouth of Mingus Creek since the 1870s, when the Mingus family constructed it to produce lumber for their new home and grist mill after the Civil War. Another sawmill was in place on Tow String by the 1880s. It was operated by Will Johnson. Bert Crisp, a Mingus Creek farmer and logger, claimed that the mill on Mingus Creek was owned by Thad Watson and was a circular saw. But a more common type of small sawmill was a sash sawmill, which used water power to move a vertical blade held within a frame—kind of like a window sash—through logs. The Tow String mill was a sash mill. In time, these mills brought frame houses and clapboard to the valley, replacing some log homes as siding became the more desirable and upscale building material. Dock Conner's family built a frame house in 1910 or 1912 on the Collins homestead and tore down the log cabin built by early Smokies guide Robert Collins, for instance. Many of the homes along Mingus Creek and its tributaries were frame houses.[2]

Residents also removed bark from chestnut oak and hemlock trees, which was called "acidwood," and sold it to tanneries.[3] Will Thomas had run a leather tannery in Qualla since before the Civil War, and by 1911, five large tanneries operated west of the Blue Ridge.[4] Forest products had long been a source of income just like ginseng, chestnuts, and animal skins. This low-volume logging had little impact on the wildlife or land, rarely causing fire, erosion, or damage to streams or woods.

SHAPE-SHIFTING LUMBER COMPANIES

Large-scale logging came to the southern Appalachians after companies exhausted the northern forests. It approached Oconaluftee from two directions.

The Big Creek area of the Smokies to the north hosted commercial logging operations as early as the 1880s, and the Cherokees introduced outside logging speculators and companies to the watershed with the lease of the timber on the Cathcart Tract in 1893. As already mentioned, the Cathcart Tract encompassed 33,000 acres in the Big Cove, Wolf Town, and Raven Fork parts of the valley as well as adjacent Soco Creek. At least one of the parties of that agreement, David L. Boyd, was from Newport, Tennessee, and likely had also been active in Big Creek. The Cherokees struck agreements with other speculators as well early in the twentieth century. Charles D. Fuller, a manufacturer from Kalamazoo, Michigan, contracted to buy the timber and minerals from a large swath of land above the Cathcart Tract boundary and west to Hughes Ridge, yet still owned by the Cherokees, in 1903. When Fuller did not come through on his part of the deal, a quit claim was executed in 1909.[5]

As commercial operations got underway, the railroad simultaneously neared the valley. Rail transport was essential to moving cut lumber to markets or mills in the quantities needed to make the enterprise profitable. As early as the mid-1880s, G. V. Litchfield and Company had constructed a lumber mill at Waynesville along the Western North Carolina Railroad line. It contracted with suppliers for more than 4 million board feet of walnut as well as large quantities of cherry and oak.[6] The Western North Carolina Railroad had been constructing a line between Asheville and Murphy since right after the end of the Civil War. It reached Dillsboro in 1883 and Bryson City the next year. By 1891, the line between Asheville and Murphy was complete, and soon it merged with other lines to become the Southern Railway Company. Once the railroad neared the Smokies, shorter rail lines owned by logging companies were able to connect with the Southern line and transport felled trees to larger mills outside Oconaluftee Valley.[7] In a key U.S. Forest Service Report on the southern Appalachian region in 1902, the authors noted that in the "largest unbroken forest areas" on the Oconaluftee, Cheoah, and Tuckasegee Rivers, "the best timber has been much culled for 20 miles from the Southern Railway, which crosses the middle of the basin."[8] So before the big logging companies even arrived on the scene in Oconaluftee, the most desirable and accessible hardwood had been taken.

As commercial logging ramped up, two main centers of operation in Oconaluftee emerged. One was the logging town of Ravensford, located on bottomland long owned by Wesley Enloe but sold after his death in 1903; this land was east of the Raven Fork tributary of the Oconaluftee River, very near the Cherokee towns of Yellow Hill and Paint Town.[9] A succession of companies located here and focused on logging up and along the Raven Fork and Straight Fork tributaries. The other logging hub encompassed the more westerly tributaries of Oconaluftee, such as Bradley Fork, Kephart Prong, Beech Flats Prong, and Collins Creek. These led downslope and downstream to Bradleytown, which became the logging town of Smokemont. Though today Ravensford is part of the Qualla Boundary, home of the Eastern Band of Cherokee Indians, at the time it was a neighboring lumber town, just across the river from Floyd Bottoms, as then the Enloe farm was known, and a couple of miles south of Smokemont. Ravensford was as much a part of the valley during the logging era as Mingus Mill. These two areas were distinct, though the individuals and companies that owned land and operated logging concerns organized into new businesses multiple times over the years. They did business separately and then together amid constantly changing company names and agreements. They opportunistically expanded, contracted, developed subsidiaries, declared bankruptcy, and reorganized into new entities in order to continue seeking a profit from the amazing timber resource of the southern Appalachians. Ultimately, the Ravensford Lumber Company and the Champion Fibre Company remained in business when the land was condemned and bought for the national park. Nonetheless, tracing the chain of company ownership and logging in the valley illustrates how the logging boom and bust from 1900 to the mid-1920s transformed the land and its small, interconnected community.

Along the western tributaries of the Oconaluftee (leading to Smokemont), Three M Lumber Company, a Wisconsin corporation, cut the hardwoods from the Beech Flats area during the early 1900s, and perhaps from Collins Creek a bit later. The Beech Flats logging included 7,000 acres up to 3,500 feet along the riversides, taking hardwoods over 16 inches in diameter. Three M built a tramroad to haul out lumber and had a mill "at the Pole Bridge" across Beech Flats. The lumber was then hauled to Whittier on wagons pulled by mules. Later, the mill was moved down to Smokemont and the logs were run down on tramcars. A tramroad was like a railroad made of lumber; its tramcars ran on interlocking log rails, and these were propelled by a team of horses or, going downhill, sometimes gravity and a brakeman.[10] In June 1906, Three M sold its Oconaluftee holdings to William S. Harvey, who was a trustee for the Southern Spruce Company, a New Jersey corporation. Harvey subsequently conveyed the acreage to Southern Spruce, which focused on cutting pulpwood. Pulpwood meant spruce, hemlock, and chestnut—high-acid woods suitable for making paper products. Another company operating in the area was the Harris-Woodbury Lumber Company of West Virginia. It bought and leased land in the upper reaches of the Oconaluftee along

Bradley Creek and to the west along Forney and Deep Creeks. It focused on cutting hardwood for saw timber.[11]

At roughly the same time, the lease on the Cathcart Tract, Cherokee land held by Harry M. Dickson and William T. Mason (who had bought it from David Boyd), was nearing its end. As mentioned, the cutting deadline was September 28, 1908, but the company continued to remove lumber until the end of 1909, when it was eventually forced to stop by a lawsuit brought by the Eastern Band of the Cherokee.[12] Attempting to improve the profit that the Cherokees were getting from their key natural resource, the Eastern Band sold the 33,000 acres above the Cathcart Tract that had been previously optioned by Charles Fuller to lumber speculator John C. Arbogast and Associates for $245,000 in 1906. Once again, speculators gained more than the Cherokees because in 1909 Arbogast sold the tract along Raven and Straight Forks to William Whitmer and Sons of Philadelphia for $630,000. Arbogast would continue to work for the new owner as a timber inspector and estimator.[13] Part of the deal was that the buyers would build a railway along a route following the Oconaluftee River to connect the Cherokee training school in Cherokee with the Southern Railway at Ela, North Carolina, which was done by 1908. The company became the Appalachian Railway, and it extended the line farther than the school to the logging town of Ravensford by 1912.[14]

Often, after a logging company or speculator had purchased timber rights or land, cutting was delayed until prices—either for lumber products or for the timber or timber rights—increased.[15] By the time sizable operations got underway there in 1918, Whitmer and Sons had deeded the Ravensford land to Parsons Pulp and Lumber Company of West Virginia. After a bankruptcy, this company eventually reorganized in 1923 as Whitmer-Parsons Pulp and Lumber Company. These changing names reveal several key points: the companies often were not profitable, the owners were interested in both pulp and hardwoods, and corporate reorganization allowed the same people to continue business with new investors.[16] Four years later, the name changed a final time to Ravensford Lumber Company, which soon ceased operations and was bought out by the state for the national park.

An important expansion of the lumber industry throughout western North Carolina but also in the Oconaluftee Valley came with the establishment in 1905 of Champion Fibre Company in Canton, North Carolina. It was a subsidiary of an established Ohio paper company and was led by Peter G. Thompson and directed by his son-in-law Reuben B. Roberson, who lived in Canton. It bought 300,000 acres in and around Canton and built a pulp mill there, which opened in 1908. Champion Fibre's business was to cut and buy pulpwood that was not desirable as saw timber but was suitable for paper and cardboard manufacturing. It was an ideal second-wave logging concern once the hardwoods were gone or of limited size. At first, in the Smokies, Champion Fibre did not engage in cutting but purchased pulp wood from other outfits for processing. Toward this end, in 1911, Thompson expanded the company's operations. Along with major partners William Whitmer and Sons—who were then operating at Ravensford—Thompson formed Champion Logging Company. The company purchased 100,000 more acres and expanded its operations into saw timber logging throughout the northwestern parts of the Smokies in both North Carolina and Tennessee. It also agreed to provide Champion Fibre with a minimum of one hundred cords of pulpwood a day at a fixed price. John Arbogast, the early investor in Whitmer and Sons, was Champion Logging's general manager.[17] To facilitate transport, Champion Fibre financed a further extension of the Appalachian Railroad to the mill at Smokemont in 1912; this extension became the Ocona Lufty Railroad in 1918.[18] The joint logging company lasted only until the last quarter of 1916, when it went bankrupt and was sold to Suncrest Lumber Company, whose center of operations was farther north, along the Pigeon River.[19]

Despite the demise of Champion Lumber Company, Thompson and Roberson's Champion Fibre Company survived and thrived. Once its subsidiary was out of the picture, and following a detailed timber survey conducted by an outside firm, it bought the holdings of Southern Spruce and Harris-Woodbury along the western Oconaluftee tributaries. Champion Fibre also sold spruce to the military during World War I for use in airplane construction.[20] Montvale Lumber Company entered into an agreement with Champion Fibre in 1917 to supply it with the "tannic acid wood from spruce, chestnut, etc." from a tract above Cherokee on the Oconaluftee River. Montvale would itself manufacture the hardwoods from the land.[21] With Champion Fibre in charge at Smokemont and in place as the owners of the highest reaches of the watershed, its operations expanded rapidly in 1917.

In addition to the centers at Ravensford and Smokemont, other companies logged parts of the valley. Most notably, Geissell and Richardson of Philadelphia bought stumpage, access, and operating rights for timber under forty-six inches in diameter along Mingus Creek and its tributaries. This land was owned by John Leonidas Floyd, his wife, Callie, and their children, heirs of the Mingus family who built the original grist mill and were early residents of the valley. The Floyds sold the timber in two contracts specifying several parcels of land; the first agreement was reached in 1915 when John Leonidas

Floyd was still alive, and the second occurred in 1917 after his death and lasted for four years. Geissell and Richardson is said to have brought the first steam-powered band mill to the valley, though its exact location is unknown. In its heyday the company employed about eighty men full time.[22] Some of the old homesites and the cemetery up Mingus Creek are remnants of the community that emerged along with this operation. About two miles up the creek, a school provided some education to the residents' children. Farmer and logger Bert Crisp said there were "around 35 or 40" families living up Mingus Creek during this time, including members of the Woody, Jenkins, McLaughlin, Watson, Ownby, Mack, Wilson, Nations, Hyatt, Mathis, Gibson, Beck, Dowdle, Knight, Parson, Everett, and Lambert families.[23]

LOGGING STEEP SLOPES AND RIVERBANKS

Despite the transience of the logging companies themselves, they cut extensively and had lasting impacts on the land. Unlike the earlier logging done by valley residents and local concerns, these companies penetrated previously inaccessible areas of the forest via switchbacks that reached high up steep slopes. Using the crosscut saw, three-man crews clearcut massive swatches of land. While this technique for felling trees was traditional, the innovative methods used to move cut timber to railroad cars were very destructive and left huge quantities of debris, tore up streams, and created conditions ripe for wildfire. Early on in the commercial period, saw timber was ball-hooted (simply rolled or slid) to a stream whose waters would convey it downstream after heavy rains. At the confluence of streams, crews would erect splash dams. These were vertical boards spread across pools where water and logs could collect; once full enough, the boards would be removed or blasted out, and the resulting torrent would carry logs downstream. With both these methods, logs would be lost upstream when water levels were low or when the current and rocks would throw them onto the stream bank.[24]

Over time timber removal shifted from tramroads and splash dams to steel rails and steam locomotives. Steel rails could accommodate much heavier loads than tramroads, and in comparison to splash dams, they lost fewer logs. They also allowed for all species to be cut at one time. The tracks followed streams uphill, though on steep slopes either a series of switchbacks or an incline railway was engineered. In coves, V-shaped log slides conveyed cut timber to railcars. Moreover, steam-powered ground and overhead skidders were used to move cut timber to railcars via cables, and a steam-powered

Champion Fibre axe men with crosscut saw, 1915–20.

GREAT SMOKY MOUNTAINS NATIONAL PARK ARCHIVES, TOWNSEND, TENN.

log loader—called a Surry (pronounced Sary) Parker—lifted logs onto cars. All of these innovations enabled faster and more complete cutting, and they provided greater access to very steep slopes. For example, overhead steam skidders could reach trees as far as 2,000 feet away from the skidder.[25] In one instance, former logger and subsequent park ranger Bill Roland claimed that an overhead skidder up from Ravensford had transported logs 5,000 feet from the mountain where the trees were cut to the one where the skidder was set.[26] These innovations made logging the steep slopes cost effective and allowed companies in the mountains to compete with companies logging less demanding topography.[27] The downside was that these technologies tore up streams and slopes and left masses of waste timber as well as other vegetation to die and dry. Incline railroads and overhead skidders even devastated areas without merchantable timber because they required removing trees that would interfere with their operation. Given seasons of heavy rain, the aftereffects of logging were increased erosion and poor regeneration of the forest. The slash made ready kindling for fires that could be started by sparks from the railroad tracks or from the engines.[28] Of course, lightning and farmers' seasonal fires to clear pastures could cause fires, too.

But the cutting itself was something. Once Champion Fibre bought out other companies after the sale of Champion Logging, it built a narrow-gauge railroad along Oconaluftee River and had a line up Kephart Prong. Logging reached almost to Mount Kephart on the state line. Carl Lambert was the son of a couple who ran a camp high up Kephart Prong. He described rail lines up Sweat Heifer Creek and to the falls. He stated that "a flume ran up the creek above the fall" to bring pulpwood to the cars. Higher up, the railroad crossed a high trestle across what Carl called Mud Creek (which must refer to today's Icewater Spring) switching back and reaching an incline at the head of the creek. At that point, overhead skidders could transport the cut spruce timber between Newfound Gap and Dry Sluice Gap to cars. Additional spur lines and switchbacks were temporarily built to reach other coves. About 2,200 acres of spruce were cut from this area. The cutting was so complete and destructive that during the dry summer of 1925 a massive fire burned up over the crest of the Smokies into Tennessee. So fierce was the fire that it consumed green trees and all ground cover, sterilizing the land.[29] Even later, heavy rains washed out the burned soil and created the popular landmark of Charlies Bunion, a famous rock outcrop along the Appalachian Trail. Shortly after its creation, park advocate Horace Kephart named the outcrop for the sore toe of his hiking companion Charlie Conner. Conner was a mountain guide, one-time logger, and son of Dock and Margaret Conner, who lived at the mouth of

Collins Creek.[30] How ironic that the great landmark, which provides sweeping views of the park, is the result of clear-cutting.

Champion's railroad on the Oconaluftee continued up Beech Flats, forking off from the line up Kephart Prong. Of course, the Beech Flats land had been previously owned by Three M and Southern Spruce, and these companies had already cut the hardwoods. Champion Fibre then cut the spruce and any remaining small hardwoods.

Along Bradley Fork and up to Hughes Ridge, good hardwoods stood on the 5,500 acres of a piece of land called the J. A. Martin tract. Champion Fibre sold the stumpage of this area to Charles Badgett and William Latham for $150,000 in the 1920s. The Badgett and Latham Lumber Company cut about 28 million feet over three years and used incline roads in conjunction with a four-mile railroad from Smokemont to transport the timber. Richland Mountain, which lies between Kephart Prong and Bradley Fork, later endured fires that burned 454 acres. Though it is impossible to calculate the total amount of timber removed from the western tributaries of the Oconaluftee River, company records show that between 1920 and 1925, Champion Fibre sawed nearly 117 million feet of timber at its mill in Smokemont. Thirty-seven percent of this timber was spruce, 34 percent hardwood, and 29 percent hemlock.[31]

On the Ravensford side of lumber operations, Parsons Pulp and Lumber Company moved up Straight Fork with a railroad all the way to Round Bottom and Balsam Corner. Parsons cut hemlock and spruce from Dan's Branch, a high tributary of Straight Fork, in 1918–19 but left standing the virgin spruce at the head of the stream. The company extended a spur line west from above Round Bottom into lower Raven Fork. It cut 144 acres just above the reservation. Yet another line followed Ledge Creek out of Round Bottom through Pin Oak Gap and into Haywood County. By the end of operations, three-fourths of the timber along Straight Fork was cut, though a lot of timber was never removed. By this time the mill at Ravensford was working night shifts to meet a production goal of 3 million feet a month, and it was selling pulpwood from cutover land to Champion Fibre for $1.50 a cord. It was racing to get as much timber out as possible before condemnation deadlines for the establishment of the park arrived.

Also on the eastern side of the valley, Suncrest Lumber Company logged Bunches Creek, Heintooga, Indian Creek, and Stillwell Creek by way of a railroad coming within a mile of the Ravensford line at Pin Oak Gap. Today, this railroad line exists as Heintooga Ridge Road and Balsam Mountain Road. The timber from this area was transported to a mill at Waynesville through Maggie Valley. It did not go to Ravensford.[32]

Though some Raven Fork areas were intensely logged, others were left to stand. Ravensford Lumber Company papers show that among the 212 million estimated board feet along Raven Fork, fewer than 1 million were cut. Similarly, by 1930, Champion Fibre Company left more spruce than it cut.[33]

SMOKEMONT AND RAVENSFORD

Up in the mountains, loggers lived in temporary camps that moved with the cutting. When the railroad reached these camps, railroad cars could be driven up to the camps and unloaded near the line as housing for the workers. These temporary camps were called string towns, and the railroad lines were colloquially called strings. Unfortunately, few accounts of these camps in Oconaluftee are available to provide more detail about what life was like there, whether they often included families or mostly just the timber cutters, teamsters, and men who worked the skidders. Local historian Carl Lambert has written that his parents ran a camp for Champion Fibre up Sweat Heifer Creek, and he commented that he "had many fond memories of fishing in this clear mountain stream . . . [and] caught my first speckled trout" there during the summer of 1924.[34] Given that this area was clear-cut, it is hard to picture how idyllic the scene may have been. Perhaps some part of the stream was not logged, at least for a time, that summer.

In any case, the resident population of the valley surged during the logging years, increasing from 1,650 to 2,724 between 1900 and 1920. About 480 men were employed in logging and railroad jobs in 1920, and the industry also brought in store clerks, people to run the boardinghouses and hotels, cooks, teachers, ministers, doctors, and a dentist—as well as their families.[35] A large portion of these new residents lived either in Smokemont or Ravensford, the company-owned mill towns built as processing plants for the timber, as business centers, transport hubs, and a community for loggers' families, mill workers, supervisors, and visiting company managers.

Both towns were located on flat bottomland that had been farms before. Ravensford land was owned by the logging company, but Smokemont was leased from Wilson Ensley Queen and his second wife, Alice Queen. The lease stipulated an annual payment of $400 for "all the level land" from the river up to the boundary line with Aden Carver's property. A large two-story Queen home and garden were excluded from the lease with a boundary just above a spring branch near the house. But the family's cornfield became the site of the sawmill.[36] The Oconaluftee Baptist Church already stood in its current place south of the Queen home. This frame structure had been built higher up

Champion Fibre employees in front of their boxcar homes, 1920.

GREAT SMOKY MOUNTAINS NATIONAL PARK ARCHIVES, TOWNSEND, TENN.

the slope than the church located on the same plot of land in the 1880s. The church's land had been previously donated by the Queen and Beck families. This new structure replaced the old log church around 1912; it soon adopted the name of the logging town and became Smokemont Baptist Church. Near the church stood the Smokemont school, also a frame building, situated just on the south side of the church grounds on a bank above the east side of the river. Today, Tow String Trail crosses this site. Smokemont school was a low-slung building with an overhanging loft at the front door. It stood on beam supports over the slope of the hillside. On the south side, five large windows were ornamented with bluebird boxes posted between each one. In time, additional schools were needed to teach all the children. At least five were near Smokemont during logging's peak. A one-room school stood at the mouth of Mingus Creek and another about two miles up; yet another served those living up Tow String.[37]

Ravensford School, 1938.

GREAT SMOKY MOUNTAINS NATIONAL PARK ARCHIVES, TOWNSEND, TENN.

Ravensford also had at least two churches, the Holiness Church and the Ravensford Church. The Ravensford school was a large, rectangular two-story building with an upstairs gymnasium that also served as an auditorium and was outfitted with a movie projector. The building featured very tall windows on the long front and back sides of the building. Like Smokemont, Ravensford also had satellite schools throughout the area; one was fancifully called the Submarine School because it was located near where a railroad bridge had fallen into Straight Fork. Ravensford high school students were taken to a Swain County school at Whittier by way of a bus converted to run on the railroad tracks. This converted bus went as far as Ela. From there students were transported in a regular bus via state road.[38]

Both Smokemont and Ravensford logging towns were constructed around large double-band sawmills, mill ponds, lumberyards, and railroad tracks. The railroad tracks of the Ocona Lufty Railroad and Appalachian Railroad, respectively, came into the mountains to the loading areas of the lumberyards. These were common carriers with passenger cars. Logging railroads extended from the mills up to the cutting areas. Once Champion Fibre was in charge of Smokemont, it bought a band mill at Waynesville and moved it to the logging town, adding to or replacing one already on the site. The band mills represented an important mechanical innovation that allowed lumber companies to handle large logs and reduce waste. Band mill blades were significantly thinner than those used in sash and circular saws; consequently, they were also more accurate. The output of the Smokemont mill was almost 117 million board feet, and its daily capacity was 80,000 board feet between 1920 and 1925. The Ravensford mill, which was a huge, barnlike structure, was capable of sawing 2 million feet of hardwoods or 3 million feet of spruce or hemlock per month.[39]

White men working in the lumber industry typically were paid a dollar for a ten-hour day, while Cherokee men were paid thirty-five cents. Often this pay was in company scrip or aluminum coins called Doog a Loo, and these were accepted at the company-owned commissaries located in the logging towns.[40] A portion of workers' wages were withheld to pay for health care from the company doctor, who visited each town periodically and could be called to a home in case of injury or sickness.[41] Mill work demanded long hours part of the year but perhaps few or none for cutters and teamsters when winter snows covered the slopes. Florence Cope Bush's account of the life of her mother, Dorie, notes that her father, who worked at the Smokemont mill, experienced both long shifts and weeks off work during the winter.[42] It is difficult to know how steady the work or adequate the pay was for most of the employees. Photographs of the mill crews at Ravensford show thirty to forty young to middle-age white men dressed in boots, overalls, shirts, and caps or hats. A photo of a Smokemont crew is similar but includes fewer laborers, only a dozen. They would have worked as sawyers, millwrights, saw filers, and laborers. Though not pictured in the photos, about three dozen Cherokee men also worked in logging, either in the mills or in the mountains as timber cutters. Most of the Cherokees worked for the Ravensford firms. Fewer than ten African Americans are listed in the 1920 census as residents in the valley and employed in logging, though an additional dozen African American residents were employed as section workers for the railroad, and four were employed as teamsters.[43]

The mill towns were far more connected to the larger society than anything previously seen in the valley. Maisie Queen Young was the granddaughter of Wilson Ensley Queen, who owned the Smokemont land. She grew up in the community and recalled the town as "booming." Both Smokemont and Ravensford had electricity and telephone lines. Each had a company commissary, a general store with a post office, an infirmary, a boardinghouse, a hotel, and a clubhouse for company managers, though none of these essential buildings was built for aesthetic appeal. They were plain and serviceable. The Ravensford commissary sold beer and soft drinks. A six-ounce Orange Crush was its most popular item, according to logging hands.[44] In Smokemont, the doctor's and dentist's offices were located in the commissary, but in Ravensford the infirmary was situated in a separate building near workers' quarters, away from the center of activity. As recreation, the towns held Cherokee stickball matches on a playing field in Ravensford, with contests between town teams and with Cherokee teams.

The candid memoir of Leonard Carson Lambert Jr., a Cherokee, provides rare insight into alcohol consumption among loggers and others at this time. He claimed that loggers and farm families (both white and Cherokee) consumed moonshine. Despite religious talk against it, folks in the valley liked alcohol but did not like "legal alcohol." His grandmother made a good living making and selling moonshine during the 1920s, and he states that someone in almost every Cherokee family did as well. Bootleggers paid off police to avoid being put out of business and jailed.[45] It seems reasonable to assume that other families besides Cherokee ones also made and sold moonshine in the valley, but I have not discovered sources stating that was the case. Certainly many farmers had grain fields and orchards that would supply ingredients for their brews.

Both towns were surrounded by a range of housing for mill workers, loggers, and company managers. A railroad map of Smokemont from 1919 shows that fourteen three- and four-room dwellings stood on the north end of town near a mill pond. An additional seven smaller dwellings were located on the south side of town, below the Queen home and the commissary. The line of these smaller homes extended as far as Smokemont Baptist Church. Three additional, larger homes lay between these small dwellings and the commissary; one was adjacent to the commissary and was occupied by its manager, and the other two were the largest—five rooms and a bath—and set apart from all others. Maisie Queen Young recalled a large clubhouse, boardinghouse, and "rows and rows" of company houses across the river from the mill. Another descendant recalled that each section of Smokemont was named, some for boroughs in New York City such as the Bronx, and others with such names as Sandtown and Pumpkintown. These must have been built later; a photograph shows a rather densely built town. Other workers lived in log cabins in the surrounding valley. For example, Lila Maples and Robert Vance Woodruff lived in a cabin on their relative Aden Carver's land for a while when Robert worked at the Smokemont mill; later the family moved closer to the father's work and rented a farm near the Cherokee Boundary.[46]

Champion Fibre's mill and town at Smokemont, 1920.

GREAT SMOKY MOUNTAINS NATIONAL PARK ARCHIVES, TOWNSEND, TENN.

The town of Ravensford was more compactly arranged than Smokemont with town buildings along the upland areas surrounding the railroad lines. It had more than seventy dwellings of various sizes; they were painted white and sported green shutters, but they were made of rough lumber. About half of these must have been small indeed because they are labeled "shacks" on a map. Others seem large enough for three or four rooms, and some of these had two stories as well as root cellars. The largest dozen homes were likely twice the size of the midsize ones.[47]

Despite their modern utilities, the towns retained some rural features. One was the proximity of fields to the town. Mescal Burke grew up near Ravensford and recalled playing with the store owner's daughter. Prominent in her memories were that her father's cornfield was right across from the store and that store customers could use a bathroom attached to the house alongside the store. The toilet, she said, had a wooden seat. Also, Hazel Caldwell

Bryson's father worked for the mill, but as a child growing up on Tight Run, she swam in the Oconaluftee River and recalled her family canning blueberries, grinding its own corn, and raising chickens. But her parents bought sugar, coffee, and flour at the store. Similarly, families used mountain remedies such as moonshine, poultices, and castor oil for illnesses. Farmers traded their surplus apples, honey, ham, and corn for store groceries. Some Cherokee women sold their handmade baskets to the stores for others to purchase for cash or in exchange for flour, sugar, and canned goods, beginning the craft trade for the Cherokees. Fishing remained a pastime and a way to supply dinner because it could be done near town. Hunting declined, though some farmers continued to hunt on occasion for game; bears were hunted to discourage them from attacking livestock.[48]

Bridges across the river and its major streams, which could be deep and fast, presented another juxtaposition of old and new. There were numerous log and swinging bridges, some stabilized with wires and handrails, some not. Stories of adults and children falling from bridges into the river in winter or in wet weather were not uncommon. Aden Carver's granddaughter told a story about Aden pulling a prank of crossing a log bridge on his hands and knees in front of city folks; she said that he could easily walk across but wanted to trick visitors into thinking he could not.[49]

Both communities eventually got bridges that could bear the weight of vehicles. In 1921, Swain County built three steel-reinforced, arched concrete Luten bridges across the river, opening the mill towns to auto traffic and providing pedestrians a broad, reliable crossing. Luten bridges were patented by Daniel Luten and the National Bridge Company in Indianapolis, Indiana, but these were constructed by the Luten Bridge Company in Knoxville, Tennessee. One bridge crossed Raven Fork and marked a swimming hole just above it, near today's park boundary. Another crossed the Oconaluftee near the Mingus home (about a half mile north of the current visitor center). This was the longest and included three spans. It was demolished in 1982. A third crossed Bradley Fork at Smokemont and stands today but is open only to foot traffic. It is located where the Smokemont Loop Trail spills into the lower end of the campground.[50] The Luten name can be seen on a relief inscribed into one of the bridge's abutments. The design of these Luten bridges was sleeker and more metropolitan than those constructed in the 1930s for the national park. They looked like they belonged in cities. Later, park-era bridges had a rustic timber or hewn stone design, which marks them as the work of the Civilian Conservation Corps.

LIVING "ON OWN ACCOUNT"

In 1910, a new question appeared on federal census sheets. In addition to recording occupation and industry, census takers began asking whether someone was an employer, a salary or wage worker, or a person working "on [one's] own account." The item appeared just in time to capture labor changes caused by logging in the park. By 1920, the number of wage workers in the valley had skyrocketed because of the influx of people for the logging companies and the railroad. Nonetheless, the established families continued to farm. Though a young man in a family might be listed as a logger and wage laborer or even as a wage earner on a farm, the male heads of the farming households were listed as working "on own account." They remained masters of their own fates. For the most part they made their living farming their own land as they had since the Civil War. As always, they sought multiple sources of revenue and subsistence, growing corn, keeping hogs and bees, raising cattle, and seasonally harvesting timber and chestnuts. Though often unrecognized and certainly undervalued, the women in these households contributed significant labor and products toward the family's health and wealth. Women processed and preserved food, wove fabric and made clothes, tended livestock and sold or bartered surplus goods at local stores—in addition to "keeping house," which included cooking, cleaning, laundry, and childcare. Most of what these families needed to survive they could raise themselves; necessities they could not produce, they could barter for or buy. In *Miners, Millhands, and Mountaineers*, historian Ronald D. Eller explained that for mountain families "land held a special meaning that combined the diverse concepts of utility and stewardship. While land was something to be used and developed to meet one's needs, it was also the foundation of daily existence, giving form to personal identity, material culture, and economic life."[51] This view helps us speculate how the farmers understood the arrival of commercial logging and the changes that industrialization brought into their lives.

Twenty-first-century park visitors cannot know if the mountain families grieved the loss of the wilderness that they had lived within. Once the clear-cutting around and upslope of their farms began, they seem to have adapted readily to changing ways to make a living. That Wilson Ensley Queen would lease his best bottomland to a logging company for a sawmill and company town can be understood in this way. Also, the Floyd family leased large tracts of land along Mingus Creek to a logging company. Bert Crisp, who had a farm along Mingus Creek, worked for Geissell and Richardson, which logged that area. Nineteen landowners in the valley agreed to right-of-way leases with Champion Fibre Company in March 1917 so that narrow-gauge railroad lines could reach timber-cutting tracts high up Bradley Fork, Kephart Prong, and Beech Flats. The Becks, Wilsons, Treadways, Conners, Gibsons, Reagans, Carvers, Bradleys, Kimseys, and others signed agreements allowing thirty-foot-wide corridors across their farmland for annual rents of five to fifty dollars. The range in rent seemed generally consistent with the anticipated length of the corridor across a particular farmer's land. The contracts included a statement that the surveyor would seek a route doing as little damage as possible to the landowner's buildings and fields but made no promises that the railroad would not disrupt the original arrangement of the houses, outbuildings, or fields and pastures.[52]

Two years after these agreements were struck, Champion saw that it needed to expand its lines and made additional agreements with the Queens and Carvers. The Queens agreed that a rail line could be built on land adjoining that of the original Smokemont lease. The track would cross a "strip of the garden," skirt the side of the Queens' barn, and approach the Queen home. This new lease was purchased for an annual rent of fifty dollars as well as two "considerations." One was that the lumber company would cover the barn's roof, two ends, and one side with a "fire-proof material." Champion would also carry a $2,500 fire insurance policy on the Queens' home and barn, with sole responsibility for paying the premiums.[53]

Champion contracted with Aden and Martha Carver to "construct and erect a dam and pipe-line on and from their land containing 199 acres, more or less, on Carver's branch a tributary of Ocona Lufty River in Swain County, N.C., through and over said lands to the reservoir and log pond now used by the Champion Fibre Company, party of the second part, at its mill yard near the mouth of Reagan's prong of the Ocona Lufty River." The arrangement allowed the company to pipe the stream's water to the reservoir at Champion's mill yard for its log pond. The cost of this agreement for a term of thirty years was "One and no/100 Dollars, and other good and valuable considerations to them in hand paid by the Champion Fibre Company."[54] It's impossible not to wonder what the unspecified considerations may have been to allow the lumber company this high level of access and impact on a family farm. In any case, they must have been desirable and not too disruptive because the Carver family remained in the valley throughout the logging years and long after Champion decamped. And even though Aden was farming in 1920 in his early seventies, his sons, Julius (age forty-three) and Mack (age twenty-four), were both cutting timber, as was Julius's son Otis (age eighteen). As further evidence of their adaptability, the 1930 census lists Aden as a renter (by then from the park service, since he had sold his land) and a sawyer working in a sawmill, likely Champion's at Smokemont.[55]

One branch of the Conner family, the one headed by the Reverend William Henry Conner and Rachel Gibson Conner, also demonstrated the ability of the established Oconaluftee families to adapt to changing times. Their son, Dock Franklin Conner, farmed at the homestead for many years, but when tourism picked up in the 1910s, he opened his home as a lodge and served as a mountain guide on occasion. In the 1930s, he paired up with Wiley Oakley, perhaps a distant cousin, who had a guide business in Gatlinburg and became the quintessential mountain guide in the years before the park was established. On the first day of an excursion from Gatlinburg, tourists would travel to Dock's home for room and board. From there, Wiley would lead a party to Cherokee the next day. The return trip included a second stay over at Dock's. Two of Dock's sons, Jaheu and Charlie, also responded to shifting opportunities in the valley. In the early 1920s, both worked as unspecified laborers for the logging industry. By 1922, Jaheu and his wife, Nellie Bradley Conner, were running the general store in Smokemont. This arrangement outlasted the logging era. Younger brother Charlie ran a meat market and supplied beef, presumably from his family's cattle, to be shipped by rail up to the logging camps. He, too, became a mountain guide, known for the sore toe that gave Horace Kephart the idea for naming Charlies Bunion. By 1930, Charlie had returned to farming.[56]

For a time in the early 1920s, a local man known as a bear hunter worked for the Conner family. Cole Cathey led the cattle to grassy areas for grazing after land had been logged. According to an article by Vic Weals, he would leave salt for the cattle as a way to anchor them to an area. Because these locations were high, they were also the haunts of bears. So Cathey always kept high-power rifle cartridges inside his waterproof coat, in case he needed to shoot a bear that was threatening the cattle. One day, Cole was helping to get hay in from a field along the river when a thunderstorm came. Dock hurried into the barn with the horses, but Cathey paused to fashion a sort of umbrella with a pitchfork and hay. This was a bad idea. When he did not come in for supper, Dock sent Charlie to look for Cathey, whom he found dead from a lightning strike. The force of the bolt shredded his clothing, exploded the rifle cartridges in his pockets, and stopped his watch at 5:30. Cathey's death certificate states that he died in the employment of D. F. Conner from an accidental lightning strike on July 12, 1922. He was six days short of his thirty-eighth birthday.[57] Somehow this tale is memorable not only for itself but also for the brevity of life and the events that characterize an era.

Perhaps the most complete account of how families continued to farm after large-scale logging began came from Dan Lambert, a resident of Tow String. During an interview conducted in 2004, Lambert provided a glimpse of home and farm economy:

> My mother was Cora Bradley Lambert. She was raised down here at what we call the Bradley place, down just below the [Tow String] church. And my father was a Lambert. He's Monroe Lambert's boy, and that's my grandpa. Of course, they lived here on the creek I reckon all their lives, and were raised here. And he farmed all of his life. And my mother gardened, made the garden, kept the house, and canned. She put up a lot of canned stuff. Blackberries was one thing and garden vegetables out of the garden. She kept a lot of chickens and we sold eggs to more or less buy our groceries or what we have to have. All we needed was flour and coffee and a little bit of sugar and lard and that's about what we bought. Most of the time, we raised our lard and kept and processed it out of the hogs.
>
> So, my dad, he farmed all the time. They'd get out wood. It was chestnut wood. We called it acid wood at that time. And they'd get out a few logs and sometimes they would cut white oak for stave timber, to make barrels out of. It sold pretty good. We sometimes cut tan bark and [used] the white oak logs, we'd take the bark and sell it for tanning material. And of course, other than that, well he pastored church about all of his life. He farmed and pastored. Even down at Bethelberry [Bethabara Church] . . . Echota, the old Echota church. And Rocksprings Baptist Church. Up at Smokemont, he was the last pastor that pastored at Smokemont.[58]

Despite the influx of new people and technologies, farmers working on their own accounts continued much as they had. In addition, they opportunistically developed ways to bring in cash that helped them buy what they could not grow or make. When it was convenient, they engaged with local businesses, but typically they did not become dependent on others. They still had their land to use as they saw fit. Is it any wonder that once they had endured logging that they felt unfairly targeted for their most precious resource, their land, when park proponents began to hold sway in public debate? The notions of wilderness preservation and outdoor recreation as legitimate purposes for their property were entirely out of keeping with their lives.

The logging era brought dramatic changes to Oconaluftee, but it was in full swing less than twenty years. The spectacle and waste of clear-cutting and wildfire raised the concerns of people who wanted to preserve the southern Appalachian forests, particularly since the northern forests were gone. For the most part, this effort was led by a group of well-off, even elite regional leaders who saw a national park as a means of social progress and economic development through tourism and the hospitality industry. Residents of the valley would have been content to keep their farms; there is no record of their desire for the establishment of a national park to protect the mountain wilderness that they had lived in for a century. Though North Carolinians initially preferred a forest preserve over a park to protect the important timber resource, eventually the idea of a national park in the East caught hold, and passionate and indefatigable park advocates such as Horace Kephart succeeded. Congress authorized the creation of the Great Smoky Mountains National Park in 1925, an act that signaled the beginning of the end for logging. Logging stopped at Ravensford in 1927 and in Smokemont in 1931. Completing the land condemnations, after complex surveys, assessments, and protracted legal wrangling, would take longer.[59] Champion Fibre negotiated a sale price for all of its property in the park boundary, a total of nearly 93,000 acres (with about 52,000 in North Carolina) for $3 million in April 1931. A final judgment in the lawsuit between the Ravensford Lumber Company and the state was announced in November 1933, paying the company $1,057,190 for its 33,000 acres (including the town of Ravensford). The company was allowed six months to remove its property from the area and use the railway to do so. However, it was not allowed to cut any additional trees or cause damage to growing timber. At the same time, the Appalachian Railway was awarded $50,000 for its land in the park and also given six months to remove property, including the "steel rails, cross ties, side tracks, switch bars, [and] switches."[60]

Once logging operations ceased, most of the mill workers and timbermen and, of course, their families were forced to leave the area, having no other means of making a living and no land to return to. Some left suddenly and neglected to pay Oscar McDonald, the Ravensford store owner, their tabs. Bryson City was the destination of some folks. Others eventually were hired by the park. Some of the houses in Ravensford were sold at auction and moved out of the park boundary within a couple of months. The hotel remained and was used for a while as a camp.[61]

The stories of those who owned farms and leased land were typically more complex. The park service assessed their land and made offers. Some accepted these offers, but others contested the assessment values in court. However, the timing of the condemnation proceedings was miserable for many. Once a price was reached and the sale was complete, the depth of the Depression was upon the nation. Bank runs, failures, and closures left former small landowners without access to funds or, in some cases, without funds at all. Maisie Queen Young claimed that her grandfather's land, which included Smokemont and more than 500 acres, averaged a price of only twenty-five dollars per acre. But "hardest part" of the whole situation was that after her family was paid, all the banks closed and they had nothing to use to buy another home.[62] This circumstance led the National Park Service to authorize lifelong leases to residents beginning in 1932. These provided the farming families the ability to stay on their land and in the homes they had built. Rents for owners who accepted the park's valuation of their property were very low, but those who contested the sale price were charged more. Smokemont Commissary clerk and postmaster George Beck was one who resisted the deal offered to him for his farm and was seen as causing "all of the problems for the North Carolina Park Commission at Smokemont." So in turn he was charged full rental for his land and home after condemnation. He eventually moved to the Qualla area of Cherokee and bought the old store that had once been owned by Will Thomas and that housed the Qualla post office. Once the park was established in 1934, leaseholders could not graze animals, fish, forage, and hunt as they had traditionally done.[63] Their ability to make a living off their own land was severely constrained. These residents took work where it was available in mills, in the CCC after it was established in 1933, and in the park service during the late 1930s and after.

Carl Lambert had lived in a logging camp high up in the Oconaluftee Valley in the 1920s when his parents ran the camp. In 1970, he visited the Sweat Heifer Creek area again to dig ramps, which the park service then allowed locals to do seasonally. His reflections on that return trip capture the dramatic change that took place at the end of logging: "Many were the stories of storms, wrecks, and people brought to mind. It seemed in my mind I could hear the old steam engines pull up those steep grades, the cry of the steam whistle, the ringing of the choppers axe, the crosscut saw and the cowbells. But these were only dreams of an era gone by."[64]

Though he rather wistfully recalled the sounds and excitement of this period, another scene checks the nostalgia for logging days. Imagine the end of the logging era as a steam locomotive pulls away from the Ravensford or Smokemont station. Alongside are trucks and automobiles, commercial signs for gasoline, and electrical lines—all the trappings of an industrialized city. What might the Oconaluftee Valley have become if the park movement had not been successful? Logging would have ended anyway once all the accessible timber had been cut, say within another decade. More mountains would be shorn of trees and likely more fire damage would have occurred, even though by the 1930s the state was becoming active in promoting fire suppression and forest management. One can wonder if Ravensford and Smokemont would have become mountain towns (or even a single town) along the lines of Bryson City. Can we really guess what the valley would look like now without the coming of the park? Some families, no doubt, would have held on and found ways to continue farming or would have found occupations in an emerging town. Could that alternative reality possibly have been preferable to the biosphere reserve that is today's park and that expands in three directions from the old Enloe farm, now the location of the visitor center?

Chapter 13

CCC TRANSFORMATIONS

FROM LOGGING CAMPS TO PARKLAND

▲ ▲ ▲

The first time I hiked Kephart Prong Trail was in the early 1990s, and I was almost rear-ended before I turned off Newfound Gap Road into the parking area. Descending from the gap, I did not know exactly when I would reach the trailhead, so I waited to signal a left turn until I saw the sign. The car behind me was pretty close and screeched to a stop just in time to avoid a crash. I count this as one of several times I've had a near miss.

Once my nerves recovered and I was parked and walking, the rest of the day was bliss. The trail offered simple joy upon understated delight, beginning with a log bridge over the Oconaluftee River and continuing with an easy incline along a broad path, flanked by wildflowers, ferns, and second-growth stands of two of my favorite trees, American beech and eastern hemlock (now threatened by an exotic insect). A few other people were around, but the way was uncrowded and the pace leisurely on a warm July Sunday. I was a hiker then, not much a student of the woods, cultural history, or park lore. Nonetheless, again and again, these disciplines presented themselves to me as I encountered evidence of earlier residents', loggers', CCC boys', and conscientious objectors' lives in my place of escape. Though not what I came for, the stone hearths, water fountain, boxwoods, cement structures, and abandoned rails made me feel as if I were finding forgotten and mysterious artifacts, kind of like my own personal Mayan temple discovery in a film about regional explorations. As an aesthetic, I was glad they were falling over and obscured by moss.

Since then, I've taken this trail a bunch of times, each one knowing more about it. Consequently, the detritus of prepark days conjures less wonder and more gratitude. I don't want the remnants removed, but I do want them overtaken by the forest, mist, and sunshine. This sentiment may seem in conflict with the endeavor of chronicling the human history of the valley, though they intertwine for me. I find the stories of the valley entertaining because of the personalities of the residents, valuable as insights into past economic times, inspiring as tales of both individual and community resourcefulness and perseverance, explanatory of "how we got here" (meaning contemporary society and its struggles to overcome tribalism), and instructive as examples of the dependence of people on the natural world, in both sustainable and exploitive ways. Still, I know that I've prioritized people and cast the flora, fauna, and land in cameo roles. Just note how I still first recall my own driving story when this trail comes to mind. I live in my own head all the time, but hiking in a park bends my thoughts. The park helps me wake up to other species, the Smokies' astonishing diversity, and human dependence on that diversity.

▲ ▲ ▲

EVEN BEFORE THE LAND condemnations and sales were complete, the National Park Service was on site and responsible for "protection and administration" of the Great Smoky Mountains National Park in 1930, after North Carolina and Tennessee conferred 150,000 acres of land to the federal government. The following January, the first superintendent, Ross Eakin, arrived to oversee the construction of park roads, trails, campgrounds, and facilities essential to accommodate the visitors who had begun to arrive in large numbers, despite the Depression.[1] The federal government recognized the terrible straits that mountain farm families and communities were placed in once their land was taken and bank runs and closures either robbed land owners of the sale proceeds or made bank funds inaccessible. Consequently, in 1932 arrangements were made—within the context of the park's establishment—to help locals survive the transition, which had been aggravated by a precipitous drop in county property taxes. With the establishment of the park, three-fourths of Swain County's taxable land was taken, and many families were forced to leave the area to find work. Congress passed a bill allowing former landowners lifetime leases on their farms so that they would have their homes and fields, at least, to live on, even though hunting, pasturing, and foraging were largely curtailed. Additionally, as part of an emergency relief act, Congress allotted $509,000 for roads, which allowed the park to hire local men to work on constructing Newfound Gap Road, the main overmountain artery of the park, connecting the primary park entrances of the two states. The North Carolina section was termed Road Project 1-B, with 1-A obviously referring to the road on the Tennessee side.[2]

These measures likely helped tide folks over, but it was not until after Franklin Delano Roosevelt took office in 1933 that significant relief programs got underway. Very quickly after the inauguration, the Roosevelt administration created Emergency Conservation Work camps, which in 1937 became known by the familiar name of the Civilian Conservation Corps. As early as April 1932, the government established enrollment quotas by county that would determine how many young men could join. Both county population and degree of destitution were considered in the formula that led to the formation of a handful of companies of 200 men each and located in Oconaluftee Valley. The park benefitted tremendously from CCC work and hosted the most companies of any national park, with the total reaching eighteen or twenty-two, depending on how the count was made. The existence of spur camps and double camps and the transfer of camps to other locations makes a simple count of camps tricky. Oconaluftee Valley was one area of the park that hosted camps throughout the CCC era.[3]

By June 1932, enrollees began arriving at Smokemont as members of NC NP-4, Company 414, also known as Camp Will Thomas, in recognition of the nineteenth-century merchant who became a Cherokee agent, state legislator, and the head of the Confederate Thomas Legion during the Civil War. The company included 132 Swain County residents. A second group, NC NP-5, Company 411, enrolled 126 North Carolina boys at Camp Kephart Prong. These regular enrollees were male, white, physically fit, unmarried, unemployed, and between the ages of eighteen and twenty-five, a range that was later expanded to seventeen to twenty-seven years of age. They agreed to remain in camp for six months and were paid thirty dollars a month. However, all except five dollars of the pay was sent to the enrollees' homes to help their families. Although some African Americans were enrolled in the CCC, local resistance prevented them from being located at Smokemont, despite plans to do so in 1935. Similarly, 150 Cherokee youth formed a separate company supervised by the Cherokees and administered through the Office of Indian

Affairs, but limited funding for the Cherokee company allowed enrollees to work only half time, significantly decreasing the aid that reached this community. Cherokee CCC men completed projects similar to those within the park, but theirs were located within the Qualla Boundary. Nonetheless, enrollees from northeastern states were placed in Oconaluftee. Within the first six months, a company of mostly Italian Americans arrived from New York, New Jersey, and Delaware. They comprised the NC NP-14, Company 1211, at Smokemont. Their lodgings were along Mingus Creek, and they became known as the "Wop Brigade" because of their heritage. Additional camps were established as time passed, including NC NP-15, Company 1215, also located at Mingus Creek. After Company 1215 was relocated to the western states in August 1935, another company arrived, Company 4484, and stayed three months before moving to Deep Creek and becoming Company NP-16. Finally, two companies were established at Ravensford, NC NP-18, Company 1259, and NC NP-19, Company 426, which was known as Camp Round Bottom. This camp, so named because the area was a round valley floor, was largely inhabited by New Yorkers.[4]

Early on, additional local relief came in the form of a program to hire older residents known as Local Experienced Men, who had local knowledge, useful skills, and relevant work experience. This expansion of the basic CCC membership brought maturity to the ranks and dampened concerns about outsiders taking work away from locals (such as those in the Wop Brigade).[5] Among these men were Oconaluftee stalwart Aden Carver, then in his early nineties, who traveled to Sugarlands to join and was sent back to the valley to serve, and Charles Bascom Queen, the son of Wilson Ensley and Alice Queen, the formerly land-rich family who leased Smokemont to Champion Fibre Company to use for its logging camp. Charles's daughter Maisie later explained that her father "worked in the shop" of Company 1211 when she was a high school senior.[6] He may have been one of the local men who helped the New Yorkers adjust. In January 1934, the associate engineer for the CCC wrote, "The work is progressing nicely in this camp [N-14]. Am happy to say that since the enrollment of the local men in this camp, the New York boys have improved two hundred percent. The health of the company is good, quarters comfortable. The men are well clothed and happy."[7] Roy Minyard Conner, the grandson of Joel and Katherine (Mingus) Conner, and Ed Bradley, a son of one of the Bradley families, were also foremen in CCC camps in Oconaluftee.[8]

The economic benefits of the CCC reached other locals as well because the camps needed large quantities of food for the men. As early as August 1933, a farmers' cooperative was formed to supply these needs in Swain County. During one week, "1,700 pounds of Irish potatoes; 20 dozen ears of corn; 250 pounds sweet potatoes; 100 pounds each of squash, turnips, tomatoes, and onions; 260 pounds of cabbage; a bushel of peppers; and 28 dozen carrots" were purchased from the cooperative for the nearby camps.[9]

When the first camps opened, the accommodations were primitive. That first summer, housing at Smokemont amounted to World War I surplus tents lined up in a field. But these were soon replaced by barracks and other military-style buildings such as a mess hall, an administration building, an infirmary, and officers' quarters. Except for the post office and store and the two-story school building, the homes and buildings in Ravensford were dismantled and their lumber was repurposed for CCC buildings. The school was also torn down in 1938.[10] The camps looked quasi-military, usually arranged around a flagpole and company sign. Interior photographs of the barracks and mess hall show long rows of bunks or tables with wood stoves for heat. A gas generator was used for cooking. The ceilings were low, and the rooms looked dark. Later photographs of the rec halls and study areas, however, look much more inviting, with the former having a pool table and the latter having desks, tables, and displays of books and magazines. Camp enrollees adapted the grounds for sports; the baseball field from the Ravensford logging town was put to use for CCC team games, and a makeshift outdoor boxing ring—mostly a level square outlined with stones—was created for matches among enrollees between camps. In 1940, a subdistrict Golden Gloves competition took place at Ravensford. The contenders in the Golden Gloves matches included names from valley families (Jenkins, Dowdle, Pressley). The Smokemont Baptist Church welcomed CCC boys for services, and Saturday "liberty parties" to nearby Sylva and Bryson City provided enrollees chances to visit these towns, shop, or go on a date.[11]

In a memoir about his time as a Smokemont enrollee, Frank Davis, who came from the central Piedmont of North Carolina, described the frequent weekend dances held at the rec hall with live orchestras playing big band music. Invitations to local young women were sent by mail. Frank met his bride, Elizabeth Sherrill of Sylva, at such a dance. Her maiden name suggests that she was a descendant of Samuel Sherrill, one of the families that settled in Oconaluftee Valley early in the nineteenth century.[12] The camps certainly provided lots of new, eligible young men for the local young women.

Life in the camps was somewhat regimented; after all, the CCC was initially administered by military officers. Even so, it provided the young men

Smokemont CCC Camp NP-4, 1933.

GREAT SMOKY MOUNTAINS NATIONAL PARK ARCHIVES, TOWNSEND, TENN.

with housing, army-issue clothing, filling meals, jobs, training opportunities, fellowship, and camaraderie. The five-day workweek began at 6:00 A.M. with reveille, included eight hours of work plus a lunch hour, and ended with lights out at 9:45 P.M.[13]

ALL MANNER OF PHYSICAL LABOR

The work projects of the CCC in Oconaluftee remain visible today; they transformed the valley into parkland, helping the land recover from the erosion, fire, and habitat destruction of the logging era, and provided landscaping, road work, and trail maintenance essential to the new park. A report for NP-4 at Smokemont from the first enrollment period of about three months claims that 8,543 "total man days" were spent on conservation work, 2,489 days on camp construction, and 2,116 on housekeeping. During the same period, this company removed fire hazards from 1,960 acres, landscaped eight acres, cleared fifteen miles of roadsides, and maintained one mile of road; the group also improved three miles of truck trails, eighteen miles of horse trails, and five miles of streams. In addition, one hundred man days were spent clearing the campground, and two were devoted to collecting a half-bushel of seeds for later cultivation.[14] This account shows that the work often included significant outdoor physical labor using saws, axes, picks, and shovels for digging, planting, and grading slopes. The days working on the campground were spent cleaning up the debris and burying the remains of the defunct sawmills and railroad lines. Champion Fibre left an old locomotive and forty railroad cars on site in Smokemont when it decamped, as well as other heavy metal equipment for sawing logs. These had to be hauled away at the park service's expense. Smaller debris was buried on site. Similar cleanup work from logging occurred at Ravensford and Mingus Creek.[15]

After the initial clearing was accomplished, more focus was placed on landscaping along Newfound Gap Road, where the NP-5 Company planted more than 11,000 trees and shrubs. NP-14 landscaped picnic areas in Oconaluftee that were being created for park visitors. Seed collection continued as part of NP-14's tasks; these northeastern seaboard natives collected fifteen bushels of hardwood seeds.[16] The seeds were taken to a CCC plant nursery in Ravensford, which was run by Eli Potter. Potter had previously been employed by the Biltmore estate in Asheville and was a big man with a bushy white mustache. Park employees later remembered him to be a keen observer of the natural world. At the nursery, Potter supervised the raising of seedlings for reforestation plantings and landscaping in the park and for pine tree seedlings used along the Blue Ridge Parkway, which also benefitted from CCC labor.[17]

In addition to these ongoing efforts, the companies located in Oconaluftee should be credited with completing three important construction projects: the rehabilitation of Mingus Mill, the creation of the fish hatchery at Kephart Prong, and the building of the Oconaluftee Ranger Station. Except for the fish hatchery, these remain intact and are key parts of the current Oconaluftee Valley experience for park visitors.

In 1931, Ed and Fred Floyd sold Mingus Mill to the park. It had been built in the late 1880s with the financing of Dr. John Mingus, their great-grandfather, and the oversight of their father, Lon Floyd, and their great-uncle Abraham Mingus. For over forty years it was one of the hubs of the community; residents came to have both corn and wheat ground. After the sale, the mill fell into disuse and disrepair. Fortunately, in 1936 and 1937, the park service architect working in the Smokies, Charles Grossman, led the effort to restore it into working order. He thoroughly evaluated the building, machinery, and

Eli Potter holding a red oak seedling at the Ravensford nursery.

GREAT SMOKY MOUNTAINS NATIONAL PARK ARCHIVES, TOWNSEND, TENN.

external features of the mill and oversaw its restoration. The repair work on the mill's component parts—dam, earthen race, timbered flume, and penstock—was extensive. Much had rotted and stopped working, so these components needed to be repaired and replaced. The mill building itself was in relatively good shape, except for the load-bearing framing of the north end. It had partially rotted and was weak from continuous exposure to water. Because the poplar and locust timber that had been originally used to frame the mill was no longer available—due to logging—chestnut timbers were used for the replacement of two plates, eight posts, and supporting braces. Grossman also dismantled and inspected the hydraulic turbine to assure that it was in running order. He found its overall condition to be acceptable. After replacing the driveshaft, the turbine was reassembled and put back into place.[18]

No doubt the mill restoration was immensely aided by Aden Carver, who had helped with the original construction of the mill under millwright Sion Early long ago. At this point, CCC "boy" Carver was over ninety. Grossman also interviewed Early, who was then retired and living in Waynesville. Younger CCC enrollees supplied the physical labor.[19]

Once the restoration was finished, the park leased the mill to John Jones to run as a tourist attraction. He hired other local help, Carrie Nations and Major McGee, as operators, and this staff ground corn for locals following the traditional standard of a one-eighth volume toll. This toll portion was then sold in Cherokee and Gatlinburg to defray expenses. Until Jones died in 1940, the mill ground 650–700 bushels of corn each year. At that point it again fell into disuse; no replacement miller was hired during the war years or even until the late 1960s, when the mill was due for another round of maintenance and restoration.[20]

At about the same time that work was underway at the mill, Superintendent Eakin received $20,000 in funds from the Works Projects Administration (WPA) to build a fish hatchery. The purpose of the hatchery was to rear fingerlings of both brook and rainbow trout to restock streams that had been overfished and were being restored after logging ceased. At this point in time, park administrators were eager to establish the park's recreational facilities with sport fishing as a primary draw. Both WPA and CCC labor were used to build the hatchery, which was located along Kephart Prong above the camp of the same name. The camp included barracks, officers' quarters, a latrine, a mess hall, educational and recreational buildings, and a woodworking shop.

The hatchery consisted of dozens of round, stone-defined rearing ponds spread across a grassy streambank as well as a small diversion dam and a pipeline for the water supply. Once fingerlings reached six inches in length, they were transported by ten-gallon milk cans to many North Carolina park streams. The brook trout were intended for streams at 3,000 feet elevation and above, and the rainbow trout were for lower-elevation streams. The current thinking by park biologists was that the native brook trout could maintain its numbers at high elevations, whereas the rainbow trout would thrive in lower streams and provide good sport fishing at the more accessible streams. Later biologists learned that elevation alone could not protect "brookies" from the larger and more aggressive rainbows, alas, and some of the stocking done in the CCC era led to losses of this native species in some streams. In any case, in the first several years, the hatchery produced between 38,000 and 250,000 trout each year, with the majority being rainbow trout. But as the operation continued, it was plagued by several instances of dramatic fish die-offs. At the time, the cause was not understood. Biologists speculated that cold water temperatures were the reason. But much later, scientists learned that the reason the hatchery became unproductive was that road construction had exposed Anakeesta rock above the tributaries that fed water into the rearing pools. When it comes into contact with air and water, Anakeesta rock creates a toxic mix of chemicals and lowers the water pH significantly. When the poisoned water reached the hatchery ponds, many fish died immediately; others were weakened and became vulnerable to disease. Eventually, the project was deemed unsustainable because of low productivity, so the park shifted its approach from rearing fish to purchasing them from local hatcheries outside the park at a cheaper cost. The hatchery was supervised during the war years by the U.S. Fish and Wildlife Service as a side camp for conscientious objectors. Later, in the 1950s, the Kephart camp was dismantled and the buildings were removed. All that remains of the camp today are boxwoods originally planted around camp buildings, a nonfunctioning stone water fountain, a brick and stone hearth and chimney, and, farther up the trail, at the hatchery area, a cistern-like cement structure.[21]

In the park's first master plan, the Oconaluftee Ranger Station was envisioned as the North Carolina park headquarters, and it was to be surrounded by a museum, residential staff buildings, and utility buildings. Consequently, the ranger station was sited at Floyd Bottoms, a large area of flat land where the river broadens and slows at the floor of the valley. This is the site of the nineteenth-century Enloe farm, first occupied by patriarch Abraham and later by his son Wesley. After Wesley's death, the land was sold to Lon Floyd, and his heirs, also owners of the Mingus Mill property. The Floyds then sold it to the state for the park. By 1938, work began on the ranger station with a Public Works Administration allotment of $18,000. The crew used stone quarried at Ravensford by CCC workers. This same stone was also quarried and transported to Tennessee, where it was used for the park headquarters at Sugarlands. The CCC transported the stone from the quarry and did all the masonry and carpentry for the ranger station. Sources credit two stonemasons for their skilled workmanship on the building: Spanish-born master stonemason Joe Troitino and T. Walter Middleton of Little Canada, North Carolina. Middleton was an enrollee whose skills improved with practice; he once told Ranger Tom Robbins that the east end of the building is rougher than the west one because they constructed the west one second.[22] The building, now situated next door to the larger, new Oconaluftee Visitor Center, which opened in 2011, included a public area for visitors seeking information as well as offices for the chief ranger and other park staff. Its design was similar to the Sugarlands headquarters, with native stone facings on exterior walls, a stone fireplace, and a full-length front porch. Though the roof was always intended to be slate, wood shingles were installed for the opening in November 1940 and replaced with slate in 1955. Once the building was complete, the CCC landscaped around it with shrubs, retaining walls, and a parking area. The other planned buildings of the complex were not built at all during the CCC era.[23] When they were built later, they were placed elsewhere.

Unfortunately, the Oconaluftee Ranger Station was not complete on September 2, 1940, for the park dedication headlined by President Roosevelt, though the headquarters at Sugarlands was open.[24] This event represented the official opening of the national park and recognized the years of effort that park proponents had invested. They had worked tirelessly to sway public opinion about the park spanning two states and then managing all the governmental, legal, and social challenges of transferring hundreds of private farms and logging company holdings to the federal government. Amid this celebration, recognition of the residents who were displaced by the park was also made. Among other local guests, the National Park Service invited two Oconaluftee Valley farmers to attend the ceremony at Newfound Gap; they were Aden Carver and Dock Conner. Also invited were two descendants of William Holland Thomas (his daughter-in-law and granddaughter) in recognition of Thomas's many efforts to secure the homeland of the Eastern Band of Cherokee Indians.[25] After the event, FDR's party drove along Newfound Gap Road into North Carolina to meet with Cherokee officials. Along the way, his motorcade passed by CCC boys lined up in formation and wearing uniforms in front of their camps' entrances. One of the leaders of the Italian American company, a First Sergeant Jackson, however, was dressed in an all-black western outfit complete with Stetson hat and cowboy boots. As a newspaper account tells it, the president noticed the man out of uniform and called him over to the limousine, asking, "What in hell are you supposed to be?" The sergeant replied that he was a CCC boy but paused and emphasized the first C for "civilian" in the acronym. This response was met with laughter and acknowledgment. After the exchange, the president gave Johnson a ride to the company's mess hall, where the head of state joined a group of enrollees for lunch.[26]

Once the United States entered World War II after the attack on Pearl Harbor, the social and economic purposes of the CCC were replaced by the need for soldiers for the war effort. Consequently, Congress ended funding for the program in the summer of 1942. Most camps closed rather quickly after that. All CCC work in the park stopped August 8, 1942, leaving many projects unfinished, including two bridges across the Oconaluftee River (one at Kephart Prong and the other at Smokemont), as well as utilities, a flume, and additional pools for the fish hatchery. Some of the men who worked in camps remained in the area, even though they were not locals. Tilghman Bass, Shelton Bradsher, Duncan Cox, Jimmy Gaither, Barry Gaither, and First Sergeant Johnson (who married a local woman) stayed in Swain County. Camp physician Dr. Roy Kirchberg went into private practice in Sylva after 1936. Ed Chambers was a CCC boy who joined at age sixteen and worked for two years, and Columbus "Clum" Cardwell, a local, also joined; later both worked for the park service. Clum was an automotive mechanic for many years.[27]

THE LAST TO LEAVE THE TOWNSHIP

It is difficult to trace how the remaining farm families departed the part of the valley that became the national park in the 1930s and 1940s, but it seems that leaseholders gradually moved on despite their great reluctance to depart. Many made homes in the nearby North Carolina counties. Oconaluftee local Carl Lambert claimed that "the Floyds, Queens, [and] Parks, moved to Virginia. Bradleys, Chambers, and Conners moved to Tennessee. Beck[s] and Conners moved to North Georgia and others to the West Coast."[28] During the CCC era, a handful of people still lived in the park. One resident, Clementine "Clem" Enloe, had a farm on Tight Run. Her husband was "Biney," a nephew of Wesley Enloe. Biney had died in October 1930, and Clem kept the farm with a lease and took care of one of their younger sons, Birtie, who was deaf and mute and then in his forties. She was known by early rangers to be ornery and resentful of new restrictions on fishing. A wiry, independent woman, she fished every day and would regularly exceed the limit. A photograph of her

Columbus "Clum" Cardwell in CCC work uniform, 1935.

GREAT SMOKY MOUNTAINS NATIONAL PARK ARCHIVES, TOWNSEND, TENN.

Clementine "Clem" Enloe going fishing, 1935–36.
Note the snuffbox in her dress pocket.

GREAT SMOKY MOUNTAINS NATIONAL PARK ARCHIVES, TOWNSEND, TENN.

shows her standing and warily staring at the camera. One hand holds a fishing pole, and in the pocket of the dress she is wearing, the shape of a snuff tin can be discerned. In 1940, at age eighty-five, Clem left her old farm and moved to a nearby asylum because of a heart condition. She died in 1945.[29] Other residents included Josh Williamson, who lived at Kephart Prong. He drove a taxi and took schoolchildren living near him down the mountain to Smokemont School. The neighboring Dowdle children were some of his regular riders. Eventually, the Williamson family moved to Whittier. Bert Crisp and his family of boys moved from their Mingus Creek farm to Tow String in the mid-1930s but then bought a farm in Whittier several years later. The Smith family, the Reagan family below Collins Creek, and Wiley Conner and his family were in residence in the 1930s, too. The Reagans had a small kerosene-powered mill for corn during this time. Tow String resident Dan Lambert, then a young boy, recalled that sometimes there would be a kerosene taste to the meal.[30]

The year 1937 marked the moment when significant changes began. Dock Conner's family at the old Collins farm began moving out of the park at that time. They had bought land in Pigeon Forge, Tennessee, long before in 1926, wisely anticipating the need to leave Oconaluftee, presumably fearing changes that the end of logging would bring. Other children of Dock's as well as a number of in-laws already lived on the Tennessee side of the park. At first, Dock, Charlie, Charlie's wife, Ella Beck Conner, and their children lived in Gatlinburg. As Gatlinburg grew into a tourist resort, they built a home and moved on to their property in Pigeon Forge. Dock had long been a widower; now that he was older, he moved in with Charlie and Ella, staying with them until his death in 1948.[31]

Distant cousin Edd Conner also died in 1937 and was at last permanently laid to rest in the white burial suit and walnut casket he had had so meticulously made for this purpose seventeen years earlier. He was seventy-three and buried in the Bryson City Cemetery. Late in the same year, Charles Bascom Queen and his wife, Mary Fisher Queen, moved out of their Smokemont home. They eventually bought "a small farm in the Olivet Community of Jackson County." Just before, their granddaughter, Agnes, was born in the family home. Agnes was the child of Maisie Queen Young and her husband, Frank.[32]

In April 1932, the Smokemont church and its 0.77 acres of land were transferred to the State of North Carolina for inclusion in the Smokies. The trustees and deacons were provided $1,100 for the value of the property. After the sale, the church continued to meet and function as the spiritual home of the families still living nearby and as a place of worship for the CCC enrollees. The Queen family had been one of the longtime supporters of the Smokemont Baptist Church. No doubt when they and others moved away, the viability of the congregation's continuing its weekly services and lease diminished. In 1939, regular services at Smokemont ended, and the park took possession of the church building. At the time, Jesse Lambert was pastor, and he led some forty members to establish Tow String Baptist Church in the Tow String Community two miles south of Smokemont.[33] Tow String was and is a pocket of privately deeded land surrounded by Cherokee land; for this reason, even though it is adjacent to the park, it was not acquired by it. Though always a part of the Oconaluftee Valley community, Tow String remained near but not within the national park, and a handful of families lived there. By the way, the origin of the name Tow String is not fully known. Former Oconaluftee park ranger Tom Robbins has suggested that the name comes from the use of flax to make fabric. The raw fiber was soaked in water to separate the tow, "the short, rougher fibers," from the finer ones. "The finer fibers were used to make linen while the tow is used for rougher materials—tow sacks."[34]

Longtime Oconaluftee residents Ben and Emma Conner Fisher were active members when the Smokemont Baptist Church closed. In fact, Emma was a descendant of Samuel Conner, who had been among the church's founders over a century earlier. In response to the strong ties that the Fishers and other members felt to each other and to the church, Emma organized a group to hold the first church reunion in 1940 by sending postcards out to members to announce the date. She maintained the church's records and mailed out letters of dismissal from Smokemont as relocating members found and joined other churches. Ben became an employee of the park service, so this couple took it upon themselves to jointly prepare the church for the homecoming revival week and Sunday reunion service every year. Their devotion to this event over the span of decades never flagged. On July 21, 1970, they were working at the church in anticipation of that year's approaching homecoming. Ben worked outside while Emma cleaned the church windows inside. During a break, Emma brought her husband water for a cool drink, and sadly Ben collapsed from a heart attack and soon died. His funeral was held at the church.[35] In time, Jesse Lambert's son, Dan Lambert, took on the task of being the preacher and organizer for the reunion; as a Tow String resident and pastor of Wright's Creek Baptist Church in Cherokee, he presided over revivals, weddings, and funerals held at the church. Even later, Raymond

Young couple outside Smokemont Baptist Church, 1930.

GREAT SMOKY MOUNTAINS NATIONAL PARK ARCHIVES, TOWNSEND, TENN.

Matthews, the pastor of Tow String Church, became the point person for the reunion, though Dan continued to preach well into the twentieth-first century. In 1976, Smokemont Baptist Church was placed on the National Register of Historic Places.[36]

As World War II approached, was fought, and ended, other icons of the community departed. The commissary in Ravensford, run by Oscar McDonald, closed in 1944. Once the CCC camps there closed, the fields were maintained as open meadow.[37] For the first time in many years, they were empty of buildings and, of course, part of the park. In 2004, the Eastern Band of Cherokee Indians gained ownership of Ravensford in a land swap with the

Two women sitting inside Smokemont Baptist Church, 1930.
GREAT SMOKY MOUNTAINS NATIONAL PARK ARCHIVES, TOWNSEND, TENN.

National Park Service and built a school complex there. The descendants of those who lost this land to the park were unhappy about the swap. It represented a broken promise: when they were forced out, they were told the land would forever be a part of the park.[38]

A month after the celebration of his 101st birthday, Aden Carver passed away on June 24, 1945. He had been living on his farm just up from Smokemont campground with his son Julius since the park came. When he died, he was the oldest known resident of Swain County. His death is significant because he had played a role in so many of the community's key events and achievements. In his teens, he helped supply food to the members of the Thomas Legion ensconced at Fort Harry over the mountain ridge. He helped build the second, grand Mingus home and Mingus Mill in the 1870s. After a number of years working as a millwright and carpenter in Tennessee, he returned to help his aging father farm the family land, which he inherited and lived on until his death. He worked for a time in the Smokemont mill during the logging years and with the CCC on the restoration of Mingus Mill in the 1930s. He was a member, deacon, and song leader of Smokemont Baptist Church. With his wife, Martha Roberts, he raised eleven children, including two sets of twins. Recognizing his status as the quintessential mountain farmer, Park Superintendent Blair Ross and other park service employees from the North Carolina side of the park attended his funeral. He was interred at the family plot behind his home. As he had for his mother, Aden carved his own tombstone. The natural upright stone includes a tracing of his granddaughter's hand at its base reaching up toward a cross. Janice Carver Mooney, who had been the child, later explained that the hand was reaching heavenward toward his eternal home.[39]

By the time Dan Lambert of Tow String returned from service after World War II, the park, its visitor centers, trails, campgrounds, and picnic areas were open and welcoming. Though a few last lessees held on, their numbers had dwindled. Following other locals, Dan joined the park service. He worked at fire towers and then on road maintenance for a total of thirty-one years, even as he served as pastor of a church in Cherokee. He rose through the ranks and eventually became a foreman with the lofty title of "equipment engineer."[40]

Jaheu Conner and his wife, Nellie Bradley Conner, were among the last remaining Oconalufty Township residents. Since logging days, they had run the store at Smokemont, living above it. After the property was sold to the park, they continued to run it with a yearly lease. The store was located near the Smokemont campground and had the first gas pumps on the North Carolina side of the park, so it got steady business, particularly in the summer. Still a general store, it sold "clothing and groceries and whatever you needed, some tools, just more or less a general merchandise store."[41] Because the park did not allow electricity, Jaheu and Nellie used oil lamps for light and block ice for refrigeration. Of course, they knew that their situation at Smokemont was tenuous, with only a yearly lease. So back in the mid-1930s they had bought property in Pigeon Forge adjoining their relatives'. Jaheu was a son of Dock Conner and a brother of Charlie Conner, who had already relocated

Conner's General Store at Smokemont, 1921.

GREAT SMOKY MOUNTAINS NATIONAL PARK ARCHIVES, TOWNSEND, TENN.

to Tennessee. A tract of sixty-two acres was put up at auction due to foreclosure, and Jaheu bought it with an $8,000 bid. In 1948, Jaheu supervised the building of a new home on this land while Nellie ran the Smokemont store. When they left Smokemont in February 1949, Jaheu was sixty, and Nellie was in her early fifties. They focused on farming their Tennessee land for a few years until Tennessee routed a new four-lane highway across it; then managing the livestock and fields across the road became difficult. So they sold the land across the road at auction in thirty-six small lots, beginning the tourist industry along Highway 321. As with both their Oconaluftee homes (at Collins Creek, and later at Smokemont), they were situated on the main road to the mountains, a road many tourists traveled. This family no doubt became one of the luckier ones displaced by the park.[42]

Once the Smokemont church and store closed, Oconalufty Township was all park. The old community was no more. In the way that people value things once they are gone, the park created a pioneer farmstead next to the ranger station, on the old Enloe farm, also known as Floyd Bottoms. It displays the way of life of late nineteenth-century farm families. In 1994, the farmstead was renamed as the Mountain Farm Museum "to better convey to visitors the open-air museum aspect of the collection of buildings."[43] This museum includes authentic farm buildings as well as a heritage garden and open fields. Though a number of the buildings were relocated from other parts of the park, the massive barn is original to the property. It is a drover's barn, with a long, narrow central passageway that goes straight through. Stalls for horses and other livestock open from the center on either side. The hayloft above reveals the barn's size; a 2,500-square-foot home could fit inside it.[44] This museum provides the best example of how the prosperous and longtime mountain families lived. It also provides a poignant testimony to the history of the valley at the central southern North Carolina park entrance. That the museum is so close to Cherokee, the home of the Eastern Band, is fitting. The histories of the Oconaluftee mountain community and that of the Cherokees who resisted removal and remained on their ancestral lands have been deeply intertwined since the early 1800s.

LESSONS OF ENDURANCE

As logging declined and the park became a reality, the Eastern Band's position in the valley changed. As early as 1914, with the first Cherokee Indian Fair in October, it began to develop a tourism business that would serve as an ongoing economic strategy to sustain its members. By the 1930s, the craft business was established. Further, by 1934 and the passage of the Indian Reorganization Act by the federal government and its approval by the EBCI—the part of the New Deal that aided Native Americans—the looming threat of allotment ended. In addition the act allowed for the establishment of tribal governments, protected and promoted Native American culture, and supported schools and business endeavors, all much needed provisions to help the band's political stability and well-being. During the same decade, the tribal council successfully negotiated land sales to the federal government for the southern segment of the Blue Ridge Parkway that would connect the park-as-highway with the Great Smoky Mountains. The council resisted early proposals of a parkway route that would disrupt the community and succeeded in gaining agreement on a favorable ridge route, with generous compensation, that skirted Cherokee farms and still provided tourists access to the park and the reservation, along with its growing attractions. Parkway construction on this segment was underway by 1940 when the park was dedicated. In the next ten years, the first Eastern Band–owned tourist complex would open at the Boundary Tree site and productions of the summertime outdoor drama *Unto These Hills* began.[45] Like all Native American communities, the Qualla Boundary continued to face citizenship, property, economic, health, and educational challenges, but by the 1930s a number of protections against future threats were firmly in place.

Some see justice in the slow unfolding of events that positioned the Qualla Boundary as a unique feature of western Carolina to be acknowledged, appreciated, and exploited for regional economic development when once the Lufty Cherokees had been pushed off their land and oppressed by white families who were, in turn, removed. Perhaps. Another idea is that the trajectories of the Eastern Band and the Oconalufty Township suggest multiple forms of resilience and strategies of adaptation when crises and change arrived, all of which are instructive. The Eastern Band endured for many reasons. Notably, the people were resourceful individually and collectively. They had a durable identity as a community while they accepted necessary internal changes. They chose capable, far-sighted, and committed leaders who appear to have learned painful lessons from the deerskin trade that ensnared them to capitalism and weakened their agency through debt. Often, they responded in time to outside threats with a unified approach. The assistance of powerful external advisers and government officials saved the day at several critical junctures. Sometimes the Cherokees were a bit lucky with timing, though they also absorbed shocks and blows that had serious impacts.

The township families were also resourceful and had a strong community spirit. Maybe because they saw themselves as part of the dominant culture of North Carolina and the United States, they were not motivated in the same way as the Cherokees to act in a unified fashion against trends that would eventually overwhelm their lives in the valley. They likely did not expect that they would become vulnerable because they perceived their status as top tier for too long. Though race was always a factor, and they had that going for them, it was not the only one. Money was and had always been. Without recognizing the threat to their community, they embraced commercial logging, which exposed them to speculators, upheaval, degradation, fire, and outside interest. If the logging companies were run by elite capitalists pursuing profits, the park proponents were a political power elite, both regional and national, seeking economic development through tourism (apparently as much as recreational options, resource restoration, and wilderness protection). Township residents were subjugated—twice—by those who wanted their land and its resources for what it could do for people outside the valley. And yet some folks still found ways to adapt and hang on. They did so alone, not collectively. They did not organize as a community to push back, which isolated the few who did resist, like George Beck and Clem Enloe, and put them to a disadvantage. But even amid their dispossession, some families got on. The Conner households who moved to Tennessee likely were the most foresighted and strategic (but then they had the resources to be so).

I am reminded of the Cherokees' precolonial identity as "the Principal People." They were the dominant indigenous group in the Southeast. That identity may not have served the Cherokees well once the Europeans arrived. Though the white valley township families did not apply such an idea to themselves, as far as I am aware, I think they may have conceived of themselves in a similar way—somewhat privileged. Those with good land occupied a sweet spot. I think this not because of the land owners' arrogance; certainly arrogance is not expressed in the records. But we humans are susceptible to self-absorption. Similar to the way in which humans are all mostly anthropocentric, we often believe in our own and our own ethnic group's edge, superiority, if not hegemony. This belief functions as self-confidence. Of course, the trouble is that it can be self-deceptive—as well as cruel, unfounded, limited, and socially counterproductive. Leaving aside the other flaws, though they are equally important, the problem with too much self-confidence is that it can blind one to events beyond one's own control, which may make it less likely to notice warnings and dangers in time to avoid them. Survival, then, may be linked to humility, even empathy.

That said, the valley should be remembered for important instances of cooperation and civility between the Cherokees and the white mountain farm families during the nineteenth century. They shared food when crops failed, provided medical help during periods of widespread disease, served together in the Thomas Legion, and undertook community projects such as roads and mills. The legacy of African Americans in the valley is more difficult to generalize about; so little is really known about this topic. Clearly, they provided labor for all sorts of efforts. The ethnic groups may not have been or behaved like kin, friend, or allies at every turn, but they managed a neighborliness that was consequential and remains inspirational. More investigation, most properly conducted by descendants, into the ways that peoples' personal lives straddled the ethnicities in the valley would yield new insights into questions of mutual esteem and daily ambiance during the nineteenth, twentieth, and current centuries. Given the scope of my work, all I can do now is point out this enticing research direction for others to explore.

The three ethnic groups—Cherokees, whites, and African Americans—continuously faced tests and opportunities in regard to the region, state, nation, and even other countries. During no period was the valley beyond the reach of outside forces. Here ethnic groups' circumstances differed considerably most of the time. Because of their different identities and status, their options were distinct as were their degrees of exposure and vulnerability. What they shared were resourcefulness and resilience when it came to major disruptions and long-term trends. I find the ability of all the valley's residents to respond to their crises heartening and instructive. Understanding that their challenges will not be those of today's places or societies, I view their stories as exemplary.

Chapter 14

CROSS JORDAN INTO CANAAN AND I WANT TO GO

REMNANTS OF A TOWNSHIP

OCONALUFTEE was the home of many mountain families, Cherokee, white, and Black. But after clearing the land for fields, after building a home, after keeping a farm going and a family fed, after years of war and hardship and growth and change, with the exception of the Cherokees and the few in Tow String, the valley was no longer theirs. Logging had changed it. Railroads had changed it. Fire had changed it. Roads had changed it. The park movement and the twentieth century had changed it. It had been their home, but the township was defunct. A good number of the longtime white families in the township still had folks on or near their homesteads. By the 1930s, some families had been on the land for over a century. Multiple generations had lived in the valley. They had scraped by and adapted.

When the state bought them out and the park came, the effort was over. They had to go as well. Some hung on with lifetime leases, limited no doubt by the Depression and its many bank closures in the early 1930s. Folks deposited the money they got from the state into banks that closed shortly afterward. Some of these banks never reopened and they lost everything. Some men worked for the CCC. Some found work with the park. Some made agreements to provide park visitors with amenities, for a while. But the era of independent farms in Oconaluftee had ended. Only the few families who bought land up

Tow String were secure; only their land was safe because it was deeded land and it was encircled by Cherokee holdings. One could say that it is ironic that the descendants of families who moved on to Cherokee land at the beginning of the nineteenth century were now removed by both state and federal government policy that favored yet another approach to land use, one fashioned for the twentieth century rather than the nineteenth. Like the Lufty Cherokees who would not leave, could not imagine abandoning their centuries-old homelands, the white mountain farming families were rooted and resisted removal, too.

Excluding the Civil War years and despite the fundamental and constant challenges of subsistence farming, Oconalufty Township in the nineteenth century represents an idyllic concept in United States history: the tight-knit farming community in the wilderness. There must have been evenings when fathers and mothers and children enjoyed moments of calm, satisfaction, and security. The day's work done, the supper over, folks would settle into the evening tasks of sewing, mending, and preparing for the next day without haste. There must have been times when there was enough good but simple food, when clothes were adequate if not fashionable, when most everything was made or grown at home and the items that had to be bought were affordable and accessible. There must have been months when sickness and death were at bay. Life would have been basic but rich. These are the times that a township descendant or a visitor can romanticize. Surely they existed—even if only fleetingly.

The yearly Smokemont Baptist Church reunion reenacts those times. It has occurred since 1940, the year the park was dedicated and a year after regular church services ended. Emma Conner Fisher is credited with creating the reunion. As the church clerk, she kept forwarding addresses of former members and sent out penny postcards to announce the event that first year. Now the pastor of Tow String Church, currently Raymond Matthews, organizes the event.[1]

For a full week each August, once again Oconaluftee seems like a community. On the week nights, the church bell rings at 7:00 P.M. By then, some folks are already seated in the pews; others make their way up the sloping, somewhat steep path to the church door. Relatives hug, friends shake hands and pat backs, and old timers and visitors smile warmly, nodding welcome and hello. People are happy, convivial, and bighearted.

Except for some children dressed overtly country-style—ringlets and checked dresses for girls or overalls with a short-sleeved shirt and bow tie for boys—attire is casual yet traditional. Women mostly wear skirts or dresses, and men have on clean jeans and short-sleeved shirts. Not many wear T-shirts. Only the preachers wear a suit and tie, but most of them remove their jackets as they warm up during their sermons. Not many people are decked out in high-tech hiking gear. Everyone is dressed to manage the warmth and humidity of the evening at the end of a hot day. They wear the everyday clothes of churchgoing people.

Evening services begin, continue, and end by singing favorite hymns and Sunday school songs, mostly of the Baptist church. Family duos and groups, child soloists, small choirs of children—accompanied (or not) with a guitar, rehearsed and impromptu, with and without a songbook or hymnal—take turns and come to the pulpit on a step-up platform to sing or lead a song. Often the performers start and the congregation joins in after a verse or two. "Greatest Friend," "Victory in Jesus," "My Name Is Written There," "Have a Little Walk with Jesus," "How Great Thou Art"—all these are sung in turn. Anyone who wishes can walk up to the pulpit and sing. Some have strong voices, but many sing not because they are talented or trained but to participate, to be fully present and back in Oconaluftee. Excellent acoustics make each voice, no matter how soft, audible to the entire room.

As the crowd sits and sings, breaths condense on the window glass, even though the windows along the long walls are all open. The air is still inside and out. The doorways stand open. No ceiling fan provides relief, but some women use paper paddle fans. Early on it is brighter outside than in; the sun reflects off of select leaves, defining a spectrum of green, from black-green to deep midtone greens to bright chartreuse. The close feeling of a shaded church dates only to more recent decades. When the church was built, the hillside was without trees. The land had long been cleared. Now, as darkness comes over the course of the evening, the room brightens, comparatively, and the bare light bulbs hanging from the ceiling provide curiously flattering incandescent light.

Kids as young as four or five sing "The Wise Man Built His House upon a Rock," "Do Lord," and "Jesus Loves Me." The children are poised, unhurried, self-confident. They receive the rapt attention of the adults as well as enthusiastic applause. One girl, probably about nine years old, comes to stand behind the pulpit and brings a big ringed binder full of songs, which she places on the lectern. With complete composure, she pages through the book for at least a minute looking for the song she wants. Everyone waits. When she finds it, she begins to sing, "Glory, Glory, Glory Somebody Touched Me," a song with verses for each day of the week. The verses for Monday through Wednesday give her a solo, but at Thursday, members of the congregation stand, clap, and join in. By the Sunday verse, everyone is up and sings through the final refrain. Then comes applause and joy.

During the singing, a visitor notices how visible everyone is. Pews are arranged to create an in-the-round experience. The raised platform for the pulpit is situated in the center of the long uphill side of the rectangular church sanctuary, rather than at a narrow end. Short pews flank the pulpit; then longer pews face the pulpit on the downhill side, with some open space for passage in front. In the corners adjacent to these front pews, additional short pews are set at angles to create an encircling effect. Even if you sit in a back pew or a corner, you see many faces throughout the church, not just the backs of others' heads. Longtime reunion preacher and Tow String resident Dan Lambert has explained that the arrangement was changed when he was a child to be "more centralized." At that time, the church was heated by a potbellied stove in the middle of the room, so that might also have been a reason for the unusual arrangement.[2]

Other physical features of the church are worth noting. The outside is covered in white painted clapboard. The interior walls and ceiling are continuous, horizontally oriented lengths of beadboard stained a dark walnut. Knots in the boards tell that the paneling is pine. According to Matthews, the wood for the church was milled at Smokemont and likely donated by Champion Fibre, the company that ran the mill. About twelve feet up, two hefty wires divide the sanctuary into three equal parts; these wires look structural but were simply used to hang curtains that would divide the space for Sunday school classes.

As the revival group warms to the singing and coalesces, a man or woman punctuates the end of a song with "Amen," "Praise the Lord," or "That's right." Others occasionally echo the exclamation. Eventually, singing gives way to testifying. Returning kin stand and talk about their happiness at being present as well as their troubles, losses, and worries over the past year. One evening, a man stands to say that his great-grandmother had belonged to the church and that "when I come here it feels like coming home. You're at home when you're saved. This family is God's family."

And so the balance between sung and spoken words tips, and a preacher rises to deliver an evangelical message about the urgency of being saved and believing in Jesus.

Often the preacher is a descendant of past preachers. Dan Lambert, now in his late eighties, is the son of Jesse Lambert, the last preacher of the church when it met regularly. He preaches several evenings of the revival week and at the Sunday service. Other Lambert relatives, including members of the

Matthews family from Tow String, preach as well. Some come to the reunion from Tennessee or other North Carolina counties. One evening, the theme of the sermon is "keeping the fire alive" for your faith. Later in the week, the preacher asks, "How is it with you?" The question encourages listeners to prepare for death and commit their souls to Jesus. Some congregants are impulsively moved to testify in agreement with this theme, and late in the week several people approach the pulpit and kneel, declaring themselves—by action if not spoken expression—saved. The deacons of Tow String Church quickly join those kneeling and join in prayer with them. Their words are impassioned but softly uttered.

After the sermon concludes, there comes a prayer. Then singing resumes. Many of the songs are nostalgic and describe the peace one gains remembering loved ones and days gone by. The lyrics anticipate a meeting of family and friends in heaven. "Precious Memories," "Little Mountain Church House," "What a Day That Will Be," and "Glad Reunion Day" have multiple meanings in the context of the reunion, suggesting both the lost Oconaluftee community and the importance of faith and belief. "Cross Jordan" is especially evocative in this way. It is sung near the end of every service. The hymn memorializes deceased family members ("Some have fathers now in glory and I want to go"), and the chorus looks forward to heavenly reunion:

Cross Jordan into glory and I want to go.
Cross Jordan into glory and I want to go.
Been a long time of suffering,
And now I want to go
To that meeting in New Jerusalem.

As each service ends, about two and a half hours later, everyone forms two circles that move in opposite directions throughout the crowded room. People greet, and hug or shake hands, often still singing. The crowd grows each night of the week as more people arrive and plan to stay for the Sunday service and picnic lunch on the grounds.

At that culmination to the week, all ages come for service and stay for lunch. Even though a fair number have traveled to attend, some from as far away as Ohio, the food is homemade. The potato salads, sliced tomatoes, fresh cucumbers and pickles, beans, casseroles, rolls, fried and baked chicken, barbecue, pies, cookies, cakes, and tea come from the gardens and kitchens of local folks. They are fresh and delicious—and ample. There's enough for all attendees as well as for the park crew who have helped with traffic and parking alongside Newfound Gap Road throughout the week. Then, it ends. The makeshift tables are folded and the chairs go back into car trunks. Folks hug and depart, smiling and waving. Promises are made to return next year.

Most days now the church is empty, dark, serenely quiet. One day I stopped by to linger for a bit. I found all in order, windows closed and doors open. A heavy white cardigan lay in a mound on one pew near the main door. I sat down by it, then folded it. I wondered whose it might be and whether I should take it to the ranger's station. I left it in hope that its owner would miss it and return to claim it. I got an ambivalent, bittersweet feeling to be in this vestige of a once resilient and vibrant community. All the sad times and the happy ones. The meetings, the marriages, the two funeral services for Edd Conner decked out in his custom-made, all-white burial suit. All the talk and stories, songs and prayers. All life's urgency gone. The park preserves the land now, a clear good, even if the overseer is an official and somewhat impersonal one. The woods keep growing back up around the church, the cleared fields and homesteads, the mills and towns, and the cemeteries. Oconaluftee, that sibilant evocation of the river's flow and continuity, that river from the crest of the Smokies—it remains. Visitors can rest "by the river," as the word "Oconaluftee" signifies, that long-ago mistaken translation of the Cherokee adjective for a village name. It is still possible to be in and near the valley township, but no longer of or from it. Visitors hold a legacy from the Cherokees, the few enslaved people, and hundreds of mountain folk and loggers who lived on this land. It is a blessing both sober and rich, with a complex origin and meaning, befitting our time.

Notes

ABBREVIATIONS USED IN THE NOTES

GSMNPA	Great Smoky Mountains National Park Archives, Townsend, Tenn.
NARA	National Archives and Records Administration, Washington, D.C.
Swain County Register	Swain County Property Records, Swain County Register of Deeds, Bryson City, N.C.
1850 Census	U.S. Bureau of the Census, Seventh Census of the United States, 1850, National Archives microfilm publication M432, NARA
1860 Census	U.S. Bureau of the Census, Eighth Census of the United States, 1860, National Archives microfilm publication M653, NARA
1870 Census	U.S. Bureau of the Census, Ninth Census of the United States, 1870, National Archives microfilm publication M593-1144, NARA
1880 Census	U.S. Bureau of the Census, Tenth Census of the United States, 1880, National Archives microfilm publication T9, NARA
1900 Census	U.S. Bureau of the Census, Twelfth Census of the United States, 1900, National Archives microfilm publication T623, NARA
1910 Census	U.S. Bureau of the Census, Thirteenth Census of the United States, 1910, National Archives microfilm publication T624, NARA
1920 Census	U.S. Bureau of the Census, Fourteenth Census of the United States, 1920, National Archives microfilm publication T625-1314, NARA
1930 Census	U.S. Bureau of the Census, Fifteenth Census of the United States, 1930, National Archives microfilm publication T626, NARA
1940 Census	U.S. Bureau of the Census, Sixteenth Census of the United States, 1940, National Archives microfilm publication, T627, NARA

INTRODUCTION

1. Moore, *Roadside Guide*, 31.

2. Mooney, "Myths of the Cherokee," 517; Wilburn, *Cherokee Landmarks around the Great Smokies*, 4.

3. Kephart, *Our Southern Highlanders*, 50, 28–32.

CHAPTER 1

1. Creswell and Guymon, "Prehistoric and Historic Background," 7.
2. Newman, "Overview," 3–5.
3. Creswell and Guymon, "Prehistoric and Historic Background," 8.
4. Creswell and Guymon, "Prehistoric and Historic Background," 8–9.
5. Creswell and Guymon, "Prehistoric and Historic Background," 8.
6. Schroedl, "Cherokee Ethnohistory and Archaeology," 206.
7. Dickens, *Cherokee Prehistory*, 12.
8. Creswell and Guymon, "Prehistoric and Historic Background," 9.
9. Newman, "Overview," 6.
10. Newman, "Overview," 6.
11. Creswell and Guymon, "Prehistoric and Historic Background," 9.
12. Creswell and Guymon, "Prehistoric and Historic Background," 9.
13. Newman, "Overview," 6; Dickens, *Cherokee Prehistory*, 11.
14. Angst, *Archaeological Investigations at Site 31SW393*, 32–34.
15. Angst, *Archaeological Investigations at Site 31SW393*, 32–34; Angst, *Archaeological Investigations of Sites 31SW393, 31SW451, 31SW459 and 31SW460*, 48–83.
16. Newman, "Overview," 9.
17. King, "History and Archeology"; Dickens, *Cherokee Prehistory*, 94.
18. King, "History and Archeology."
19. Angst, *Archaeological Investigations at Site 31SW393*, 134.
20. Newman, "Overview," 9.
21. Newman, "Overview," 9; Dickens, *Cherokee Prehistory*, 100–101; Bense, *Archaeology of the Southeastern United States*, 218–19.
22. Creswell and Guymon, "Prehistoric and Historic Background," 10; Dickens, *Cherokee Prehistory*, 207.
23. Kreusch, *Report on Archeological Investigations*, 11.
24. Keel, "Ravensford Tract Archeological Project," 9–11.
25. Wilburn, "Nununyi, the Kituhwas," 55; and "Archeological Overview," 6–8.
26. Angst, *Archaeological Investigations at Site 31SW393*, 138.

CHAPTER 2

1. Mooney, "Myths of the Cherokee," 232.
2. King, "Introduction," ix.
3. McLoughlin, *Cherokees and Christianity*, 130–35; Mails, *Cherokee People*, 18.
4. McLoughlin, *Cherokees and Missionaries*, 346.
5. McLoughlin, *Cherokees and Missionaries*, 346.
6. Dickens, *Cherokee Prehistory*; Dickens, "Origins and Development of Cherokee Culture," 3–32.
7. Whyte, "Proto-Iroquoian Divergence," 134–44.
8. Whyte, "Proto-Iroquoian Divergence," 141.
9. Mooney, *Myths of the Cherokee*, 182.
10. Peterson, "Defining Cultural Landscapes through Human Ecology," 101.

11. Polhemus, *Toqua Site*, 1221.

12. Schroedl, "Cherokee Ethnohistory and Archaeology," 220; Rodning, "Architectural Symbolism and Cherokee Townhouses," 62.

13. Schroedl, "Cherokee Ethnohistory and Archaeology," 214.

14. Peterson, "Defining Cultural Landscapes," 101.

15. Peterson, "Defining Cultural Landscapes," 102.

16. Cumfer, *Separate Peoples, One Land*, 25; Perdue, *Slavery and the Evolution of Cherokee Society*, xii.

17. Perdue, *Slavery and the Evolution of Cherokee Society*, 12–15.

18. Perdue, *Slavery and the Evolution of Cherokee Society*, 14.

19. McLoughlin, *Cherokee Renascence in the New Republic*, 15.

20. Mooney, *Myths of the Cherokee*, 242–45.

21. Peterson, "Defining Cultural Landscapes," 101.

22. Perdue, *Slavery and the Evolution of Cherokee Society*, 11, 17–18.

23. Mooney, *Myths of the Cherokee*, 250–51, 263–64.

24. Mooney, *Myths of the Cherokee*, 425.

25. Mooney, *Myths of the Cherokee*, 325–29, 472–74.

26. Duncan and Riggs, "Cherokee Heritage Trails Guidebook," 77.

27. Mooney, *Myths of the Cherokee*, 321–22.

28. Mooney, *Myths of the Cherokee*, 327–29.

29. Mooney, *Myths of the Cherokee*, 425; Garrett and Garrett, *Medicine of the Cherokee*, 114.

30. Purdue, *Slavery and the Evolution of Cherokee Society*, 4.

31. Reid, "Perilous Rule," 33–45.

32. Mooney, *Myths of the Cherokee*, 250; Perdue, *Slavery and the Evolution of Cherokee Society*, 5–6.

33. Mooney, *Myths of the Cherokee*, 245–49.

34. Zogry, *Anetso*, 33–44, 52.

35. Zogry, *Anetso*, 188.

36. Mooney, *Myths of the Cherokee*, 286–87.

37. Zogry, *Anetso*, 188–90.

38. Gaillard, *As Long as the Waters Flow*, 29–30.

CHAPTER 3

1. McDowell, *Documents Relating to Indian Affairs, 1754–1765*, xii.

2. King, "Introduction," x.

3. Dunaway, *First American Frontier*, 32.

4. Schroedl, "Cherokee Ethnohistory and Archaeology," 204.

5. Schroedl, "Cherokee Ethnohistory and Archaeology," 204.

6. Greene, *Cherokee Out Towns*, 38.

7. Greene, *Cherokee Out Towns*, 38.

8. Greene, *Cherokee Out Towns*, 40.

9. Dunaway, *Women, Work, and Family*, 55.

10. Dunaway, *First American Frontier*, 32.

11. Thornton, *Cherokees*, 29–40.

12. McDowell, *Documents Relating to Indian Affairs, May 21, 1750–August 7, 1754*, 84–85.

13. King, "Introduction," xii.

14. Greene, *Cherokee Out Towns*, 38.

15. Greene, *Cherokee Out Towns*, 42.

16. McDowell, *Documents Relating to Indian Affairs, 1754–1765*, xvi.

17. McDowell, *Documents Relating to Indian Affairs, May 21, 1750–August 7, 1754*, 74–75.

18. McDowell, *Documents Relating to Indian Affairs, May 21, 1750-August 7, 1754*, 172.

19. McDowell, *Documents Relating to Indian Affairs, May 21, 1750–August 7, 1754*, Vol. 1, 76.

20. McDowell, *Documents Relating to Indian Affairs, 1754–1765*, xvi.

21. McDowell, *Documents Relating to Indian Affairs, May 21, 1750–August 7, 1754*, xvi–xvii.

22. McDowell, *Documents Relating to Indian Affairs, May 21, 1750–August 7, 1754*, 194.

23. Greene, *Cherokee Out Towns*, 49.

24. McDowell, *Documents Relating to Indian Affairs, 1754–1765*, 13–14.

25. McDowell, *Documents Relating to Indian Affairs, 1754–1765*, 22.

26. McDowell, *Documents Relating to Indian Affairs, 1754–1765*, xxii–xxiv; Conley, *Cherokee Encyclopedia*, 166.

27. McDowell, *Documents Relating to Indian Affairs, 1754–1765*, xxiv–xxv.

28. McDowell, *Documents Relating to Indian Affairs, 1754–1765*, xxvi–xxx.

29. McDowell, *Documents Relating to Indian Affairs, 1754–1765*, xxxv; Hatley, *Dividing Paths*, 114–33; Tortora, *Carolina in Crisis*, 101–34; Conley, *Cherokee Encyclopedia*, 166–69.

30. Greene, *Cherokee Out Towns*, 53–54.

31. Greene, *Cherokee Out Towns*, 54.

32. Greene, *Cherokee Out Towns*, 54–55.

33. Greene, *Cherokee Out Towns*, 55–56.

34. Schroedl, "Cherokee Ethnohistory and Archaeology," 222–23.

35. Greene, *Cherokee Out Towns*, 57.

36. Greene, *Cherokee Out Towns*, 63.

37. Greene, *Cherokee Out Towns*, 60.

38. Greene, *Cherokee Out Towns*, 60–63.

39. Colonel Moore to General Rutherford, November 17, 1776, quoted in Greene, *Cherokee Out Towns*, 61.

40. Greene, *Cherokee Out Towns*, 61.

41. Greene, *Cherokee Out Towns*, 62–63.

42. Greene, *Cherokee Out Towns*, 66–67.

43. Schroedl, "Cherokee Ethnohistory and Archaeology," 223–25.

44. McLoughlin, *Cherokee Renascence*, 64–66; Dunaway, *Women, Work, and Family*, 59–63.

45. King, "Introduction," xiii.

46. Schroedl, "Cherokee Ethnohistory and Archaeology," 225–25; Peterson, "Defining Cultural Landscapes," 106.

47. Peterson, "Defining Cultural Landscapes," 106.

48. Greene, *Cherokee Out Towns*, 68–69; Dunaway, *First American Frontier*, 53–54.

49. Peterson, "Defining Cultural Landscapes," 113; Dunaway, *Women, Work, and Family*, 60.

50. Peterson, "Defining Cultural Landscapes," 113.

CHAPTER 4

1. Parris, "Boundary Tree Still Lives in Memory."

2. Wigginton, "Rufus A. Morgan," 403.

3. State Library of North Carolina, "NC Land Records before 1800."

4. Arthur, *Western North Carolina History*, 138–39.

5. Lambert, "Oconaluftee River," 8; Dunaway, *First American Frontier*, 72–86.

6. Peterson, "Two Early Boundary Lines," 21.

7. Peterson, "Two Early Boundary Lines," 29.

8. McCarter and Kelley, *Meigs Line*, 130.

9. Thomas Freeman's Journal, in Records of the Cherokee Agency in Tennessee, 1801–1835, National Archives microfilm publication M208, RG 75, roll 1, p. 549, NARA.

10. Thomas Freeman's Journal, 549–50.

11. McCarter and Kelley, *Meigs Line*, 146; Conley, *Cherokee Encyclopedia*, 130.

12. Thomas Freeman's Journal, 549–50.

13. McCarter and Kelley, *Meigs Line*, 151.

14. Ellison, *Mountain Passages*, 69.

15. Godbold and Russell, *Confederate Colonel*, 10; Mooney, "Myths of the Cherokee," 162.

16. Thomas Freeman's Journal, 549–50.

17. Return J. Meigs to secretary of war, October 20, 1802, cited in Peterson, "Two Early Boundary Lines," 42n32.

18. Meigs to secretary of war, October 22, 1802, cited in Peterson, "Two Early Boundary Lines," 43n32.

19. Meigs to secretary of war, n.d., cat. no. 15656, Meigs Post Papers, GSMNPA.

20. Webb, Leigh, and Benyshek, *Ravensford Land Exchange Tract*, 38.

21. Arthur, *Western North Carolina History*, 208.

22. Webb, Leigh, and Benyshek, *Ravensford Land Exchange Tract*, 48.

23. McLoughlin and Conser, "Cherokees in Transition," 687.

24. Frizzell, "Native American Experience," 41.

25. Dykeman and Stokely, *Highland Homeland*, 44–45.

26. Dykeman and Stokely, *Highland Homeland*, 24.

27. Carl G. Lambert, "Oconaluftee River," 7.

28. See Cathey, *Genesis of Lincoln*; Coggins, *Eugenics of President Abraham Lincoln*; and Coggins, *Abraham Lincoln*.

29. Edward C. Conner, "Manuscript of Edward C. Conner," unpublished manuscript, November 17, 1937, Conner folder, DDC 390.92, p. 36–38, Edd Conner Manuscript, GSMNPA. This manuscript seems to be an early version of a more polished memoir by Edward Clarence Conner, also probably completed in 1937. It is a disorganized typescript that contains some passages that appear in the memoir, but it also contains anecdotes and information about Oconaluftee residents that appear nowhere else. In addition, it is highly repetitive as if it is a collection of draft pages that the author or an assistant intended to revise and polish later. Cook, "Sketches of Haywood County," 71.

30. Cook, "Sketches of Haywood County," 71–72.

31. Ed Trout, "Mingus Mill," unpublished manuscript, 1990, Mingus Family Papers, GSMNPA.

32. Dunaway, *First American Frontier*, 47–48.

33. Finger, *Eastern Band of Cherokees*, 11; Owl, "Eastern Band of Cherokee Indians," 106; "Register of Persons Who Wish Reservation under the Treaty of July 8, 1817," document 1987.091.001, Reservations under 1817 Treaty Collection, Museum of the Cherokee Indian Archives, Cherokee, N.C.

34. "Register of Persons Who Wish Reservation under the Treaty of July 8, 1817," Reservations under 1817 Treaty Collection.

35. Mooney, "Myths of the Cherokee,"163; Finger, *Eastern Band of Cherokees*, 71; Godbold and Russell, *Confederate Colonel*, 10–11, 49.

36. Mooney, "Myths of the Cherokee," 163.

37. Dunaway, *Women, Work, and Family*, 102–4.

38. Frizzell, "Native American Experience," 43.

39. Quoted in Finger, *Eastern Band of Cherokees*, 11.

40. Mooney, "Myths of the Cherokee," 163. Interestingly, Willnotah does not mention the topic of alcohol in his account of the trance and vision.

41. Wilburn, "Indian Gap Trail," 1–2.

42. Minutes of Haywood County Court of Pleas and Quarter Sessions, 1809–1834, microfilm 2A, 2:189, quoted in Jenkins, *Gass*, n.p., n10; Dunaway, *First American Frontier*, 108–10.

43. Wilburn, "Indian Gap Trail," 8–9.

44. Robert S. Lambert, "The Pioneer History of the Great Smoky Mountains National Park: A Report to the Superintendent Based upon Documentary Sources," June 15–October 1, 1957, p. 67, Robert S. Lambert Papers, GSMNPA.

45. W. H. Thomas to Jas. P. H. Porter, June 24, 1839; Thomas to Elizabeth and John Welch, September 6, 1839; and Thomas to H. P. King, September 28, 1839, all reproduced in Wilburn, "Indian Gap Trail," 23–26.

46. "Representations of the value of the Qualla Town store as made out by J. W. King," January 1, 1837, and December 31, 1838, MS 80–3, folder 75, William Holland Thomas Papers, Special Collections, Western North Carolina University, Cullowhee.

47. "Robert Collins Road Book: Smoky Mountain Head of Oconalufty River Heading towards Tennessee," June, no year, 1897.157.012, folder 12, William Holland Thomas Collection I, Museum of the Cherokee Indian Archives, Cherokee, N.C.

48. Lambert, "Oconaluftee Valley," 424.

49. Kendall, *Rifle Making*, 10.

50. Jenkins, "Mining of Alum Cave," 78–87; Inscoe, *Mountain Masters*, 89–104; Dunaway, *First American Frontier*, 184–85.

51. McLoughlin, *Cherokees and Missionaries*, 383.

52. Arthur, *Western North Carolina*, 224.

53. Bush, *Ocona Lufta Baptist*, 11.

54. Bush, *Ocona Lufta Baptist*, 17.

55. Bush, *Ocona Lufta Baptist*, 11–12. Bush names John H. Beck, but he may have been John C. Beck.

56. Bush, *Ocona Lufta Baptist*, 18–19, 25; Alma Matney Francis, "Jacob Mingus, Sr. Family: Refuted Data," unpublished manuscript, Iowa Park, Tex., 1985, cat. no. 15658, p. 2, Mingus Family Papers, GSMNPA.

57. Bush, *Ocona Lufta Baptist*, 4.

58. Cook, "Sketches of Haywood County," 88.

59. Mooney, "Myths of the Cherokee," 163.

60. McLoughlin, *Cherokees and Missionaries*, 163.

CHAPTER 5

1. Memorial of citizens of Haywood and Macon Counties, January 31, 1836, roll 2, William Holland Thomas Papers, David M. Rubenstein Rare Book and Manuscript Library, Duke University, Durham, N.C.

2. Mooney, "Myths of the Cherokee," 163.

3. Finger, *Eastern Band of Cherokees*, 18.

4. "Letter from General W. Scott to War Department"; Jurgelski, "New Light on the Tsali Affair," 133–64.

5. "Washington's Account as Related to Molly Sequoyah," 224.

6. Jurgelski, "New Light on the Tsali Affair," 138.

7. Ellison, "Will Thomas, Tsali & Tsali's Rock," 25–26.

8. "Letter from General W. Scott to War Department."

9. Conley, *Cherokee Encyclopedia*, 250.

10. Ellison, "Will Thomas, Tsali & Tsali's Rock," 22.

11. "Petition of Area Whites to Col. Foster."

12. "Newspaper Clipping from the Scrapbook of Col. W. S. Foster's Wife."

13. Jurgelski, "New Light on the Tsali Affair," 139, 153.

14. Lanman, *Letters from the Alleghany Mountains*, 112–14.

15. King and Evans, "Tsali," 194–99.

16. Reagan, *Smoky Mountain Clans*, 2:149.

17. Kent Cave, "Reminiscences of Mrs. Gerald Mooney," September 1981, interview transcript, p. 1, Carver Family Papers, GSMNPA.

18. Ellison, "Will Thomas, Tsali & Tsali's Rock," 26.

19. Godbold and Russell, *Confederate Colonel*, 12–13.

20. Hill, "East Is East and West Is West," 57–58; Finger, *Eastern Band of Cherokees*, 29.

21. Thomas and Savage, "William Holland Thomas," 36–47.

22. Thomas and Savage, "William Holland Thomas," 41; Conley, *Cherokee Encyclopedia*, 91–92.

23. Godbold and Russell, *Confederate Colonel*, 12–13, 40.

24. Paul T. Atteridg, "The Descendants of Abraham Enloe," unpublished manuscript, n.d., Enloe Family Papers, GSMNPA; Tom Robbins Papers, Mingus Family folder, GSMNPA.

25. Lambert, "Oconaluftee Valley," 422–23, 425.

26. 1850 Census, Slave Schedule, Haywood County, N.C., p. 2; 1860 Census, Slave Schedule, Jackson County, N.C., p. 2.

27. Lambert, "Oconaluftee Valley," 421.

28. Lambert, "Oconaluftee Valley," 423; Robert S. Lambert, "The Pioneer History of the Great Smoky Mountains National Park: A Report to the Superintendent Based upon Documentary Sources," June 15–October 1, 1957, p. 59, Robert S. Lambert Papers, GSMNPA.

29. Cook, "Sketches of Haywood County," 77.

30. Lambert, "Oconaluftee Valley," 423.

31. Finger, *Eastern Band of Cherokees*, 28–40.

32. Mooney, "Myths of the Cherokee," 168.

33. Godbold and Russell, *Confederate Colonel*, 42; Wilburn, "Memorandum for the Superintendent," March 22, 1939, Mingus Family folder, cat. no. 15658, GSMNPA; Lambert, "Oconaluftee River," 8; Frizzell, "Native American Experience," 46–57.

34. Kilpatrick and Kilpatrick, "Chronicles of Wolftown," 1–111.

35. Kilpatrick and Kilpatrick, "Chronicles of Wolftown," 58–60.

36. Lanman, *Letters from the Alleghany Mountains*, 85–87.

37. Cook, "Sketches of Haywood County," 73.

38. John Mingus to David Ring, March 20, 1845, 2012.321.0001.1, Museum of the Cherokee Indian Archives, Cherokee, N.C.

39. T. H. Welch, Note regarding John Mingus, May 29, 1868, 2012.366.0001.1, Museum of the Cherokee Indian Archives.

40. Lanman, *Letters from the Alleghany Mountains*, 88.

41. Lanman, *Letters from the Alleghany Mountains*, 89.

42. Lanman, *Letters from the Alleghany Mountains*, 90.

43. Lanman, *Letters from the Alleghany Mountains*, 92.

44. Lanman, *Letters from the Alleghany Mountains*, 85.

45. Lanman, *Letters from the Alleghany Mountains*, 93–114.

46. Lanman, *Letters from the Alleghany Mountains*, 93–95.

47. Lanman, *Letters from the Alleghany Mountains*, 96.

48. Lanman, *Letters from the Alleghany Mountains*, 100–104.

49. Lanman, *Letters from the Alleghany Mountains*, 104–5.

50. Dykeman and Stokeley, *Highland Home*, 51; Webb, Leigh, and Benyshek, *Ravensford Land Exchange Tract*, 49; Cook, "Sketches of Haywood County," 88.

51. Kilpatrick and Kilpatrick, "Chronicles of Wolftown," 46–47.

52. Bush, *Ocona Lufta Baptist*, 48–60.

53. Dunaway, *Women, Work, and Family*, 86–88.

54. Bush, *Ocona Lufta Baptist*, 34–37; Weals, "Saga of the Dock Conner Family," part 3.

55. Bush, *Ocona Lufta Baptist*, 44, 48.

56. Lambert, "Oconaluftee Valley," 425.

CHAPTER 6

1. Fink, "Early Explorers in the Great Smokies," 63–64.

2. Fink, "Early Explorers in the Great Smokies," 64; Ward, "People Names in Plant Names."

3. Frome, *Strangers in High Places*, 104.

4. Avery and Boardman, "Arnold Guyot's Notes," 263.

5. Fink and Avery, "Arnold Guyot's Explorations," 255.

6. Avery and Boardman, "Arnold Guyot's Notes," 252.

7. Avery and Boardman, "Arnold Guyot's Notes," 264n39, 288.

8. Fink, "Early Explorers in the Great Smokies," 67.

9. Fink and Avery, "Arnold Guyot's Explorations," 256, 259–61; Guyot, "Guyot's Measurement of the Mountains of Western N.C.," 1; Ablon, "Tribal Council Supports Changing NC Mountain's name."

10. Frome, *Strangers in High Places*, 109.

11. Fink, "Early Explorers in the Great Smokies," 66.

12. Fink and Avery, "Arnold Guyot's Explorations," 255; Avery and Boardman, "Arnold Guyot's Notes," 251–318.

13. Avery and Boardman, "Arnold Guyot's Notes," 263–64.

14. Avery and Boardman, "Arnold Guyot's Notes," 289.

15. Avery and Boardman, "Arnold Guyot's Notes," 284.

16. Avery and Boardman, "Arnold Guyot's Notes," 290.

17. Avery and Boardman, "Arnold Guyot's Notes," 291.

CHAPTER 7

1. Crow, *Storm in the Mountains*, 3; Fisher, *Civil War in the Smokies*, 22–23.

2. Inscoe, *Mountain Masters*, 105–14.

3. Bush, *Ocona Lufta Baptist*, 3.

4. "Hamilton T. Mingus," roll 0245; "Thomas G. Enloe," roll 0243; "Benjamin M. Enloe," roll 0315; "Benjamin F. Enloe," roll 0315; "William A. Enloe," roll 0352; "Joseph A. Collins," roll 0314, all in Civil War Service Records, Confederate, North Carolina, National Archives microfilm publication M270, RG 109, NARA.

5. Hamilton T. Mingus to Abraham Mingus, Asheville, N.C., August 23, 1861, Jenkins and Sossamon, *Heritage of Swain County*, 14.

6. "Thomas Enloe," roll 0243, "Benjamin M. Enloe," roll 0315, "William A. Enloe," roll 0352, all in Civil War Service Records, Confederate; Lambert, "Oconaluftee River," 6.

7. Mooney, "Myths of the Cherokee," 168–69.

8. Crow, *Storm in the Mountains*, 1–13; Fisher, *Civil War in the Smokies*, 45–46; Thomsen, *Rebel Chief*, 161–76; Godbold and Russell, *Confederate Colonel*, 93–100.

9. "Asaph T. Enloe," roll 0569; "Sevier S. Enloe," roll 0569; "John T. Enloe," roll 0569; "John T. Collins," roll 0568; "Ephraim S. Conner," roll 0568; "Benjamin Carver," roll 0568; "James H. Bradley," roll 0568; "Osborn Bradley," roll 0568; "William A. Beck," roll 0567; "John A. Beck," roll 0567; "Stephen J. Beck," no roll number; "S. Carson Beck," roll 0567; "Jarrett M. [*sic.*] Smith," roll 0573, all in Civil War Service Records, Confederate; Crow, *Storm in the Mountains*, 20; Fisher, *Civil War in the Smokies*, 42–43; Bush, *Dorie*, 141. Curiously, Bush notes that Benjamin Carver was about seventeen years younger than Aden Carver.

10. Crow, *Storm in the Mountains*, caption to illustrations following p. 96.

11. Crow, *Storm in the Mountains*, 14–15, 198; Stringfield, "Sixty-Ninth Regiment," 729–31.

12. Finger, *Eastern Band of Cherokees*, 84.

13. Quoted in Crow, *Storm in the Mountains*, 5.

14. Crow, *Storm in the Mountains*, 5–8, Fisher, *Civil War in the Smokies*, 47, Finger, *Eastern Band of Cherokees*, 85–86.

15. Crow, *Storm in the Mountains*, 16–17; Finger, *Eastern Band of Cherokees*, 91–94; Stringfield, "Sixty-Ninth Regiment," 736–37.

16. Fisher, *Civil War in the Smokies*, 48; Crow, *Storm in the Mountains*, 29–30.

17. Quoted in Inscoe and McKinney, *Heart of Confederate Appalachia*, 110.

18. Prince, "Fort Harry," 2–6; McMahan, "Upland Chronicles"; Wilburn, "Indian Gap Trail," 11–12.

19. Prince, "Fort Harry," 2–3; Robert S. Lambert, "The Pioneer History of the Great

Smoky Mountains National Park: A Report to the Superintendent Based upon Documentary Sources," June 15–October 1, 1957, p. 25, Robert S. Lambert Papers, GSMNPA.

20. "Benjamin Carver," roll 0568, Civil War Service Records, Confederate; Civil War "Widows' Pensions," National Archives microfilm publication RG 15, NARA; Beckwith, "Narcissus Carver"; Prince, "Fort Harry," 3–4.

21. Parker, "25th North Carolina Infantry Regiment"; "Fredericksburg," American Battlefield Trust.

22. Benjamin Franklin Enloe to John Mingus, December 18, 1862, in Jenkins and Sossamon, *Heritage of Swain County*, 14.

23. "Benjamin F. Enloe," roll 0315, Civil War Service Records, Confederate.

24. "Joseph A. Collins," roll 0314, Civil War Service Records, Confederate; Jenkins, *Gass*, n.p., n31.

25. Fisher, *Civil War in the Smokies*, 61.

26. Inscoe and McKinney, *Heart of Confederate Appalachia*, 115; Stringfield, "Sixty-Ninth Regiment," 738.

27. Fisher, *Civil War in the Smokies*, 88.

28. Fisher *Civil War in the Smokies*, 85.

29. Mooney, "Myths of the Cherokee," 170.

30. "Joe Welch," roll 0574, Civil War Service Records, Confederate; Crow, *Storm in the Mountains*, 40–46; Stringfield, "Sixty-Ninth Regiment," 738–42.

31. Inscoe and McKinney, *Heart of Confederate Appalachia*, 103.

32. Crow, *Storm in the Mountains*, 51; Inscoe and McKinney, *Heart of Confederate Appalachia*, 111.

33. Reagan, "Asoph Hughes Family," 184; Carl G. Lambert, "Oconaluftee River," 6; "Asoph Hughes," U.S. Find a Grave Index, 1600s–Current, 2013, www.findagrave.com/memorial/111271426/Asoph-Hughes.

34. Donald B. Reagan, *Smoky Mountain Clans*, 2:129–57. The chapter on the Bradley family shows that James and Osborn, who enlisted in 1862, were brothers and sons of James Holland and Martha Grant Bradley. William B. ("William Bradley," roll 0568) and Andrew Jackson Bradley Jr. (listed as "A. Jackson Bradley," roll 0568) were also brothers and sons of Andrew Jackson Bradley and Mary Elvira Trentham Bradley. They enlisted in March 1863 but on different days, which may explain why Andrew Jackson Jr. was enrolled in Company K rather than Company F. Thomas Bradley ("Thomas Bradley," roll 0568) was the son of Isaac and Mida Ledbetter Bradley. Finally, Wilson Bradley ("Wilson Bradley," roll 0568) was either a half-brother to James Holland Jr. and Osborn, as the son of James Holland Bradley and his first wife, name unknown, or he was the son of Wilson and Jane Bright Bradley. If he was the former, he married Elizabeth T. Mingus and moved with her family to Missouri; he would have been thirty-seven when he enlisted. If he was the son of Wilson and Jane Bradley, he was a Wilson Jr. and would have been twenty-six years old at enlistment. All citations are to Civil War Service Records, Confederate.

35. "William Bradley," roll 0568; "A. Jackson Bradley," roll 0568; "Thomas Bradley," roll 0568; "Wilson Bradley," roll 0568, all in Civil War Service Records, Confederate.

36. "William T. Bradley," roll 0014; "Thomas Bradley," roll 0014; "James Bradley," roll 0014, all in Civil War Service Records, Union, North Carolina, National Archives microfilm publication M 401, RG 94, NARA.

37. Crow, *Storm in the Mountains*, 50–54; Fisher, *Civil War in the Smokies*, 123–25.

38. Crow, *Storm in the Mountains*, 56; Godbold and Russell, *Confederate Colonel*, 118.

39. Arthur, *Western North Carolina*, 610.

40. Crow, *Storm in the Mountains*, 56–58; Fisher, *Civil War in the Smokies*, 126–27.

41. Finger, *Eastern Band of Cherokees*, 95–97; Crow, *Storm in the Mountains*, 131–32.

42. Quoted in Crow, *Storm in the Mountains*, 116.

43. Crow, *Storm in the Mountains*, 114–16; Fisher, *Civil War in the Smokies*, 135–36.

44. Crow, *Storm in the Mountains*, 64–93; Shenandoah Valley Battlefields, "Battle of Piedmont,"; Cooling, "Monocacy"; Stringfield, "Sixty-Ninth Regiment," 743–56.

45. Dougherty, "A Bad Time Was Had by All"; Crow, *Storm in the Mountains*, 94–98; Adelman, "Third Battle of Winchester"; Dunn, "Battle of Third Winchester."

46. Crow, *Storm in the Mountains*, 97–102.

47. Bush, *Ocona Lufta Baptist*, 4.

48. Crow, *Storm in the Mountains*, 121–25; Fisher, *Civil War in the Smokies*, 137–39; Stringfield, "Sixty-Ninth Regiment," 758–59; Fisher, "Colonel George W. Kirk," 37–38.

49. Wilburn, "Indian Gap Trail," 17.

50. Jenkins, *Gass*, n.p., n31; Wilburn, "Indian Gap Trail," 14; Prince, "Fort Harry," 3–5. Prince dates the incident of Kirk's passage over Oconalufty Turnpike as the winter of 1864, but it actually occurred in February 1865.

51. Crow, *Storm in the Mountains*, 123.

52. Crow, *Storm in the Mountains*, 125–41; Fisher, *Civil War in the Smokies*, 141–42; Stringfield, "Sixty-Ninth Regiment," 760–61.

53. Fisher, *Civil War in the Smokies*, 148.

54. Bush, *Ocona Lufta Baptist*, 4.

55. Bush, *Ocona Lufta Baptist*, 4.

CHAPTER 8

1. Zeigler and Grosscup, *Heart of the Alleghanies*, 129.

2. Edward C. Conner, "Manuscript of Edward C. Conner," unpublished manuscript, November 17, 1937, Conner folder, DDC 390.92, p. 2–3, Edd Conner Manuscript, GSMNPA.

3. 1880 Census, Oconalufty Township, Swain County, N.C., Enumeration District 183, pp. 1–19.

4. Zeigler, "On Foot across the Mountains."

5. Davis, "Qualla," 581.

6. Kephart, *Our Southern Highlanders*, 445.

7. Davis, "Qualla," 577.

8. Godbold and Russell, *Confederate Colonel*, 130.

9. Charles Grossman, "0–67 Mingus Creek Mill," unpublished notes, November 26, 1935, pp. 1–2, Mingus Family Papers, GSMNPA.

10. Conner, "Manuscript of Edward C. Conner," 71.

11. 1860 Census, Slave Schedule, Jackson County, N.C., pp. 1–5.

12. 1860 Census, Slave Schedule, Jackson County, N.C., p. 2; 1870 Census, Qualla Township, Jackson County, N.C., p. 271B; 1880 Census, Ocona Lufty, Swain County, N.C., Enumeration District 183, p. 210B; 1900 Census, Oconalufty, Swain County, N.C., Enumeration

District 109, p. 3; Howell, "Life of Berry Howell," 182–83; Woodford, *When All God's Children Get Together*, 14–17.

13. 1880 Census, Ocona Lufty, Swain County, N.C., Enumeration District 183, p. 202C. This family is particularly confusing because a note appears below its 1880 Census listing that is only partly legible. It says, "This last family here is obscurity had like to have been forgotten. is the last one taken there being no place in place it with the proper numbers use the acres [illegible]." Further, Abram Mingus was the census enumerator in 1880, so one would expect that he would correctly list a household that he likely knew and that shared his last name.

14. 1860 Census, Slave Schedule, Jackson County, N.C., p. 2; 1870 Census, Qualla Township, Jackson County, N.C., p. 271B; 1880 Census, Ocona Lufty, Swain County, N.C., Enumeration District 183, p. 202C; 1900 Census, Oconalufty, Swain County, N.C., Enumeration District 108, p. 6.

15. Bush, *Ocona Lufta Baptist*, 63–64; Alma Matney Francis, "Jacob Mingus, Sr. Family: Refuted Data," unpublished manuscript, Iowa Park, Tex., 1985, cat. no. 15658, pp. 3–4, Mingus Family Papers, GSMNPA; "Clarinda Trentham," August 24, 1926, no. 22683, Tennessee State Library and Archives, Nashville; Tennessee Death Records, 1908-1958, roll 10, Tennessee State Library and Archives; "C.J. Mingus, age 28, married William R. Trentham, of Gatlinburg, Tenn., 21, on June 2, 1883, in Swain County, N.C.," U.S. Marriage Records, 1741–2011, RG 048, North Carolina County Registers of Deeds, State Archives of North Carolina, Raleigh; 1880 Census, Gatlinburg, Sevier County, Tenn., Enumeration District 188, p. 454B.

16. Santoro, *Myself When I Am Real*, 15–16; "Charles Mingus," Army Register of Enlistments, 1798–1914, National Archives microfilm publication M233, RG 94, NARA; "Charles Mingus, Sr.," U.S. Find a Grave Index, 1600s–Current, 2011, www.findagrave.com/memorial/80898521/Charles-Mingus. See also Gabbard, *Better Git It in Your Soul*, 13–17; Mingus, *Beneath the Underdog*, 124–33.

17. 1860 Census, Slave Schedule, Jackson County, N.C., p. 2; 1870 Census, Qualla Township, Jackson County, N.C., p. 266B; 1880 Census, Qualla Township, Jackson County, N.C., Enumeration District 102, pp. 254A–55B; 1900 Census, Quallatown, Jackson, N.C., Enumeration District 56, p. 8.

18. 1860 Census, Slave Schedule, Jackson County, N.C., pp. 1–2; 1870 Census, Qualla Township, Jackson County, N.C. p. 274A; 1880 Census, Qualla Township, Jackson County, N.C., Enumeration District 102, p. 253A; Eastern Cherokee Census Rolls, 1835–1844, National Archives microfilm publication T496, M1773, RG 75; Enumeration and Enrollment Censuses, 1893–1905, RG 75, NN-371-22, p. 11, Records of the Bureau of Indian Affairs, 1793–1999, National Archives at Atlanta, Ga.

19. 1880 Census, Ocona Lufty, Swain County, N.C., Enumeration District 183, pp. 199–208.

20. 1880 Census, Ocona Lufty, Swain County, N.C., Enumeration District 183, pp. 199–208; 1900 Census, Oconalufty, Swain County, N.C., Enumeration District 109, p. 1–36; Swain County Register, vol. 6 (1876): 274–75; 19: 10–12; 13: 244; 20: 6.

21. 1900 Census, Oconalufty, Swain County, N.C., Enumeration District 109, p. 304A; Howell, "Life of Berry Howell," 182–83; Swain County Register, vol. 7 (1884): 91–92; 18 (1894): 178–79; 20 (1904): 550; 31 (1908): 205; 31 (1909): 447; 41 (1913): 69; 42 (1915): 16; 42 (1916):

269; 48 (1920): 454; 62 (1936): 200; "Chrisenberry Napoleon Haynes Howell," U.S. Find a Grave Index, 1600s–Current, 2014, www.findagrave/memorial/139261445/Chrisenberry-Napoleon-Haynes-Howell; "Sarah 'Sally' Powell Howell," U.S. Find a Grave Index, 1600s–Current, 2015, www.findagrave/memorial/143938571/Sarah-Sally-Powell-Howell; Woodford, *When All God's Children Get Together*, 14–17.

22. 1900 Census, Quallatown, Jackson, N.C., Enumeration District 56, p. 183B; 1910 Census, Charleston, Swain County, N.C., Enumeration District 147, p. 10B; 1920 Census, Charleston, Swain County, N.C., Enumeration District 175, p. 12B; 1930 Census, Charleston, Swain County, N.C., Enumeration District 1, p. 8B; 1940 Census, Bryson City, Swain County, N.C., Enumeration District 87-1, p. 18A; "William Moses Powell, March 6, 1969, 11586, Death Certificate, Bryson City, Swain County, N.C.," North Carolina Death Certificates, 1909–1976, S.123, rolls 19-242, 280, 313-682, 1040-1297, North Carolina State Board of Health, Bureau of Vital Statistics, State Archives of North Carolina, Raleigh; "Anna Powell Thomas, August 10, 1950, 24192, Death Certificate, Charleston, Swain County, N.C.," North Carolina Death Certificates; "Beulah Powell Sudderth," U.S. Find a Grave Index, 1660s–Current, 2011, www.findagrave/memorial/65931820/Beulah-Powell-Sudderth; Swain County Register, vol. 32: 61; 35: 469; 42: 539; 45: 395; 50: 251, 425; 51: 351; "James and Lizzie P. Powell," 258.

23. 1860 Census, Slave Schedule, Jackson County, N.C., p. 2; "Statistics of Birdtown Indians taken in the year 1899," North Carolina, Native American Census, selected tribes 1894–1913, Eastern Cherokee Census Rolls, 1835–1844, M1773, RG 75 T496, p. 5, Records of the Bureau of Indian Affairs, 1793–1999, National Archives at Atlanta, Ga.; 1900 Census, Oconalufty, Swain County, N.C., Enumeration District 109, p. 4B; 1904 Indian Census, roll 22, line 5, Indian Census Rolls, 1885–1941, M595, RG 75, NARA; 1910 Indian Census, roll 22, line 14, Indian Census Rolls, 1885–1941; 1910 Census, Oconalufty, Swain County, N.C., Enumeration District 153, p. 9A; 1920 Census, Ocanalufty, Swain County, N.C., Enumeration District 182, p. 6A; 1923 Indian Census, roll 4, line 4, Indian Census Rolls, 1885–1941; 1930 Census, Oconalufty, Swain County, N.C., Enumeration District 10, p. 4A; 1940 Census, Beaverdam, Haywood County, N.C., Enumeration District 44-8, p. 5A; Guion, "Hester Roll, 1884," record 987, p. 16, Records Relating to Enrollment of Eastern Cherokee by Guion Miller, 1908–1910, M685, RG 75, 12 rolls, Records of the Bureau of Indian Affairs, 1793-1999, NARA; "Churchill Roll 1908," North Carolina, Native American Census, selected tribes 1894–1913, Eastern Cherokee Census Rolls, 1835–1844, M1773, RG 75, T496, p. 72; Report of Guion Miller on Exceptions to his Report of May 28, 1909, January 5, 1910, record 9333, Records Relating to Enrollment of Eastern Cherokee by Guion Miller, 1908–1910; United States Department of the Interior, *Indian Field Service Eastern Cherokee Enrolling Commission*, 150–64; "Harrison Coleman Death Certificate, January 1, 1923, 182," North Carolina Death Certificates; "Roll of Deceased Eastern Cherokee Annuitants Whose Right to Enrollment with the Eastern Band of Cherokee Indians of North Carolina Were Challenged by the Tribal Council, Who Left Estates Consisting of Suspended Per Capita Payments and Accrued Interest, and Who Died prior to June 4, 1924," Final Roll of the Eastern Band of Cherokee Indians of North Carolina, under Act of June 4, 1924, 1928 Baker Roll and Records of the Eastern Cherokee Enrolling Commission, 1924–1929, National Archives microfilm publication M2104, RG 75, pp. 457–59, Records of the Bureau of Indian Affairs, NARA; "Mourning Emmaline Coleman," U.S. Find a Grave Index, 1600s–Current, 2011,

www.findagrave.com/memorial/80287806/Mourning-Emmaline-Coleman; "Gibsontown Cemetery Memorials," U.S. Find a Grave Index, 1600s–Current, 2011, www.findagrave.com/cemetery/2352000/memorial-search?page=1sr129495137.

24. 1870 Census, Qualla Township, Jackson County, N.C., p. 284B; 1880 Census, Ocona Lufty, Swain County, N.C. Enumeration District 183, p. 208D; 1900 Census, Oconalufty, Swain County, N.C., Enumeration District 109, pp. 1A–16B.

25. Thornton, *Cherokees*, 130.

26. Thornton, *Cherokees*, 125.

CHAPTER 9

1. Hiram C. Wilburn, "Types of Architectures in the Great Smoky Mountains National Park: The More Pretentious Two-Story House," unpublished manuscript, n.d., cat. 15658, p. 1, Mingus Family Papers, GSMNPA.

2. Wilburn, "Types of Architecture," 1.

3. Cook, "Sketches of Haywood County," 79–81.

4. 1880 Census, Ocona Lufty, Swain County, N.C., Enumeration District 183, p. 202C.

5. "John Mingus," U.S. Find a Grave Index, 1600s–Current, 2007, www.findagrave.com/memorial/17274331/John-Mingus; "Mary 'Polly' Enloe Mingus," U.S. Find a Grave Index, 1600s–Current, 2007, www.findagrave.com/memorial/17274348/Mary-Polly-Enloe-Mingus; 1900 Census, Oconalufty, Swain County, N.C., Enumeration District 108, p. 6.

6. Ed Trout, "Mingus Mill," unpublished manuscript, 1990, pp. 2–3, Mingus Family Papers, GSMNPA.

7. Trout, "Mingus Mill," 2–3.

8. Trout, "Mingus Mill," 3–6.

9. Charles Grossman, "0–67 Mingus Creek Mill," unpublished notes, November 26, 1935, p. 2, Mingus Family Papers, GSMNPA. The identity of the "Bill Bradley" who helped with the mill is not known.

10. Trout, "Mingus Mill," 1–3.

11. "P. Suie, early marriage record, February 8, 1885, North Carolina," U.S. Marriage Records, 1741–2011, RG 048, North Carolina County Registers of Deeds, State Archives of North Carolina, Raleigh.

12. 1880 Census Ocona Lufty, Swain County, N.C., Enumeration District 183, p 201B.

13. Alexander, "The Big Smoky Mountains," 10. Thanks to Don Casada for information about Alexander's professorship.

14. Howell, "Life of Berry Howell," 183.

15. 1900 Census, Oconalufty, Swain County, N.C., Enumeration District 109, p. 3; Sale of 108 acres more or less from J. M. Enloe and wife, M. A. Enloe, to J. L. Floyd, December 18, 1905, registered March 11, 1907, Swain County Register, vol. 31 (1905): 11.

16. 1880 Census, Ocona Lufty, Swain County, N.C., Enumeration District 183, pp. 201B, 203B, 208D; 1900 Census, Oconalufty, Swain County, N.C., Enumeration District 109, pp. 1–3; 1910 Census, Oconalufty, Swain County, N.C., Enumeration District 152, p. 1A; 1920 Census, Ocanalufty, Swain County, N.C., Enumeration District 181, p. 4B; "Joseph Johnson 'Joe' Enloe," U.S. Find a Grave Index, 1600s–Current, 2010, www.findagrave.com/memorial/52407441/Joseph-Johnson-Joe-Enloe; "Lula Hayes Enloe," U.S. Find a Grave Index, 1600s–Current, 2015, www.findagrave.com/memorial/153271467/Lula-Hayes-Enloe;

"Malinda Lollis Enloe," U.S. Find a Grave Index, 1600s–Current, 2011, www.findagrave/memorial/71088294/Malinda-Lollis-Enloe; "Wesley Matthew Enloe," U.S. Find a Grave Index, 1600s–Current, 2011, www.findagrave/memorial/71088227/Wesley-Matthew-Enloe; Record of Appointment of Postmasters, 1832–Sept. 30, 1971, roll 95, p. 557, Records of the Post Office Department, M841, RG 28, NARA.

17. Reagan, *Smoky Mountain Clans*, 2:190; Alma Matney Francis, "Jacob Mingus, Sr. Family: Refuted Data," unpublished manuscript, Iowa Park, Tex., 1985, cat. no. 15658, p. 3, Mingus Family Papers, GSMNPA.

18. Bush, *Ocona Lufta Baptist*, 135.

19. Mrs. R. L. Creal, "'Doc' Conner Has Lived 62 Years in Smokies," unpublished manuscript, n.d., box 2, folder 25, Casada Collection, Special Collections Library, University of Tennessee, Knoxville; Swain County Register, vol. 2 (1880): 390–92.

20. Weals, "Saga of the Dock Conner Family," 4–5.

21. Bush, *Ocona Lufta Baptist*, 34–35.

22. Reagan, *Smoky Mountain Clans*, 2:182–200; Ida Reagan, "Asoph Hughes Family," 185.

23. Reagan, *Smoky Mountain Clans*, 1:15; Donald B. Reagan, *Smoky Mountain Clans*, 2:190; Burr, *Map of North and South Carolina Exhibiting the Post Offices, Post Roads, Canals, Rail Roads, &c*, in Burr and Arrowsmith, *American Atlas*, 6; *Daily Bulletin of Orders*.

24. Zeigler and Grosscup, *Heart of the Alleghanies*, 130.

25. Jenkins, *Gass*, 2–10.

26. Jenkins, *Gass*, 19; Bush, *Ocona Lufta Baptist*, 58.

27. Edward C. Conner, "The Conner Manuscripts: Story of the Life of Edward Clarence Conner," unpublished manuscript, n.d., Conner folder, no. 33980, p. 1, Edd Conner Manuscript, GSMNPA. This is the second of the two unpublished Edd Conner memoirs. Both are typescripts. This one appears better organized and is formatted in double columns. The title page is on National Park Service letterhead with Arno B. Cammerer named as director, so it would have been created during Cammerer's tenure between 1933 and 1940, probably in 1937.

28. "John C. Beck," U.S. Find a Grave Index, 1600s–Current, 2010, www.findagrave.com/memorial/53474208/john-beck; "Jane M. Swearinggen Beck," U.S. Find a Grave Index, 1600s–Current, 2021, www.findagrave.com/memorial/221913849/Jane-M-Beck.

29. "Samuel Beck," U.S. Find a Grave Index, 1600s–Current, 2010, www.findagrave.com/memorial/53454062/Samuel-Beck; Crow, *Storm in the Mountains*, 178.

30. Bush, *Ocona Lufta Baptist*, 44, 127–29.

31. The cause of death as childbirth comes from the U.S. Federal Census Mortality Schedule, 1850–85, National Archives microfilm T655, NARA.

32. Bush, *Ocona Lufta Baptist*, 127–29.

33. Maples, *Smoky Mountains Cemeteries*, 133–36; Great Smoky Mountains National Park, "Cemeteries within Great Smoky Mountains National Park," 5; "Beck Cemetery Memorials." U.S. Find-a-Grave Index, 1600s–Current, 2000, www.findagrave.com/cemetery/46827/memorial-search?page+1#sr-71928272.

34. Reagan, *Smoky Mountain Clans*, 2:129–57.

35. Reagan, *Smoky Mountain Clans*, 2:149.

36. Reagan, *Smoky Mountain Clans*, 2:137–38; Jackson County Register of Deeds, vol. 1 (1848): 586.

37. Reagan, *Smoky Mountain Clans*, 2:139, 155.

38. Reagan, *Smoky Mountain Clans*, 2:149–50.

39. 1870 Census, Qualla Township, Jackson County, N.C., pp. 271A–73A.

40. Reagan, *Smoky Mountain Clans*, 2:145–50.

CHAPTER 10

1. Sossamon, "Aseph Hamilton Hughes Family," 183–84; Ida Reagan, "Asoph Hughes Family," 184–85; Carpenter, "Thomas Irvin Hughes," 185–86; Sparks, "William Self and Mary Lugene Moody Hughes," 187–88; Williams, "Agriculture."

2. Edward C. Conner, "The Conner Manuscripts: Story of the Life of Edward Clarence Conner," unpublished manuscript, n.d., Conner folder, no. 33980, pp. 1, 2, Edd Conner Manuscript, GSMNPA.

3. "Conner Manuscripts," 2–9.

4. In his memoir, Edd Conner states that the Sunday preacher was "Henery Conner" and the one who called him to his conversion was "John Harvy Conner." But this variance in names seems to be a feature of the manuscript rather than an indication that the man was any other than William Henry Conner. "Conner Manuscripts," 1, 2.

5. "Conner Manuscripts," 15–17.

6. "Conner Manuscripts," 18.

7. "Conner Manuscripts," 19.

8. "Conner Manuscripts," 26–64; Cook, "Sketches of Haywood County," 92.

9. Sale of land from W. A. Enloe and his wife, M. C. Enloe, to M. E. Hayes, February 15, 1900, registered March 2, 1901, Swain County Register, vol. 22 (1900): 171–72.

10. Cook, "Sketches of Haywood County," 92.

11. "Conner Manuscripts," 65–68.

12. "Conner Manuscripts," 68–69.

13. "Conner Manuscripts," 69.

14. Bush, *Ocona Lufta Baptist*, 141; Florence Cope Bush, "Mary Bradley Carver," unpublished manuscript, n.d, p. 2, Carver Family Papers, GSMNPA.

15. Smith, "Aden Carver—Mountaineer," 5.

16. Joseph Hall, "Aden Carver Interview," Smokemont, N.C., 1939, transcript, pp. 118–21, Carver Family Papers, GSMNPA.

17. 1880 Census, Harrisburg, Sevier County, Tenn., Enumeration District 181, p. 343B.

18. Charles Grossman, "0-67 Mingus Creek Mill," unpublished notes, November 26, 1935, p. 1, Mingus Family Papers, GSMNPA; Cook, "Sketches of Haywood County," 80; Bush, *Ocona Lufta Baptist*, 52, 143.

19. Hall, "Aden Carver Interview," 119; Brad Free notes on Aden Carver, n.d., p. 2, Carver Family Papers, GSMNPA.

20. Bush, "Mary Carver Bradley," 3.

21. Kent Cave, "Reminiscences of Mrs. Gerald Mooney," September 1981, interview transcript, p. 1, Carver Family Papers, GSMNPA.

22. Cave, "Reminiscences of Mrs. Gerald Mooney," 1.

23. Sale of land from A. K. Bradley and Sarah Bradley to J. L. Queen, October 28, 1881, registered October 29, 1881, in Swain County Register, vol. 3 (1881): 165–66.

24. Bush, *Ocona Lufta Baptist*, 68.

25. Young, "Wilson Ensley and Amanda Catherine Queen," 260; "Alice Bradley Queen, death May 22, 1948, 9997, Valleytown, N.C.," North Carolina Death Certificates, 1909–1976, S.123, rolls 19-242, 280, 313-682, 1040-1297, North Carolina State Board of Health, Bureau of Vital Statistics, State Archives of North Carolina, Raleigh; 1920 Census, Oca-nalufty, Swain County, N.C., Enumeration District 182, p. 11A.

26. Bush, *Ocona Lufta Baptist*, 12.

27. Swain County Register, vol. 3 (1882): 183–84.

28. Bush, *Ocona Lufta Baptist*, 12.

29. Bush, *Ocona Lufta Baptist*, 27.

30. Swain County Register, vol. 27 (1906): 513–14.

31. 1880 Census, Ocona Lufty, Swain County, N.C., Enumeration District 183, pp. 199–208D; 1900 Census, Oconalufty, Swain County, N.C., Enumeration Districts 108 and 109; pp. 287A–301B, 302A–17B. These numbers are based on a hand count of the 1880 and 1990 census sheets for Oconalufty township, excluding both "Indian" and Black (or mulatto) families. The number for 1900 also excludes Quallatown, which was located in Jackson County and counted as a separate census district that year.

32. Carpenter, "Thomas Irvin Hughes," 186.

CHAPTER 11

1. Frizzell, "Native American Experience," 48; Godbold and Russell, *Confederate Colonel*, 131; Thomsen, *Rebel Chief*, 221.

2. Finger, *Eastern Band of Cherokees*, 102–5; Owl, "Eastern Band of Cherokee Indians," 136–42.

3. "Agreement between W. H. Thomas and Abraham Mingus," March 6, 1866, William H. Thomas Collection I, 1987.157009, Museum of the Cherokee Indian Archives, Cherokee, N.C.; Temple, *Map Showing the Chief Location and Lands of the Eastern Band of Cherokees*; Thomsen, *Rebel Chief*, 225.

4. Godbold and Russell, *Confederate Colonel*, 132–33; Thomsen, *Rebel Chief*, 223–25; Finger, *Eastern Band of Cherokees*, 119; Owl, "Eastern Band of Cherokee Indians," 126–30.

5. Finger, *Eastern Band of Cherokees*, 108–10; Owl, "Eastern Band of Cherokee Indians," 136–42.

6. Finger, *Eastern Band of Cherokees*, 125; Frizzell, "Politics of Cherokee Citizenship," 211–12.

7. Donaldson, *Extra Census Bulletin*, 18.

8. Frizzell, "Politics of Cherokee Citizenship," 206.

9. Frizzell, "Native American Experience," 48–50.

10. Finger, *Eastern Band of Cherokees*, 125–34.

11. Davis, "Qualla," 584.

12. Davis, "Qualla," 583–84.

13. Davis, "Qualla," 584.

14. Davis, "Qualla," 586.

15. Finger, *Eastern Band of Cherokees*, 131–34; Owl, "Eastern Band of Cherokee Indians," 154–56.

16. Young, "Sketch of the Cherokee People," 171.
17. Carrington, "Eastern Band of Cherokees," 16.
18. Carrington, "Eastern Band of Cherokees," 16.
19. Carrington, "Eastern Band of Cherokees," 16; Young, "Sketch of the Cherokee People," 171–72.
20. Carrington, "Eastern Band of Cherokees," 16; Donaldson, *Extra Census Bulletin*, 9.
21. Zeigler and Grosscup, *Heart of the Alleghanies*, 36.
22. Finger, *Eastern Band of Cherokees*, 147–49.
23. Zeigler and Grosscup, *Heart of the Alleghanies*, 38; Finger, *Eastern Band of Cherokees*, 114, 139–42.
24. Zeigler and Grosscup, *Heart of the Alleghanies*, 38–39.
25. Zeigler and Grosscup, *Heart of the Alleghanies*, 39.
26. Finger, *Eastern Band of Cherokees*, 156–58.
27. Oakley, *New South Indians*, 9–10; Perdue, *Cherokee*, 91.
28. Greene, *Cherokee Out Towns*, 84; Ward and Davis, *Time before History*, 6–7; Valentine, "Our Mission and History."
29. Mann S. Valentine, "Report on Excavations at the Sawnooke Mound, Swain County, North Carolina in 1882," 1883, MS C 57, archaeological notes, Valentine Family Papers, Valentine Archives, Richmond, Va.
30. Valentine, "Report on Excavations," Valentine Family Papers, 1–2.
31. Valentine, "Report on Excavations," Valentine Family Papers, 2.
32. Valentine, "Report on Excavations," Valentine Family Papers, 5.
33. Greene, *Cherokee Out Towns*, 84.
34. Edward Valentine to Mann Valentine, July 18, 1883, Valentine Family Papers.
35. Ward and Davis, *Time before History*, 7.
36. Moses, *Indian Man*, 18–22.
37. Moses, *Indian Man*, 22–36.
38. Colby, "Routes to Rainy Mountain," 600.
39. Mooney, "Sacred Formulas of the Cherokee," 310–19.
40. Mooney, "Sacred Formulas of the Cherokee," 311.
41. Mooney, "Sacred Formulas of the Cherokee," 312.
42. Mooney, "Sacred Formulas of the Cherokee," 313.
43. Mooney, "Myths of the Cherokee"; Mooney, "Swimmer Manuscript"; Kilpatrick and Kilpatrick, "Chronicles of Wolftown," 1–111.
44. Speck and Broom, *Cherokee Dance and Drama*, xv–xxiv.
45. Mooney, "Sacred Formulas of the Cherokee," 332.
46. Mooney, "Sacred Formulas of the Cherokee," 329.
47. Mooney, "Sacred Formulas of the Cherokee," 330.
48. Colby, "Routes to Rainy Mountain," 94–97, 107.
49. Colby, "Routes to Rainy Mountain," 76, 85, 108–9.
50. Moses, *Indian Man*, 40.
51. Mooney, "Sacred Formulas of the Cherokee," 318–19.
52. "James Mooney," 211.
53. Mooney, "Sacred Formulas of the Cherokee," 313.
54. Mooney, "Sacred Formulas of the Cherokee," 314–18.

55. Donaldson, *Extra Census Bulletin*, 8.

56. The area of the Cathcart Tract is outlined on Temple's map: *Map Showing the Chief Location and Lands of the Eastern Band of Cherokees.*

57. Finger, *Eastern Band of Cherokees*, 162, 169.

58. Colby, *Routes to Rainy Mountain*, 75.

59. Spaulding, "Expenses of Timber Experts," 3.

60. Spaulding, "Expenses of Timber Experts," 4–6.

61. W. W. Wortherspoon, quoted in Williams, "Merger of Apaches," 242.

62. *United States et al. v. W. T. Mason Lumber Co.*, 714–22.

63. James, "Myths of the Cherokee," 179; Finger, *Eastern Band of Cherokees*, 171.

64. Finger, *Eastern Band of Cherokees*, 171–72; Mooney, "Myths of the Cherokee," 179.

65. *United States et al. v. W. T. Mason Lumber Co.*, 722.

66. Robert S. Lambert, "Logging in the Great Smoky Mountains National Park: A Report to the Superintendent," October 1, 1958, p. 30, Great Smoky Mountains National Park Library, Gatlinburg, Tenn.

67. Finger, *Eastern Band of Cherokees*, 174–75; Perdue, *Cherokee*, 90–99.

68. Oakley, *New South Indians*, 42–47.

69. Owl, "Eastern Band of Cherokee Indians," 142.

70. Mooney, "Sacred Formulas of the Cherokee," 328–31; Young, "Sketch of the Cherokee People," 173.

71. Young, "Sketch of the Cherokee People," 171.

72. Donaldson, *Extra Census Bulletin*, 9.

73. Donaldson, *Extra Census Bulletin*, 12.

74. Donaldson, *Extra Census Bulletin*, 13.

75. Donaldson, *Extra Census Bulletin*, 14; Young, "Sketch of the Cherokee People," 170.

CHAPTER 12

1. Robert S. Lambert, "The Pioneer History of the Great Smoky Mountains National Park: A Report to the Superintendent Based upon Documentary Sources," June 15–October 1, 1957, p. 9, Robert S. Lambert Papers, GSMNPA.

2. Lambert, "Oconaluftee River," 7; Robert R. Madden, "Interview with Bert Crisp," tape 42–69 with transcript, 1968–69, pp. 29, 37–41, Oral History Collection, GSMNPA; Mrs. R. L. Creal, "'Doc' Conner Has Lived 62 Years in Smokies," unpublished manuscript, n.d., box 2, folder 25, p. 1, Casada Collection, Special Collections Library, University of Tennessee, Knoxville, University of Tennessee Special Collection Library; Weals, "Saga of the Dock Conner Family," part 2.

3. Lambert, "Report to the Superintendent," 9.

4. Holmes, *Forest Conditions in Western North Carolina*, 70.

5. Swain County Register, vol. 24 (1903): 357–63; 33 (1909): 277–79. See also *Southern Lumberman*, July 15, 1902, 7; July 1, 1903, 27.

6. Lambert, "Logging in the Great Smokies," 351–52.

7. Poole, *History of Railroading in Western North Carolina*, 9–46; Lambert, "Logging in the Great Smokies," 354; Eller, *Miners, Millhands, and Mountaineers*, 99–100.

8. *Message from the President Transmitting a Report of the Secretary of Agriculture*, 81–82.

9. Wesley M. Enloe died in 1903; his will named J. F. Enloe and Andrew J. Patton as executors and instructed them to sell his land "across the river and all my mountain lands" (September 1, 1902, Swain County, County Clerk's Office). This land was sold to J. L. Floyd in 1906 and then again to logging concerns in 1909. See Swain County Register, vol. 29 (1906): 488–90; 31 (1909): 476.

10. Lambert, "Report to the Superintendent," 35; George Beck interview, July 23, 1958, in Robert S. Lambert Papers, box 4, folder 8, GRSM 13217, GSMNPA; Poole, *History of Railroading*, 141.

11. Lambert, "Report to the Superintendent," 33–35; Swain County Register, vol. 29 (1906): 1–14; 30 (1907): 437–43.

12. *United States et al. v. W. T. Mason Lumber Co.*, 722.

13. Robert S. Lambert, "Logging in the Great Smokies," 354; "The Champion Lumber Company," *St. Louis Lumberman*, 58; "Along the Smoky Mountain Range," *Lumber World*, 21; statement of John C. Arbogast, "Expect to Prove: Champion Fibre Co," n.d., p. 14-6, Champion Fibre Company Papers, GSMNPA; untitled note, Robert S. Lambert Papers, box 4, folder 7, GSMNPA.

14. Lambert, "Report to the Superintendent," 29–31; Poole, *History of Railroading*, 172–73; Swain County Register, vol. 33 (1908): 80–85; 34 (1910): 381–85.

15. Mastran and Lowerre, *Mountaineers and Rangers*, 5.

16. Statement of John C. Arbogast, "Expect to Prove: Champion Fibre Co," cited in untitled note, Robert S. Lambert Papers, box 4, folder 7, GSMNPA.

17. "Champion Lumber Company," *St. Louis Lumberman*, 58; "In the Mountains of Western North Carolina," *American Lumberman*, 43; "Expect to Prove: Champion Fibre Company," cited in untitled note, Robert S. Lambert Papers, box 4, folder 8, GSMNPA; Eller, *Miners, Millhands, and Mountaineers*, 108–10.

18. Coleman, *Railroads of North Carolina*, 15, 37.

19. Lambert, "Logging in the Great Smokies," 360; "Receiver Asked for William Whitmer and Sons, Inc.," *New York Lumber Trade Journal*, 26.

20. Lambert, "Logging on the Little River," 358; untitled note, Robert S. Lambert Papers, box 4, folder 8, GSMNPA; Swain County Register, vol. 44 (1917): 76–79, 80–89, 420–28.

21. "R. E. Wood Buys in North Carolina," *Hardwood Record*, 36.

22. Lambert, "Coming of the Railroad," 15; Shipman, *Thirty-First Report of the Department of Labor*, 217, 265; Swain County Register, vol. 41 (1915): 340–42; 44 (1917): 429–31.

23. Madden, "Interview with Bert Crisp," 15–16, 37–41.

24. Eller, *Miners, Millhands, and Mountaineers*, 110; Lambert, "Logging in the Great Smokies," 355–59; Lambert, "Oconaluftee River," 8.

25. Korstian, "Southern Appalachian Spruce Forest," 9–11.

26. Untitled note, Robert S. Lambert Papers, box 4, folder 7, GSMNPA; Lambert, "Logging in the Great Smokies," 18.

27. "Mountains of Western North Carolina," *American Lumberman*, 43.

28. Poole, *History of Railroading in Western North Carolina*, 140–43; Lambert, "Logging in the Great Smokies," 359.

29. Lambert, "Report to the Superintendent," 34; Lambert, "Coming of the Railroad," 16.

30. Coggins, *Place Names of the Smokies*, 45–46; Weals, "Saga of the Dock Conner Family," 8.

31. Lambert, "Report to the Superintendent," 34.

32. Lambert, "Report to the Superintendent," 31–33; Lambert, "Oconaluftee River," 8.

33. Lambert, "Logging in the Great Smokies," 362.

34. Lambert, "Coming of the Railroad," 16.

35. 1900 Census, Oconalufty, Swain, N.C., Enumeration District 108, pp. 287A–301B; Enumeration District 109, pp. 302A–17B; 1920 Census, Oconalufty, Swain, N.C. Enumeration District 181, pp. 237A–49B; Enumeration District 182, pp. 250A–65A.

36. Tom Robbins, personal communication with author, August 2, 2017.

37. Lambert, "Oconaluftee River," 7; Young, "Wilson Ensley and Amanda Catherine Queen," 260; Swain County Register, vol. 44 (1917): 434–36; Bush, *Ocona Lufta Baptist*, 104.

38. Lambert, "Oconaluftee River," 8; Bush, *Ocona Lufta Baptist*, 97.

39. Lambert, "Logging in the Great Smokies," 355–60; Lambert, "Report to the Superintendent," 31–32, 36.

40. "Doogaloo" is an alternate spelling; "Commissary," *Sylva (N.C.) Herald*, 1; Perdue, *Cherokee*, 96; Ross Fuqua, "Interview of Mescal Burke and Ruth Floyd Hill," August 28, 2004, History no. 13, transcript, 9, 12–13, 68–69, Ravensford Oral History Project, GSMNPA; Burns and Schmitt, *Ravensford*.

41. Fuqua, "Interview of Mescal Burke," 68–69.

42. Bush, *Dorie*, 10–11.

43. 1920 Census, Ocanalufty, Swain County, N.C., Enumeration Districts 181 and 182, pp. 237A–49B, 250A–65A.

44. "Commissary," 1; Young, "Wilson Ensley and Amanda Catherine Queen Family," 260; Lambert, "Oconaluftee River," 8; Fuqua, "Interview of Mescal Burke," 50–51.

45. Lambert, *Up from These Hills*, 12–21.

46. Grimshawe, *Map Showing the Location of the Dwellings and Commissary*; Young, "Wilson Ensley and Amanda Catherine Queen Family," 260; Kent Cave, "Reminiscences of Mrs. Gerald Mooney," September 1981, interview transcript, 4, Carver Family Papers, GSMNPA.

47. Keel, "Ravensford Tract Archeological Project," 14.

48. Fuqua, "Interview of Mescal Burke," 9–13; Burns and Schmitt, *Ravensford*.

49. Cave, "Reminiscences of Mrs. Gerald Mooney," 8.

50. Sikora, *Luten Bridges in Great Smoky Mountains National Park*.

51. Eller, *Miners, Millhands, and Mountaineers*, 38.

52. Swain County Register, vol. 44 (1917): 196–416; 44 (1918): 593–94; 48 (1920): 352–53; Madden, "Interview with Bert Crisp," 15.

53. Swain County Register, vol. 46 (1919): 193–95.

54. Swain County Register, vol. 48 (1919): 350–51.

55. 1920 Census, Ocanalufty, Swain County, N.C., Enumeration District 182, pp. 262B–63B; 1930 Census, Oconalufty, Swain County, N.C., Enumeration District 107, p. 3A.

56. Jaheu Conner's name is highly variable in government documents. It seems that his full formal name was John Samuel Conner, but his nickname was Jaheu, Jeheu, and Jay Hugh. In some documents, he is referred to as John G. Conner, which seems an error. Charlie Conner's full name was Charles Wiley Conner. Weals, "Saga of the Dock Conner Family," parts 2 and 3: 7.

57. Weals, "Saga of the Dock Conner Family," part 3: 9; "Andrew Coleman Cathey,"

North Carolina Death Certificates, 1909–1976, S.123, rolls 19-242, 280, 313-682, 1040-1297, North Carolina State Board of Health, Bureau of Vital Statistics, State Archives of North Carolina, Raleigh.

58. Phillip E. Coyle, "Dan Lambert Interview," January 19, 2004, transcript, p. 2, Ravensford Oral History Project, GSMNPA.

59. Burns and Schmitt, *Ravensford*; Lambert, "Report to the Superintendent," 31–36.

60. Swain County Register, vol. 61 (1933): 1–3; 61 (1934): 29–30.

61. Burns and Schmitt, *Ravensford.*

62. Young, "Wilson Ensley and Amanda Catherine Queen Family," 260.

63. Pierce, *Great Smokies*, 163; "Commissary," 1; Coyle, "Dan Lambert Interview," 21; Lambert, "Oconaluftee River," 8.

64. Lambert, "Coming of the Railroad," 16.

CHAPTER 13

1. J. R. Eakin, "Memorandum for the Director," December 23, 1930, box 1081, file 201-006, RG 79, National Archives, cited in Pierce, *Great Smokies*, 175; Catton, "Gift for All Time," 63.

2. Catton, "Gift for All Time," 63, 73; Robbins, "Great Smoky Mountains National Park," 11–12.

3. Jolley, *"That Magnificent Army,"* 16–17; Charlotte Pyle, "CCC Camps in Great Smoky Mountains National Park," unpublished manuscript, April 1979, 2, GSMNPA; Catton, "Gift for All Time," 64.

4. Jolley, *"That Magnificent Army,"* 16–18, 33–36, 109, 121–27, 139; Pyle, "CCC Camps," 2, 7–9; Ross Fuqua, "Interview of Mescal Burke and Ruth Floyd Hill," August 28, 2004, History no. 13, transcript, p. 11, Ravensford Oral History Project, GSMNPA; Burns and Schmitt, "Ravensford"; Oakley, *New South Indians*, 59.

5. Jolley, *"That Magnificent Army,"* 22, 28.

6. Young, "Wilson Ensley and Amanda Catherine Queen," 260.

7. Robert P. White, "Narrative Report on Emergency Conservation Work, Great Smoky Mtns. National Park," January 1934, p. 5, GSMNPA.

8. Catton, "Gift for All Time," 67.

9. Jolley, *"That Magnificent Army,"* 28.

10. Davis, *My CCC Days*, 12; Burns and Schmitt, *Ravensford.*

11. Davis, *My CCC Days*, 23–55; Jolley, *"That Magnificent Army,"* 44; Burns and Schmitt, *Ravensford*; Phillip E. Coyle, "Dan Lambert Interview," January 19, 2004, transcript, p. 4, Ravensford Oral History Project, GSMNPA.

12. Davis, *My CCC Days*, 27–30, 57.

13. Davis, *My CCC Days*, 31–32; Jolley, *"That Magnificent Army,"* 39.

14. R. H. Montony, "General Report on ECW for First Enrollment Period," September 1933, Civilian Conservation Corps Papers, GSMNPA.

15. Pierce, *Great Smokies*, 177–78; Jill Breit, "Interview of Tom Robbins," June 15, 2005, transcript, p. 4, Ravensford Oral History Project, GSMNPA.

16. Jolley, *"That Magnificent Army,"* 60–62; Breit, "Interview of Tom Robbins," 17.

17. Cook, "Sketches of Haywood County," 111–12; Burns and Schmitt, *Ravensford*; Eli Potter, "Eli Potter 4/1/35," Eli Potter Papers, GSMNPA.

18. Ed Trout, "Mingus Mill," unpublished manuscript, 1990, pp. 3–10, Mingus Family Papers, GSMNPA.

19. "A. A. Carver, Smokemont, Marks, 100th Birthday," *Asheville Citizen*; Fuqua, "Interview of Mescal Burke," 55.

20. Trout, "Mingus Mill," 3.

21. Pierce, *Great Smokies*, 180; Catton, "Gift for All Time," 223–24; Brown, *Wild East*, 137; Brill, "Smokies' Conscientious Objector (CO) Work Camp," 14.

22. Tom Robbins, personal communication with author, August 2, 2017.

23. Catton, "Gift for All Time," 72; Jolley, *"That Magnificent Army,"* 64; Burns and Schmitt, "Ravensford."

24. Catton, "Gift for All Time," 72.

25. Hiram C. Wilburn, "Letter to the Superintendent," June 6, 1939, Hiram C. Wilburn Papers, GSMNPA.

26. Jolley, *"That Magnificent Army,"* 33.

27. Catton, "Gift for All Time," 70; "Commissary," *Sylva (N.C.) Herald*, 1; Burns and Schmitt, Ravensford; National Conference on State Parks, "Truck Tire-Changing Dolly," 38; and "Safety Device for Roller's Trailing Wheels," 29.

28. Lambert, "Oconaluftee Valley," 8; see also Bush, *Ocona Lufta Baptist*, 145–46.

29. "Elmina Clementine 'Clem' Conley Enloe," U.S Find a Grave Index, 1600s–Current, 2008, www.findagrave/memorial/25301882/Elmina-Clementine-Enloe.

30. Coyle, "Dan Lambert Interview," 19–23; Robert R. Madden, "Interview with Bert Crisp," tape 42–69 with transcript, 1968–69, p. 25, Oral History Collection, GSMNPA.

31. Weals, "Saga of the Dock Conner Family," 4–5.

32. "Edward Clarence Conner," U.S Find a Grave Index, 1600s–Current, 2012, www.findagrave/memorial/92149407/Edward-Clarence-Conner; Young, "Wilson Ensley and Amanda Catherine Queen Family," 260.

33. Bush, *Ocona Lufta Baptist*, 5–7.

34. Tom Robbins, personal communication with author, August 1, 2017.

35. Bush, *Ocona Lufta Baptist*, 8–9; "Certificate of Death for Ben Clingham Fisher, August 6, 1970, no. 25781, Cherokee, Swain County, N.C.," North Carolina Death Certificates, 1909–1976, S.123, rolls 19–242, 280, 313–682, 1040–1297, North Carolina State Board of Health, Bureau of Vital Statistics, State Archives of North Carolina, Raleigh.

36. Bush, *Ocona Lufta Baptist*, 5; "National Register of Historic Places Inventory."

37. Breit, "Interview of Tom Robbins," 9.

38. Burns and Schmitt, *Ravensford*; Fuqua, "Interview of Mescal Burke," 43–44.

39. Kent Cave, "Reminiscences of Mrs. Gerald Mooney," September 1981, interview transcript, p. 3, Carver Family Papers, GSMNPA; Bush, *Ocona Lufta Baptist*, 138–43.

40. Coyle, "Dan Lambert Interview," 7.

41. Coyle, "Dan Lambert Interview," 4.

42. Weals, "Saga of the Dock Conner Family," part 3: 8–9.

43. Pridemore, F. D., "Memo H3015," April 21, 1994, Tom Robbins Papers, Vertical Files, Oconaluftee Ranger Station, Great Smoky Mountains National Park, Cherokee, N.C.

44. Trout, *Historic Buildings of the Smokies*, 46–47.

45. Finger, *Cherokee Americans*, 75–97; Oakley, *New South Indians*, 36–76; Whisnant, *Super-Scenic Motorway*, 183–213.

CHAPTER 14

1. This account of the Smokemont Baptist Church Reunion is based on the author's attendance, August 7–10, 2014.

2. Phillip E. Coyle, "Dan Lambert Interview," January 19, 2004, transcript, p. 12, Ravensford Oral History Project, GSMNPA.

Bibliography

MANUSCRIPT AND ARCHIVAL COLLECTIONS

- Atlanta, Ga.
  - National Archives at Atlanta (microfilm, accessed through Ancestry.com)
    - Records of the Bureau of Indian Affairs, 1793–1999
      - Eastern Cherokee Census Rolls, 1835–1884, M1773, RG 75, T496
        - North Carolina, Native American Census, selected tribes 1894–1913
      - Enumeration and Enrollment Censuses, 1893–1905, RG 75, NN-371-22

- Bryson City, N.C.
  - Swain County Register of Deeds
    - Swain County Property Records

- Cherokee, N.C.
  - Museum of the Cherokee Indian Archives
    - Reservations under 1817 Treaty Collection
    - William Holland Thomas Collection I
  - Oconaluftee Ranger Station, Great Smoky Mountains National Park
    - Vertical Files
      - Tom Robbins Papers

- Cullowhee, N.C.
  - Special Collections, Western North Carolina University
    - William Holland Thomas Papers

- Durham, N.C.
  - David M. Rubenstein Rare Book and Manuscript Library, Duke University
    - William Holland Thomas Papers

- Gatlinburg, Tenn.
  - Great Smoky Mountains National Park Library

- Knoxville, Tenn.
  - Special Collections Library, University of Tennessee
    - Casada Collection

- Nashville, Tenn.
  - Tennessee State Library and Archives

- Raleigh, N.C.
  - State Archives of North Carolina (microfilm, accessed through Ancestry.com)

North Carolina County Register of Deeds
U.S. Marriage Records, 1741–2011, RG 048
North Carolina State Board of Health, Bureau of Vital Statistics
North Carolina Death Certificates, 1909–1976, S.123

Richmond, Va.
Valentine Archives
Valentine Family Papers

Sylva, N.C.
Jackson County Register of Deeds

Townsend, Tenn.
Great Smoky Mountains National Park Archives
Carver Family Papers
Champion Fibre Company Papers
Civilian Conservation Corps Papers
Edd Conner Manuscript
Eli Potter Papers
Enloe Family Papers
Hiram C. Wilbur Papers
Land Acquisition Records
Meigs Post Papers
Mingus Family Papers
Oral History Collection
Ravensford Oral History Project
Robert S. Lambert Papers

Washington, D.C.
National Archives and Records Administration (microfilm, accessed through Ancestry.com and Fold3.com)
Army Register of Enlistments, 1798–1914, M233, RG 94
Civil War Service Records, Confederate, North Carolina, M270, RG 109
Civil War Service Records, Union, North Carolina, M401, RG 94
Civil War "Widows' Pensions," RG 15
Records of the Bureau of Indian Affairs, 1793–1999
Indian Census Rolls, 1885–1941, M595, RG 75
1928 Baker Roll and Records of the Eastern Cherokee Enrolling Commission, 1924–1929, M2104, RG 75
Records Relating to Enrollment of Eastern Cherokee by Guion Miller, 1908–1910, M685, RG 75, 12 rolls
Records of the Cherokee Agency in Tennessee, 1801–1835, M208, RG 75, roll 1
Records of the Post Office Department, M841, RG 28
Record of Appointment of Postmasters, 1832–Sept. 30, 1971, roll 95
U.S. Bureau of the Census, Seventh Census of the United States, 1850, M432
U.S. Bureau of the Census, Eighth Census of the United States, 1860, M653
U.S. Bureau of the Census, Ninth Census of the United States, 1870, M593-1144

U.S. Bureau of the Census, Tenth Census of the United States, 1880, T9
U.S. Bureau of the Census, Twelfth Census of the United States, 1900, T623
U.S. Bureau of the Census, Thirteenth Census of the United States, 1910, T624
U.S. Bureau of the Census, Fourteenth Census of the United States, 1920, T625-1314
U.S. Bureau of the Census, Fifteenth Census of the United States, 1930, T626
U.S. Bureau of the Census, Sixteenth Census of the United States, 1940, T627
U.S. Bureau of the Census, U.S., Federal Census Mortality Schedule, 1850–85, T655

PRIMARY AND SECONDARY SOURCES

Ablon, Matthew. "Tribal Council Supports Changing NC Mountain's Name from Confederate General to Original Cherokee Name." WCNC.com, July 21, 2022. www.wcnc.com/article/news/regional/cherokee-tribal-council-kuwahi-north-carolina/275-2285e915-5b39-4e01-bcda-9adb9d4fa4b7.

Adelman, Gary. "The Third Battle of Winchester." American Battlefield Trust. Accessed May 27, 2014. www.battlefields.org/learn/articles/third-battle-winchester.

Alexander, Eben. "The Big Smoky Mountains." *New York Evening Post*. August 11, 1888, 10.

American Lumberman. "In the Mountains of Western North Carolina." October 7, 1911, 43.

Ancestry.com. "U.S. Find A Grave Index, 1600s–Current." Accessed May 2015–July 2022. http://ancestry.com.

Angst, Michael G., ed. *Archaeological Investigations at Site 31SW393, Smokemont, Swain County, North Carolina*. Knoxville: University of Tennessee Archaeological Research Laboratory, 2012.

———. *Archaeological Investigations of Sites 31SW393, 31SW451, 31SW459 and 31SW460 in the Great Smoky Mountains National Park, Swain County, North Carolina*. Knoxville: University of Tennessee Archaeological Research Laboratory, 2008.

Arthur, John Preston. *Western North Carolina History from 1730–1913*. Johnson City, Tenn.: Overmountain Press, 1914.

Asheville Citizen. "A. A. Carver. Smokemont, Marks, 100th Birthday." May 25, 1944.

Avery, Myron H., and Kenneth S. Boardman, eds. "Arnold Guyot's Notes on the Geography of the Mountain District of Western North Carolina." *North Carolina Historical* Review 15 (July 1938): 251–318.

Beckwith, David L. "Narcissus Carver." *Smoky Mountain Ancestral Quest.com*. 1995–2014.

Bense, Judith A. *Archaeology of the Southeastern United States: Paleoindian to World War I*. San Diego, Calif.: Academic Press, 1994.

Brill, David. "The Smokies' Conscientious Objector (CO) Work Camp." *Smokies Life* 3, no. 2 (2009): 10–20.

Brown, Margaret Lynn. *The Wild East: A Biography of the Great Smoky Mountains*. Gainesville: University Press of Florida, 2000.

Burns, Christie, and Sarah Schmitt. *Ravensford: The Story of Our Land: A Documentary about the History and Future of Ravensford*. Bowling Green: Western Kentucky Department of Folk Studies and Anthropology, 2006. DVD.

Burr, David H., and John Arrowsmith. *The American Atlas, Exhibiting the Post Offices, Post*

Roads, Rail Roads, Canals, and the Physical and Political Divisions of the United States of America, 15. [London?]: John Arrowsmith, [1839].

Bush, Florence Cope. *Dorie: Woman of the Mountains*. Knoxville: University of Tennessee Press, 1992.

———. *Ocona Lufta Baptist: Pioneer Church of the Smokies, 1836–1939*. Concord, Tenn.: Misty Cove Press, 1990.

Carpenter, Dina D. "Thomas Irvin Hughes." In Jenkins and Sossamon, *Heritage of Swain County*, 185–86.

Carrington, Henry B. "Eastern Band of Cherokees of North Carolina." In *Extra Census Bulletin: Indians: Eastern Band of Cherokees of North Carolina*, Thomas Donaldson, 6–7. Washington, D.C.: U.S. Census Printing Office, 1892.

Cathey, James H. *The Genesis of Lincoln*. Canton, N.C.: B. H. Cathey, 1939.

Catton, Theodore. "A Gift for All Time: Great Smoky Mountains National Park Administrative History." Environmental History Workshop: October 10, 2008. http://npshistory.com/publications/grsm/adhi.pdf.

Coggins, Allen R. *Place Names of the Smokies*. Gatlinburg, Tenn.: Great Smoky Mountains Natural History Association, 1999.

Coggins, James Caswell. *Abraham Lincoln: A North Carolinian, with Proof*. Gastonia, N.C.: Carolina Printing, 1927.

———. *The Eugenics of President Abraham Lincoln: His German-Scotch Ancestry Irrefutably Established by Recently Discovered Documents*. Elizabethton, Tenn.: Goodwill, 1940.

Colby, William Munn. "Routes to Rainy Mountain: A Biography of James Mooney, Ethnologist." Ph.D. diss., University of Wisconsin–Madison, 1977.

Coleman, Alan. *Railroads of North Carolina*. Charleston, S.C.: Arcadia, 2008.

Conley, Robert J. *A Cherokee Encyclopedia*. Albuquerque: University of New Mexico Press, 2007.

Cook, Alice R. "Sketches of Haywood County and the Smokies." Unpublished manuscript, ca. 1983. Canton, N.C.

Cooling, B. Franklin. "Monocacy." American Battlefield Trust. Accessed May 30, 2014. www.battlefields.org/learn/civil-war/battles/monocacy.

Creswell, Bradley A. and Gail L. Guymon. "Prehistoric and Historic Background." In *Archaeological Investigations of Sites 31SW393, 31SW451, 31SW459 AND 31SW460 in The Great Smoky Mountains National Park, Swain County, North Carolina*, by Michael G. Angst. Knoxville: University of Tennessee Archaeological Research Laboratory, 2008.

Crow, Vernon H. *Storm in the Mountains: Thomas' Confederate Legion of Cherokee Indians and Mountaineers*. Cherokee, N.C.: Press of the Museum of the Cherokee Indian, 1982.

Cumfer, Cynthia. *Separate Peoples, One Land: The Minds of Cherokees, Blacks, and Whites on the Tennessee Frontier*. Chapel Hill: University of North Carolina Press, 2007.

Daily Bulletin of Orders Affecting the Postal Service, vol. 1, no. 100 (June 29, 1880); vol. 8, no. 2199 (May 21, 1887); vol. 10, no. 2913 (21 Sept. 1889); vol. 10, no. 2948 (November 1, 1889). *Jim Forte Postal History*. www.postalhistory.com.

Davis, Frank C. *My CCC Days: Memories of the Civilian Conservation Corps*. Boone, N.C.: Parkway, 2006.

Davis, Rebecca Harding. "Qualla." *Lippincott's Magazine of Popular Literature and Science* 16, no. 95 (November 1875): 576–86.

Dickens, Roy S., Jr. *Cherokee Prehistory: The Pisgah Phase in the Appalachian Summit Region*. Knoxville: University of Tennessee Press, 1976.

———. "The Origins and Development of Cherokee Culture." In *The Cherokee Indian Nation: A Troubled History*, edited by Duane H. King, 3–32. Knoxville: University of Tennessee Press.

Donaldson, Thomas. *Extra Census Bulletin: Indians. Eastern Band of Cherokees of North Carolina*. Washington, D.C.: U.S. Census Printing Office, 1892.

Dougherty, Patrick T. "A Bad Time Was Had by All." American Civil War Story. Updated 2012–16. www.americancivilwarstory.com/a-bad-time-was-had-by-all.html.

Dunaway, Wilma A. *The First American Frontier: Transition to Capitalism in Southern Appalachia, 1700–1860*. Chapel Hill: University of North Carolina Press, 1996.

———. *Women, Work, and Family in the Antebellum Mountain South*. Cambridge: Cambridge University Press, 2008.

Duncan, Barbara R., and Brett H. Riggs. *Cherokee Heritage Trails Guidebook*. Chapel Hill: University of North Carolina Press, 2003.

Dunn, Krissy. "The Battle of Third Winchester." American Battlefield Trust. Accessed June 17, 2014. www.battlefields.org/learn/articles/battle-third-winchester.

Dykeman, Wilma, and Jim Stokely. *Highland Homeland: The People of the Great Smokies*. Washington, D.C.: National Park Service, 1978.

Eller, Ronald D. *Miners, Millhands, and Mountaineers: Industrialization of the Appalachian South 1880–1930*. Knoxville: University of Tennessee Press, 1982.

Ellison, George. *Mountain Passages: Natural and Cultural History of Western North Carolina and the Great Smoky Mountains*. Charleston, S.C.: History Press, 2005.

———. "Will Thomas, Tsali & Tsali's Rock." *Journal of Cherokee Studies* 24 (2005): 25–26.

Finger, John R. *Cherokee Americans: The Eastern Band of Cherokees in the Twentieth Century*. Lincoln: University of Nebraska Press, 1991.

———. *Eastern Band of Cherokees, 1819–1900*. Knoxville: University of Tennessee Press, 1984.

Fink, Paul. "Early Explorers in the Great Smokies." *East Tennessee Historical Society's Publications* 5 (January 1933): 63–64.

Fink, Paul M., and Myron H. Avery. "Arnold Guyot's Explorations in the Great Smoky Mountains." *Appalachian* (December 1936): 253–61.

Fisher, Noel. *The Civil War in the Smokies*. Gatlinburg, Tenn.: Great Smoky Mountains Association, 2005.

———. "Colonel George W. Kirk: Villain or Hero?" *Smokies Life* 7, no. 1 (2013): 30–39.

"Fredericksburg." American Battlefield Trust. Accessed June 23, 2014. www.battlefields.org/learn/articles/fredericksburg.

Frizzell, George E. "The Native American Experience." In *The History of Jackson County*, edited by Max R. Williams, 33–66. Sylva, N.C.: Jackson County Historical Society, 2001.

———. "The Politics of Cherokee Citizenship, 1898–1930." *North Carolina Historical Review* 61, no. 2 (April 1984): 205–30.

Frome, Michael. *Strangers in High Places*. Knoxville: University of Tennessee Press, 1980.

Gabbard, Krin. *Better Git It in Your Soul: An Interpretive Biography of Charles Mingus*. Berkeley: University of California Press, 2016.

Gaillard, Frye. *As Long as the Waters Flow: Native Americans in the South and East*. Winston-Salem, N.C.: John F. Blair, 1998.

Garrett, J. T., and Michael Garrett. *Medicine of the Cherokee: The Way of Right Relationship*. Rochester, Vt.: Bear, 1996.

Godbold, E. Stanly, Jr., and Mattie U. Russell. *Confederate Colonel and Cherokee Chief*. Knoxville: University of Tennessee Press, 1990.

Great Smoky Mountains National Park. Cemeteries within Great Smoky Mountains National Park, 2001. www.interment.net/data/us/nc/great-smoky-mountains-national-park-cemeteries.pdf.

Greene, Lance K. *The Archaeology and History of the Cherokee Out Towns*. Volumes in Historical Archaeology, vol. 40, edited by Stanley South. Columbia: University of South Carolina, 1999.

Grimshawe, T. D. *Map Showing the Location of the Dwellings and Commissary, Also the Railway and Sidings at Smokemont NC*. September 1918, rev. January 11, 1919. GRSM 20640, Great Smoky Mountains National Park Archives, Townsend, Tenn.

Guyot, Arnold. "Guyot's Measurement of the Mountains of Western N.C." *Asheville News*, July 18, 1860.

Hardwood Record. "R. E. Wood Buys in North Carolina." August 10, 1917.

Hatley, Tom. *The Dividing Paths: Cherokees and South Carolinians through the Era of Revolution*. New York: Oxford University Press, 1993.

Hill, Sarah. "East Is East and West Is West: Cherokee Women after Removal." *Journal of Cherokee Studies* 20 (1999): 57–58.

Holmes, J. S. *Forest Conditions in Western North Carolina*. North Carolina Geological and Economic Survey Bulletin no. 23. Raleigh, N.C.: Edwards and Broughton, 1911.

Howell, Elvira. "The Life of Berry Howell." In Jenkins and Sossamon, *Heritage of Swain County*, 182–83.

Inscoe, John C. *Mountain Masters, Slavery, and the Sectional Crisis in Western North Carolina*. Knoxville: University of Tennessee Press, 1989.

Inscoe, John C., and Gordon B. McKinney. *The Heart of Confederate Appalachia: Western North Carolina in the Civil War*. Chapel Hill: University of North Carolina Press, 2000.

"James and Lizzie P. Powell." In Jenkins and Sossamon, *Heritage of Swain County*, 258.

Jenkins, Gary Claude. *Gass: A Family of the Great Smoky Mountains*. Chattanooga, Tenn.: published by the author, 2010.

———. "Mining of Alum Cave." *East Tennessee Historical Society's Publications* 60 (1988): 78–87.

Jenkins, Hazel C., and Ora Lee Sossamon, eds. *The Heritage of Swain County, North Carolina, 1988*. Bryson City, N.C.: Swain County Genealogical and Historical Society; Winston-Salem, N.C.: Hunter, 1988.

Jolley, Harley E. *"That Magnificent Army of Youth and Peace": The Civilian Conservation Corps in North Carolina, 1933–1942*. Raleigh: North Carolina Department of Cultural Resources, 2007.

Jurgelski, William Martin. "New Light on the Tsali Affair." In *Light on the Path: The Anthropology and History of the Southeastern Indians*, edited by Thomas J. Pluckhahn and Robbie Ethridge, 133–64. Tuscaloosa: University of Alabama Press, 2006.

Keel, Bennie C. "The Ravensford Tract Archeological Project." 2007. http://npshistory.com/series/archeology/seac/air/ravensford-tract.pdf.

Kendall, Arthur I. *Rifle Making in the Great Smoky Mountains*. Popular Study Series. History no. 13. Washington, D.C.: National Park Service, U.S. Department of the Interior, 1940.

Kephart, Horace. *Our Southern Highlanders*. 1922. Reprint, Knoxville: University of Tennessee Press, 1984.

Kilpatrick, Anna, and Jack Frederick Kilpatrick. "Chronicles of Wolftown: Social Documents of the North Carolina Cherokees, 1850–1862." Anthropological Papers no. 75. *Bureau of American Ethnology Bulletin* 196 (1966): 1–112.

King, Adam. "History and Archeology: Mississippian Period: Overview." *New Georgia Encyclopedia*. Athens: Georgia Humanities Council and University of Georgia Press, 2002, www.georgiaencyclopedia.org/nge/Article.jsp?id=h-707.

King, Duane H., ed. "Introduction." In *The Cherokee Indian Nation: A Troubled History*, ed. King, ix–xvii. Knoxville: University of Tennessee Press, 1979.

King, Duane H., and E. Raymond Evans. "Tsali: The Man behind the Legend." *Journal of Cherokee Studies* 4, no. 4 (1979): 194–99.

Korstian, C. F. "The Southern Appalachian Spruce Forest as Affected by Logging and Fire." *Technical Bulletin*, U.S. Department of Agriculture, 1930.

Kreusch, Erik Skot. *Report on Archeological Investigations at 31SW240/GRSM 152 "Wild Turkey."* Gatlinburg, Tenn.: Great Smoky Mountains National Park, 2010.

Lambert, Carl G., Sr. "The Coming of the Railroad." In Jenkins and Sossamon, *Heritage of Swain County*, 15–16.

———. "The Oconaluftee River and the First White Settlers." In Jenkins and Sossamon, *Heritage of Swain County*, 8.

Lambert, Leonard Carson. *Up from these Hills: Memories of a Cherokee Boyhood*. Lincoln: University of Nebraska Press, 2011.

Lambert, Robert S. "Logging in the Great Smokies, 1880–1930." *Tennessee Historical Quarterly* 20, no. 4 (December 1961): 350–63.

———. "Logging on the Little River, 1890–1940." *East Tennessee Historical Society Publications* 33 (1961): 32–42.

———. "The Oconaluftee Valley, 1800–1860." *North Carolina Historical Review* 35, no. 4 (October 1958): 415–26.

Lanman, Charles. *Letters from the Alleghany Mountains*. New York: Putnam, 1849.

"Letter from General W. Scott to War Department, November 6, 1838." *Journal of Cherokee Studies* 4, no. 4 (1979): 217.

Lumber World. "Along the Smoky Mountain Range." April 15, 1911, 21.

Mails, Thomas E. *The Cherokee People: The Story of the Cherokees from Earliest Origins to Contemporary Times*. Tulsa, Okla.: Council Oak Books, 1992.

Maples, Mike. *Smoky Mountains Cemeteries: Cemeteries of the Great Smoky Mountains*. Charleston, S.C.: Createspace, 2017.

Mastran, Shelley Smith, and Nan Lowerre. *Mountaineers and Rangers: A History of Federal Forest Management in the Southern Appalachians, 1900–81*. FS-380. Washington, D.C.: USDA Forest Service, 1983.

McCarter, Dwight, and Joe Kelley. *Meigs Line: Rangers Rediscover a Two-Century-Old*

Disputed Boundary between the U.S. and Cherokee Nation. Asheville, N.C.: Grateful Steps, 2009.

McDowell, William L., Jr. *Documents Relating to Indian Affairs, May 21, 1750–August 7, 1754*. Vol. 1 of *The Colonial Records of South Carolina*. Columbia: South Carolina Archives Department, 1958.

——, ed. "Introduction." In *Documents Relating to Indian Affairs, 1754–1765*, ix–xlii. Vol. 2 of *The Colonial Records of South Carolina*. Columbia: University of South Carolina Press, 1970.

McLoughlin, William G. *Cherokee Renascence in the New Republic*. Princeton, N.J.: Princeton University Press, 1986.

——. *The Cherokees and Christianity, 1794–1874: Essays on Acculturation and Cultural Persistence*. Athens: University of Georgia Press, 1994.

——. *Cherokees and Missionaries, 1789–1839*. Norman: University of Oklahoma Press, 1995.

McLoughlin, William G., and Walter H. Conser. "Cherokees in Transition: A Statistical Analysis of the Federal Cherokee Census of 1835." *Journal of American History* 64, no. 3 (December 1977): 678–703.

McMahan, Carroll. "Upland Chronicles: Controversy Surrounds the Legend of Fort Harry." *Mountain Press.com*, January 18, 2014. www.themountainpress.com/lifestyles/upland-chronicles-controversy-surrounds-the-legend-of-fort-harry/article_724c5182-df4e5996-8228-0e1fa072dd35.html.

Message from the President of the United States Transmitting a Report of the Secretary of Agriculture in Relation to the Forests, Rivers, and Mountains of the Southern Appalachian Region. 57th Cong., 1st sess. S. Doc. 84. Washington D.C.: Government Printing Office, 1902.

Mingus, Charles. *Beneath the Underdog: His World as Composed by Mingus*. Edited by Nel King. New York: Alfred A. Knopf, 1971.

Mooney, James. "Myths of the Cherokee." *Nineteenth Annual Report of the Bureau of American Ethnology*, part 1. Washington, D.C.: Government Printing Office, 1900.

——. "Sacred Formulas of the Cherokee." *Seventh Annual Report of the Bureau of American Ethnology*. Washington, D.C.: Government Printing Office, 1891.

——. "The Swimmer Manuscript: Sacred Formulas and Medicinal Prescriptions." Revised, completed, and edited by Frans M. Olbrechts. *Bureau of American Ethnology Bulletin* 99. Washington, D.C.: Government Printing Office, 1932.

Moore, Harry L. *A Roadside Guide to the Geology of the Great Smoky Mountains National Park*. Knoxville: University of Tennessee Press, 1988.

Moses, L. G. *The Indian Man: A Biography of James Mooney*. Urbana: University of Illinois Press, 1984.

National Conference on State Parks. "Safety Device for Roller's Trailing Wheels." *Grist* 18, no. 4 (July/August 1974): 29.

——. "Truck Tire-Changing Dolly." *Grist: Park Practice* 4, no. 5 (September/October 1960): 38.

"National Register of Historic Places Inventory – Nomination Form for Smokemont Baptist Church." United States Department of Interior, National Park Service. January 1, 1976. http://npshistory.com/publications/grsm/nr-smokemont-baptist-church.pdf.

Newman, T. Stell. "An Overview of the Probable Indian Culture History, Great Smoky Mountains National Park." GRSM 32009. Denver, Colo.: Denver Service Center, National Park Service, ca. 1974.

"Newspaper Clipping from the Scrapbook of Col. W. S. Foster's Wife, Betty." *Journal of Cherokee Studies* 4, no. 4 (1979): 234.

New York Lumber Trade Journal. "Receiver Asked for William Whitmer and Sons, Inc." October 1, 1916.

Oakley, Christopher Arris. *New South Indians: Tribal Economics and the Eastern Band of Cherokee in the Twentieth Century*. Knoxville: University of Tennessee Press, 2018.

Owl, Henry M. "The Eastern Band of Cherokee Indians before and after the Removal." M.A. thesis, University of North Carolina, Chapel Hill, 1929.

Palmer, Gail. *Cemeteries of the Smokies*. Unpublished manuscript, 2015.

Parker, Matthew D. "25th North Carolina Infantry Regiment." *ThomasLegion.net*. 2005–15. Accessed August 20, 2014. www.thomaslegion.net/25th.html (page discontinued).

Parris, John. "Boundary Tree Still Lives in Memory," *Asheville (N.C.) Citizen-Times*, May 21, 1987, pp. 1, 12.

Perdue, Theda. *The Cherokee*. New York: Chelsea House, 1989.

———. *Slavery and the Evolution of Cherokee Society, 1540–1866*. Knoxville: University of Tennessee Press, 1979.

Petersen, Ronald H. "Two Early Boundary Lines with the Cherokee Nation." *Journal of Cherokee Studies* 6, no. 1 (Spring 1981): 14–33.

Peterson, Shane C. "Defining Cultural Landscapes through Human Ecology: A Case Study from the 1819 Citizen Cherokee Reservations in Western North Carolina." *North Carolina Archaeology* 56 (October 2007): 96–117.

"Petition of Area Whites to Col. Foster, Nov. 18, 1838." *Journal of Cherokee Studies* 4, no. 4 (1979): 228.

Pierce, Daniel S. *The Great Smokies: From Natural Habitat to National Park*. Knoxville: University of Tennessee Press, 2000.

Polhemus, Richard R. *The Toqua Site – 40MR6: A Late Mississippian Dallas Phase Town*. Vol. 2. *Report of Investigations no. 41*. Knoxville: Department of Anthropology, University of Tennessee, 1987.

Poole, Cary Franklin. *A History of Railroading in Western North Carolina*. Johnson City, Tenn.: Overmountain Press, 1995.

Prince, Pete. "Fort Harry, Tennessee: A Phenomenon in the Great Smoky Mountains National Park." *Smoky Mountain Historical Journal* 29, no. 1 (Spring 2003): 2–6.

Reagan, Donald B. *Smoky Mountain Clans*. 3 vols. Rev. ed. [Knoxville, Tenn.]: Published by the author, 1978–83.

Reagan, Ida. "Asoph Hughes Family." In Jenkins and Sossamon, *Heritage of Swain County*, 185.

Reid, John Phillip. "Perilous Rule: The Law of International Homicide." In *The Cherokee Indian Nation: A Troubled History*, edited by Duane H. King, 33–45. Knoxville: University of Tennessee Press, 1979.

Robbins, Tom. "Great Smoky Mountains National Park." In Jenkins and Sossamon, *Heritage of Swain County*, 11–12.

Rodning, Christopher B. "Architectural Symbolism and Cherokee Townhouses." *Southeastern Archaeology* 29, no. 1 (Summer 2010): 59–79.

Santoro, Gene. *Myself When I Am Real: The Life and Music of Charles Mingus*. Oxford: Oxford University Press, 2000.

Schroedl, Gerald F. "Cherokee Ethnohistory and Archaeology from 1540 to 1838." In *Indians of the Greater Southeast: Historical Archaeology and Ethnohistory*, edited by Bonnie G. McEwan, 204–41. Gainesville: University Press of Florida, 2000.

Shenandoah Valley Battlefields. "Battle of Piedmont, June 5–6, 1864." Shenandoah Valley Battlefields National Historic District. Accessed June 20, 2014. www.shenandoahatwar.org/battle-of-piedmont.

Shipman, M. L. *Thirty-First Report of the Department of Labor and Printing of the State of North Carolina, 1917–18*. Raleigh, N.C.: Edwards and Broughton, 1918.

Sikora, Dorota. *Luten Bridges in Great Smoky Mountains National Park, Great Smoky Mountains National Park Roads & Bridges, Luten Bridges, Gatlinburg, Sevier County, TN*. Map, 1996, Washington, D.C., Library of Congress Prints and Photographs Division.

Smith, Cindy. "Aden Carver—Mountaineer." *Mountain Trails*. January 1989.

Sossamon, Ora Lee. "Aseph Hamilton Hughes Family." In Jenkins and Sossamon, *Heritage of Swain County*, 183–84.

Southern Lumberman (Nashville). July 15, 1902, 7.

Southern Lumberman (Nashville). July 1, 1903, 27.

Sparks, Billie Montez Scott. "William Self and Mary Lugene Moody Hughes Family." In Jenkins and Sossamon, *Heritage of Swain County*, 187–88.

Spaulding, O. L. "Expenses of Timber Experts: Letter from the Acting Secretary of the Treasury," no. 151. *The Executive Documents of the House of Representatives for the Second Session of the Fifty-second Congress 1892–93*. Washington, D.C.: Government Printing Office, 1893.

Speck, Frank G., and Leonard Broom. *Cherokee Dance and Drama*. Norman: University of Oklahoma Press, 1851.

State Library of North Carolina. "NC Land Records before 1800: Land Grant Process." North Carolina: Government and Heritage Library, 2017. https://statelibrary.ncdcr.libguides.com/nclandrecords1800/grants.

St. Louis Lumberman. "The Champion Lumber Company." April 15, 1911, 58.

Stringfield, W. W. "Sixty-Ninth Regiment." In *Histories of the Several Regiments and Battalions from North Carolina in the Great War, 1861–65*, vol. 3, edited by Walter Clark, 729–31. Goldsboro: State of North Carolina and Nash Brothers, 1901.

Sylva (N.C.) Herald. "Commissary." July 14, 1977.

Temple, M. E. *Map Showing the Chief Location and Lands of the Eastern Band of Cherokees, in Cherokee, Jackson, Graham, and Swain Counties, North Carolina*. U.S. Land Office, 1876, in 47th Cong., 1 Sess., House Ex. Doc. 196, Ser. 2031. Washington, D.C.: Government Printing Office, 1882. https://dc.lib.unc.edu/cdm/singleitem/collection/ncmaps/id/1053/rec/.

Thomas, Elizabeth Avery, and Kirk Savage. "William Holland Thomas and the Myth of the White Chief." *Journal of Cherokee Studies* 34 (Summer 2019): 36–47.

Thomasson, Lillian Franklin. *Swain County: Early History and Educational Development*. Unpublished manuscript, Bryson City, N.C., 1965.

Thomsen, Paul A. *Rebel Chief: The Motley Life of Colonel William Holland Thomas, C.S.A.* New York: Tom Doherty Associates, 2004.

Thornton, Russell. *The Cherokees: A Population History.* Lincoln: University of Nebraska Press, 1990.

Tortora, Daniel J. *Carolina in Crisis: Cherokees, Colonists, and Slaves in the American Southeast, 1756–1763*. Chapel Hill: University of North Carolina Press, 2015.

Trout, Ed. *Historic Buildings of the Smokies.* Gatlinburg, Tenn.: Great Smoky Mountains Association, 1995.

United States Department of the Interior. *Indian Field Service Eastern Cherokee Enrolling Commission: Miscellaneous Testimony in Enrollment Cases Under the Act of June 4, 1924*, Vol. 3. 1926–28. Ancestry.com.

United States et al. v. W. T. Mason Lumber Co. 81 S.E. 1064 (N.C. 1914), 647, reprinted in Federal Reporter, *Cases Argued and Determined in the Circuit Courts of Appeals and Circuit and District Courts of the United States.* Vol. 172, October–November 1909. Saint Paul, Minn.: West, 1910.

Valentine. "Our Mission and History." The Valentine. 2015. https://thevalentine.org/about/history-mission/.

Ward, Bill. "People Names in Plant Names, Part VI—The Geologists Connection." Native Plant Society of Texas, Boerne Chapter, 2011. http://npsot.org/wp/boerne/files/2011/01/People_Names_in_Plant_Names_Part_VI.pdf.

Ward, H. Trawick, and R. P. Stephen Davis Jr. *Time before History: The Archaeology of North Carolina*. Chapel Hill: University of North Carolina Press, 1999.

"Washington's Account as Related to Molly Sequoyah." *Journal of Cherokee Studies* 4, no. 4 (1979): 224.

Weals, Vic. "The Saga of the Dock Conner Family." *Knoxville Journal*, August 16, 30, September 13, 1976 (repr. *Skagit River Journal*, edited by Noel v. Bourasaw), parts 1–3.

Webb, Paul A., David S. Leigh, and Tasha Benyshek. *Cultural and Historical Resource Investigations of the Ravensford Land Exchange Tract, Great Smoky Mountains National Park, Swain County, North Carolina*. Vol. 1. Durham, N.C.: TRC Garrow Associates, 2002.

Whisnant, Anne Mitchell. *Super-Scenic Motorway: A Blue Ridge Parkway History.* Chapel Hill: University of North Carolina Press, 2006.

Whyte, Thomas R. "Proto-Iroquoian Divergence in the Late Archaic–Early Woodland Period Transition of the Appalachian Highlands." *Southeastern Archaeology* 26, no. 1 (Summer 2007): 134–44.

Wigginton, Eliot. "Rufus A. Morgan." In *Foxfire 4*, 394–441. New York: Anchor Books, 1977.

Wilburn, Hiram C. *Cherokee Landmarks around the Great Smokies.* Asheville, N.C.: Stephens Press, 1966.

———. "The Indian Gap Trail." Historical Paper no. 5. Washington, D.C.: U.S. Department of the Interior, 1940.

———. "Nununyi, the Kituhwas, or Mountain Indians and the State of North Carolina." *Southern Indian Studies* 2 (1950): 54–64.

Williams, Fred C. "Agriculture." Encyclopedia of Arkansas Online. Last updated September 11, 2020. https://encyclopediaofarkansas.net/entries/agriculture-385/.

Williams, Walter L. "The Merger of Apaches with Eastern Cherokee: Qualla in 1893." *Journal of Cherokee Studies* 2 (Spring 1977): 240–45.

Woodford, Ann Miller. *When All God's Children Get Together: A Celebration of the Lives and Music of African American People in Far Western North Carolina*. Andrews, N.C.: Ann Miller Woodford and One Dozen Who Care, 2015.

Young, Maisie Queen. "Wilson Ensley and Amanda Catherine Queen Family." In *The Heritage of Swain County North Carolina*, edited by Ora Lee Sossamon, 260. Winston-Salem, N.C.: Hunter Publishing Company, 1988.

Young, Virginia D. "A Sketch of the Cherokee People on the Indian Reservation of North Carolina." *Woman's Progress*, January 1894, 169–74.

Zeigler, Wilbur G. "On Foot Across the Mountains." *Asheville Citizen*, May 22, 1879.

Zeigler, Wilbur G., and Ben S. Grosscup. *Heart of the Alleghanies; Or, Western North Carolina, Comprising Its Topography, History, Resources, People, Narratives* . . . . Raleigh, N.C.: Alfred Williams, 1883.

Zogry, Michael J. *Anetso, the Cherokee Ball Game: At the Center of Ceremony and Identity.* Chapel Hill: University of North Carolina Press, 2010.

Index

Page numbers in italics refer to illustrations.